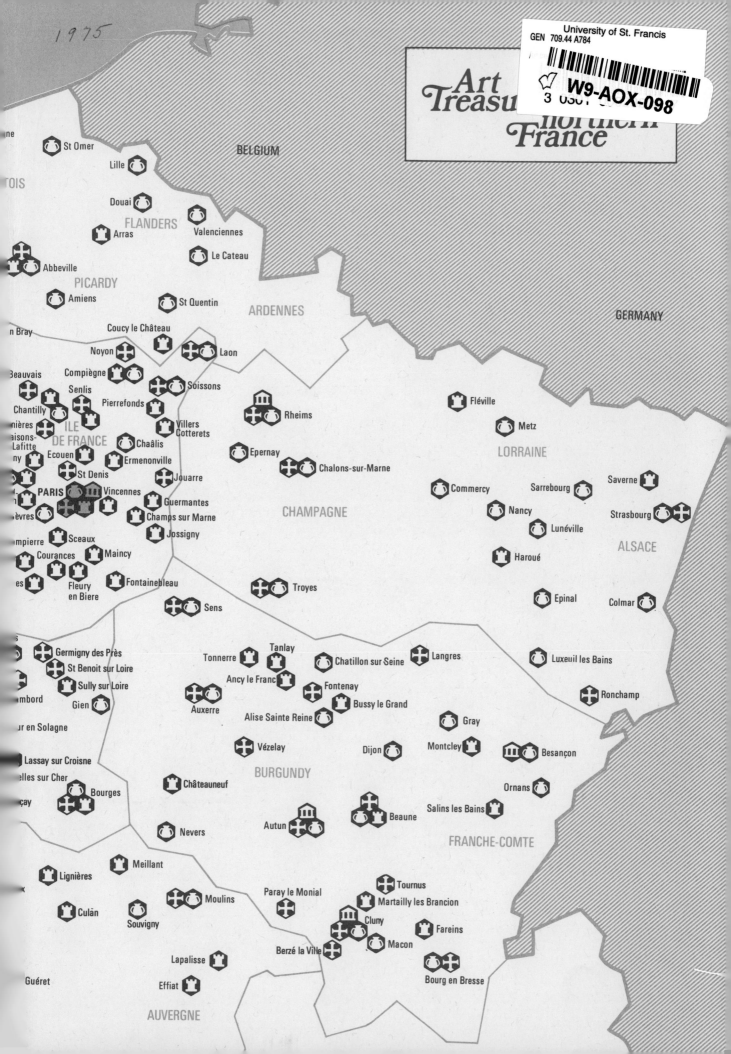

Art Treasures in France

Art Treasures in France

Monuments, Masterpieces, Commissions and Collections

Introduced by Germain Bazin
Conservateur en chef at the Louvre, Paris

Paul Hamlyn
London   Sydney

General Editors
Trewin Copplestone
London
Bernard S. Myers
New York

The Art Treasures series:
France
Italy
The British Isles
Spain
Germany
Russia
Egypt
India
Japan
**The United States
of America**

Half title illustration:
Jade covered cup, sixteenth century;
Louvre, Paris
Frontispiece:
Louis XIV at the establishment of
the Academy of Science and
Foundation of the Observatory
1667 *detail* by Henri Testelin;
Versailles
Opposite:
Virgin and child, *c* 1400, by
Claus Sluter, from the Chartreuse de
Champmol, Dijon

Published jointly by
The Hamlyn Publishing Group Limited,
Hamlyn House, The Centre, Feltham, Middlesex
and McGraw-Hill Book Company, New York and Toronto
© The Hamlyn Publishing Group Limited, 1969. All rights reserved
Printed in Italy by Officine Grafiche Arnoldo Mondadori, Verona
Phototypeset by BAS Printers Limited, Wallop, Hampshire

Contents

7   **Introduction** by Germain Bazin

9   **The art of Prehistoric Man**
Desmond Collins

21   **Celts and Romans in Gaul**
c 600 BC−AD 500
Martin Henig

33   **Christian France and the Monastic Churches**
500−1144
Sabrina Mitchell

51   **Church, King and Court in the Gothic Age**
1144−1500
Sabrina Mitchell

73   **Princely Patrons and the French Renaissance**
1500−1600
Anthony Radcliffe

93   **Versailles and the Age of the Cardinals**
1600−1700
Mary Whiteley

113   **The Last Years of the Monarchy**
1700−1789
Anthony S. G. Green

127   **The Founding of the National Museums**
1789−1871
Charles Harrison

141   **The State and the Individual**
1871 to the present day
Nicholas Wadley

164   **Museums and Monuments**

172   **Acknowledgements**

173   **Index**

Introduction

It is in France that art offers the traveller the most distant horizons; it was there that primitive man felt, surging up in him, an imperative need to express in pictures his idea of the world. Born in the depths of caves like Lascaux, the artistic epic of France has followed its course without interruption to the present day. French art created some styles and borrowed others invented by other nations; it was also the source of a number of artistic revolutions which radically altered the development of western art.

The French are tempted to see the beginnings of their humanist tradition not in the great monuments of Arles or Nîmes but in the work of Gallo-Roman sculptors. The reliefs of these native craftsmen show a naturalism which moderates the more rhetorical classicism of Rome. Long after the barbarian invasions, the relief figure was born again in France and a fusion of sculpture and architecture was attempted in the Romanesque style, to be triumphantly achieved in the Gothic – the most original contribution in the history of styles since the Greeks. We can see at Chartres and Rheims how the heavy walls have become weightless in order to admit the fantastic imagery of stained glass; but on the exterior the architecture affirms its strength and the statuary brings to this affirmation the steady equilibrium of its masses. The native classicism which had flowered in the Gallo-Roman figures reappeared on the portals of the cathedrals.

At about this time patrons in France began to encourage foreign artists. The Fleming Claus Sluter brought new ideas to his sculpture for the dukes of Burgundy, but a far greater force was to come from Italy. Louis XII and Francis I invited Italian artists and craftsmen to embellish their courts and thus Renaissance principles spread into France, firmly guiding French art towards a new classicism which was never entirely to be relinquished. This style, and the way of life which reflected it at Versailles, was to be the model for all Europe.

Collectors soon became discerningly eclectic. While Marie de Medici had opened her Luxembourg palace to the paintings of Rubens, Louis XIV sought the work of the great Italian masters as well as of contemporary French painters. The wealthy merchants and financiers collected Italian, Flemish and Dutch pictures, and at the end of the ancien régime the Comte d'Angivillier, preparing the public museum which he was never able to open, deliberately set out to acquire foreign masterpieces for a museum which he conceived in the image of Europe.

This is the museum which was opened at the Louvre by the Convention in 1793. The policy of artistic conquest inspired by the European aspirations of the Convention was later to be confirmed in the name of Napoleon, whose victories filled not only the Louvre but museums throughout the Empire with a wide range of works. The Louvre kept faith with the spirit of its founders and today contains some of the most famous works of art in the world, such as the *Mona Lisa* and the *Venus de Milo*. Foreign acquisitions like these are an important part of France's art collections.

Although France was slow to recognise the work of her own revolutionary young painters in the late nineteenth century, the Impressionists now hold pride of place in her public galleries. Today we can see links with the past in their work, for Degas sometimes reminds us of Ingres, Monet evokes Claude and Renoir is related to the eighteenth century.

The purpose of this book is to survey the ebb and flow of conservatism and revolution in French art and to give an account of the changing tastes of patrons and collectors. The main text is followed by an alphabetical list of the important museums and monuments in the country which will enable the reader or the traveller to find his way among the superb art treasures of France. Germain Bazin

THE CHATEAU OF VERSAILLES
1668
Pierre Patel the Elder, c. 1620–1676
oil on canvas
Musée de Versailles

This painting shows the château of Versailles during the early stages of the transformation of Louis XIII's small hunting lodge by the architect Louis Le Vau. The approach and grouped buildings were planned to lead up towards the centre of the palace, the old Cour de Marbre, while behind stretch the great vistas of formal tree-lined avenues and sheets of water designed by André Le Notre.

France is one of the great treasure houses of art in the world and custodian of examples of all cultures. The story of her collections begins with the days of Greek Massilia, now the thriving port Marseilles, but the history of art indigenous to France goes back even further.

Some of the earliest, most famous and finest examples of the art of early man in Europe are located in France. The caves at Lascaux are the best known of many prehistoric sites in the country. The vast majority of the evidence for cave man and his art has been recovered from the picturesque limestone gorge of the Vézère valley and the surrounding areas of south-west France, sometimes called Aquitaine. This evidence is found through excavation, or, as in the case of Lascaux, through chance discovery. What is revealed is evocative of the early life of man; but only the patient work of archaeologists can begin to reconstruct a picture of that life. The terms used to describe the periods of pre-history are archaeological; hence the time-honoured divisions into Stone Age, Bronze Age and Iron Age. The earliest and by far the longest period is the Stone Age which is subdivided into the Old Stone Age (Palaeolithic), the Middle Stone Age (Mesolithic), and the New Stone Age (Neolithic).

The later part of the Palaeolithic, immensely significant in the context of the history of art, is sharply distinguished from the earlier Palaeolithic by a number of innovations. In stone technology these are the regular use of flint blades and a tool called the burin, which is probably a chisel and may well have been the ancient artistic engravers' main piece of equipment. This period, in which there was an almost universal occurrence of art, is marked by the introduction of standardised bone tools. The artistic content of the Leptolithic cycle, characterised by a refinement of tool making, is painting and engraving, often of cave interiors and sometimes in occupation strata, and the most outstanding examples in France come from this cycle. They are usually classified in various culture contexts or phases which take their names from the type site where evidence of the phase was first found. Thus for example Aurignac, a cave in the foothills of the Pyrenees, gives its name to a whole cultural period.

During this Aurignacian culture the first representations of animals appear. Even in the later stages of the Aurignacian culture there are paintings of animals which are still extremely crude. The early artists of this period used to engrave as well, and the outline of an animal thought to be a reindeer from the 'Renne' rock shelter at Belcayre indicates how simple was the technique employed in this first known phase of artistic representation. Several material cultures have been found overlying the Aurignacian; by far the most widespread is named after de Noailles in the Corrèze department.

De Noailles

The de Noailles culture is important because of the large number of art objects associated with it, and because it is the second main occurrence of art in the archaeological record. Both simple paintings and engravings are known from the Labattut rock shelter a few yards from Castanet where a crude painting was found. These show more skill and confidence than was found, for instance, in the Belcayre engraving or the Castanet painting of the preceding Aurignacian period. Only in the latest Aurignacian stage is there any indication of a sureness of hand and fineness of line, while the best of the de Noailles engraving is very fine, although there remains a tendency to mis-shapenness and distortion of parts of the animal.

One of the best known types of Palaeolithic art is the small human female statuette known as a 'venus', several of which have been found in France. Only one example can be assigned to an undoubted and known

I

STATUE-MENHIR FROM AVEYRON

Neolithic, c. 2000 BC
stone
about 30 in (76 cm)
Musée des Antiquités Nationales,
Saint-Germain-en-Laye

These statues known as 'menhirs' which look rather like milestones, are common in France. They are usually thought to represent goddesses; some have breasts, indicating female sex. This example from Aveyron has short hands shown as though reaching over the shoulders, and hand-like pendants hanging from the belt. Under the chin is a curious forked object which may be a neck ornament.

culture context; it comes from Tursac and is from a de Noailles layer. The *Lespugue venus*, which is a masterpiece of carving, is very probably from **4** the same context. In view of the detailed stylistic similarities to Tursac of other venuses, notably Sireuil and 'la Poire'–the headless venus from **2** Brassempouy–these examples should probably be regarded as de Noailles. This in turn would suggest that the famous girl's head from Brassempouy **7** was of the same age. Also from the de Noailles phase, and closely related to the venus statuettes are some bas-reliefs from Laussel, the best known of **12** which is a relief of a woman holding a bison horn.

At this point two important caves should be considered where there are paintings on the walls although no art has been found in strata actually excavated by archaeologists–the caves of Pech-Merle and Cougnac. At **3, 5** Pech-Merle a remarkable series of smeared designs survive on a low ceiling with finger marks in the soft clay still visible. One design clearly reproduces the stylistic features of the venus series, and one suggests that the panel may be of de Noailles date. This detective work can be extended;

2

'LA POIRE' VENUS

Leptolithic, 30,000 to 20,000 BC
carved in ivory
3 in (8 cm)
Musée des Antiquités Nationales,
Saint-Germain-en-Laye

This fragmentary figurine was one of seven found in 1892 by Edouard Piette in the Grotte du Pape near Brassempouy. The extreme obesity of the stomach can only really be explained as pregnancy, which is indicated in several other similar figures. The treatment of the stomach and groin is close to that of a relief carving from Terme Pialat, a de Noailles site in the Dordogne.

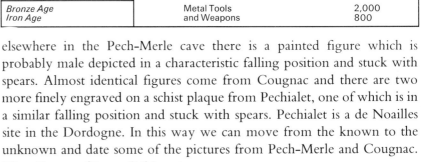

Main Divisions of Prehistory		Way of Life		Names of Culture Stages	Beginning of Stage in Years BC
Stone Age	Early Palæolithic	*Hunting and Gathering*	Stone Tools	Acheulian	500–250,000
				Mousterian Complex	70,000
	Later (upper) Palæolithic or Leptolithic		Earliest Art	Early Perigordian	35,000
			Stone and Bone Tools	Aurignacian	32,000
				Later Perigordian including de Noailles Culture	25,000
				Protomagdalenian Final Aurignacian	20,000 19,000
				Solutrian Magdalenian	18,500 16,000
	Mesolithic		Miniature Stone Tools	Azilian	9,000
	Neolithic	*Farming*	Pottery	Chassean	4,000
			Megalithic Monuments		
Bronze Age *Iron Age*			Metal Tools and Weapons		2,000 800

elsewhere in the Pech-Merle cave there is a painted figure which is probably male depicted in a characteristic falling position and stuck with spears. Almost identical figures come from Cougnac and there are two more finely engraved on a schist plaque from Pechialet, one of which is in a similar falling position and stuck with spears. Pechialet is a de Noailles site in the Dordogne. In this way we can move from the known to the unknown and date some of the pictures from Pech-Merle and Cougnac.

The climax of Leptolithic art

The large mural paintings and engravings of the interiors of caves such as **6,** Lascaux, Niaux, Font de Gaume, Les Combarelles, Teyjat and Gabillou **13** are with good reason regarded as the main treasures of Leptolithic art, and indeed of all prehistoric art in France. Large numbers of small carved bones and utilitarian objects, often of surpassing beauty, indicate that the **8,** climax of hunting art was the Magdalenian culture, which takes its name from the site of la Madeleine, especially the stages which fall in the remarkably short time span from about 14,000 to 11,000 B.C. This is a mere moment by prehistoric standards, but covers the extent of the whole of western civilization.

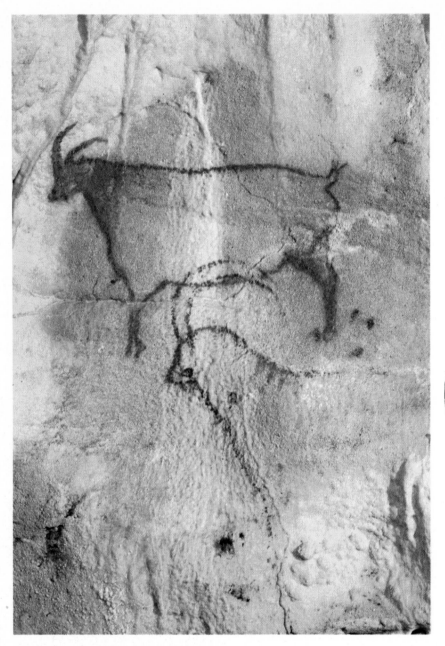

3
IBEXES
Leptolithic,
possibly de Noailles culture 25,000–22,000 BC
19·25 in (49 cm long)
The Cougnac cave near Gourdan (Lot)

The Cougnac cave was discovered in 1949. Most of the paintings, like this pair of ibexes, are in red ochre, and almost all are in outline. The head of the upper (probably female) ibex is filled in in colour but the head itself is disproportionately small as is common in earlier Leptolithic art. The motif of one animal of each sex shown close together is also common, and fits the idea of fertility symbolism.

4
THE LESPUGUE VENUS
Leptolithic, c. 25,000 to 22,000 BC
carved in mammoth ivory
h. 5·75 in (14·6 cm)
Musée de l'Homme, Paris

This figurine, found in 1922 by René de St Perier in the Rideaux cave near Lespugue, is a classic example of the 'venus' series which are characteristic of this period, especially the de Noailles culture. These figurines have strongly emphasised middle regions and breasts, and are generally thought to signify a pre-occupation with the fertility of the tribe or perhaps of their game. Other examples from Kostenki in Russia and Willendorf in Austria are similar in style. The significance of the triangular object under the buttocks is not known, it may be a kind of tray for the infant to fall into in childbirth.

11

5

DAPPLED HORSES

Leptolithic, possibly late Perigordian
in the main chamber of
Pech-Merle cave near Cabrerets (Lot)

The cave was discovered in 1922, and the
pictures were studied by the Abbé Lemozi.
The overlapping horses are surrounded by
six hand silhouettes in black, some of them
very indistinct, of a kind common in other
caves in the Pyrenees and northern Spain.
They are made by blowing the paint over
the hand – probably through a tube of bone
or reed. This technique produces the blobs
which make the dappling of the horse and
its surround, so the horse and hands are
probably contemporary. Even the outline
of the horse seems to be made in this way.

6

THE CHINESE HORSE

Leptolithic; possibly 15,000 – 13,000 BC
painted in black and yellow
59 in (149 cm)
in the axial gallery of the Lascaux cave
near Montignac, Dordogne

This fine naturalistic painting is accompanied by a number of signs; the linear
designs in front of and over the stomach
of the horse seem to represent spears or
arrows and are often thought to indicate
ritual magic. The pattern of parallel lines
above is more enigmatic. Similar designs
occur in other Lascaux paintings and elsewhere; they are sometimes called scuti-
forms (shield shapes) but they are more
often interpreted as traps or huts.

Since its relatively recent discovery in 1940, Lascaux has been the object of more controversy concerning its dating than any other cave. Positive evidence has recently come to hand from occupation strata found surprisingly in a deep shaft in the cave. These have a radiocarbon age in the bracket 15,000–13,000 B.C. Decorative motifs from these deposits can be matched on the walls, and this evidence suggests that much or all of the art from this site dates from the early Magdalenian phase.

The paintings of Lascaux are executed in a flowing naturalistic style. Near the entrance is a round hall and from this radiate two passages with numerous pictures. The majority of these paintings and engravings are of animals, but there are also enigmatic squared signs known as 'tectiforms', which can possibly be interpreted as traps. The animals are in side view, some merely outlined or with only the head coloured in. A few are more finely shaded. Probably some brush technique was used by this time, rather than the smearing and paint blowing found earlier. Extreme fineness of the engraved line is a characteristic which runs right through Magdalenian art, both on dated objects from such sites as Laugerie and Couze, and on the big murals of Lascaux, Les Combarelles and Teyjat. Preservation was good until a sharp deterioration was noticed in 1962 and the cave was closed.

If Lascaux is a good cave to choose when describing early Magdalenian art, then Font de Gaume is probably the best example of the polychrome painting of middle to late middle Magdalenian art. The skill of the artists of Font de Gaume in sketching mammoths, reindeer and bison, and the felicitous effect of the shading of brown, red and black colours into one another has been much admired. Unfortunately the Font de Gaume paintings are never easily distinguishable although they have been cleaned in recent years.

Although not as colourful as Lascaux, the Pyrenean cave of Niaux is probably as rewarding; its bison and ibexes are executed with great skill and are found in a large chamber set dramatically deep in the cave. Other Pyrenean sites reiterate a theme found at Niaux which is usually regarded as hunting magic. It takes the form of spears painted or engraved on the animals or adjacent to them, and can be clearly seen at Niaux and on a statuette from Isturitz accurately datable to the late middle Magdalenian. In the caves of Montespan and le Portel, however, there are indications of ritual of a more positive kind. A horse crudely traced in the soft clay adhering to the walls of Montespan has been speared many times all over its body with a pointed object. In this cave the carcass of a bear modelled in clay had, judging by the bear skull found in the head position, been disguised in a bear pelt and ritually speared. Les Trois Frères, a third cave in the vicinity, reveals the famous picture of a man in animal disguise; he can reasonably be interpreted as the shaman or witch doctor who would officiate in such magical hunting ceremonies.

These indications of hunting ritual are clear enough to permit a tentative reconstruction of the kind of circumstances under which Magdalenian art was created. Hunting societies would usually consist of small bands of individuals whose time was mainly taken up with the business of daily survival. More advanced hunting peoples such as those of North America would have shamans or other religious officials and a complicated code of beliefs involving rituals and myths firmly held by the tribe. The perpetuation of such rituals would be regarded very seriously because the hunters believed that these would ensure their success in hunting. The position of shaman was one carrying great prestige and perhaps occasionally some immunity from everyday tasks. Ritual painting would be carried out

7
THE BRASSEMPOUY HEAD
Leptolithic, 30,000–20,000 BC
carved in ivory
h. 1·5 in (3·8 cm)
Musée des Antiquités Nationales,
Saint-Germain-en-Laye

This small head was found with other statuettes in the Grotte du Pape at Brassempouy in 1892. The mammoth ivory is better preserved in this specimen than in the others as it was protected by an overlying clay layer. The head is thought to be that of a girl, possibly wearing a hood, though the cross hatching may have been intended as hair. The features could be regarded as Caucasoid or even Mongoloid, and the high pronounced cheeks indicate the presence of a layer of fat which would be an adaption to the tundra climate.

under his supervision, perhaps by 'novices' or trainees. With the prestige would go great responsibility or power, but also the possibility of material benefit and the necessary leisure to perform their esteemed duties.

The Magdalenian phase is above all known by the numerous small art objects in bone and ivory from the cave occupations. Some are functional objects, notably spear throwers and perforated batons. Others do not seem to have had any function, as in the case of the beautiful bison and hyena from la Madeleine. Perhaps the highest point of cave art is in the engravings from the cave of Teyjat. Here the aurochs, horses and reindeer are executed with a magnificent fineness and accuracy of line. Another cave at Teyjat produced a baton with small engraved human-like figures called 'diablotins', which is typical of the way humans are often shown in half-animal and cartoon-like character in the Magdalenian. By the close of the last stage of the Magdalenian in southern France it seems that both the economy and culture had broken down in the face of a drastic altera-tion of the environment as the climate changed.

The extension of the Leptolithic phase is conventionally set apart under the name Mesolithic and has little art except skilfully made implements similar to those of the Leptolithic but often smaller. This was followed by the second major cycle of art in France which, although much more recent, is not represented by any comparable profusion of art. It may be called the Megalithic cycle because it is best represented in the great stone-constructed tombs called megaliths. The difference between the art of the Leptolithic and of the Megalithic eras is not only stylistic, but is reinforced by the fundamentally different nature of the communities which produced them. The Leptolithic peoples were hunters, living mostly in tundra and steppe where the winters were rigorously cold. The Megalithic communities were completely dependent on farming for their livelihood. They belonged mainly to the Neolithic or agricultural Stone Age, but their Megalithic tradition was still strong as metal objects arrived and while metallurgy was being established some 2000 years B.C.

The kinds of society in which the two cycles of art–Leptolithic and Megalithic–were created were radically different. The hunters would have been members of a tribal society, who followed their game over vast, sparsely populated territories. The farmers, who were more numerous and settled, used their collective Megalithic tombs over centuries. Although very little is known of their settlements, the growing of corn and the rearing of herds imposed a quite different sort of stamp on these communities, which were compelled to stay for most of the time with their cultivated plots. Tribal society was drastically modified as simple farming made possible the accumulation of wealth, and trading of varied goods led to a scale of material values. The respected hunter chief characteristic of hunting societies was giving way to the rich cattle owner and the warlords of an efficient food producing and metal using economy. Class barriers were cutting across and destroying tribal loyalties. The kind of shaman who had presided over the hunting rituals was giving way to a class of priests who were supported by a society increasingly concerned with the afterlife and the elaboracies of burial. The archaeologist, Childe, has spoken of this as the spread of a Megalithic religion, which is well represented in France.

The Megalithic art cycle

With the end of the last ice age, the hunters did not cease to exist, but probably became much more scattered. Some may have followed the animal herds north, other tribes probably died out, while others took to fishing and fowling–a food gathering existence with little of the glamour

8
STAFF WITH LEAPING HORSE
Magdalenian, c. 1300 BC
carved in reindeer antler
11 in (28 cm)
Musée des Antiquités Nationales,
Saint-Germain-en-Laye

This piece, a typical utilitarian art object, was found by B. Betirac about 1955 in the Montastruc rock shelter near Bruniquel, a rich Magdalenian site. It is almost certainly a spear thrower, even though the hook at the weighted end is missing. The perfora-tion at the grip end is presumably for suspension from the belt or a thong. The position of the horse is partly determined by the shape of the antler, but it is a most effective and elegant piece of sculpture.

of the mammoth and reindeer hunters.

The spread of agriculturalists across Europe, bringing ceramics with them, marks one of the most decisive changes in Europe's history. The primitive cultures of central and eastern Europe had a limited folk art, known to us mainly from their painted pottery. In France no such painted ceramics have been commonly found. New styles of art are associated with the spread of the building of Megalithic tombs, which involve rock engraving, but are otherwise quite unlike the Leptolithic. These tombs usually consist of stone-lined passages or galleries leading to chambers in which the dead were interred. The main designs of Megalithic art are axes; stylised human figures, especially in the form of 'menhirs'; rows of meandering lines often of inverted U-shape; spirals and double spirals or circles grading into 'oculi' or eye designs.

The axe designs reflect the fact that one of the most important pieces of equipment of the early farmers was the polished stone axe. Such axes were sometimes works of art themselves made of a beautiful green jadeite. The axe was essential in felling the woodlands prior to the cultivation of food plants. Although a few surviving tribes of hunter-gatherers, such as the Tardenoisians, did turn to agriculture by borrowing domestic grains and animals, the great majority of the unprecedentedly numerous settlers of the Neolithic age were immigrants from elsewhere in Europe bringing with them new equipment such as the polished stone axe.

Statue menhirs were laboriously carved in hard rocks and show curiously stylized people with their arms folded flat across their bodies and the features compressed into the typical milestone-like shape. The example from St Sernin in Aveyron is especially good and other characteristic examples are known from Gard.

Megalithic tombs and constructions are important to us not only because they have been used as canvases for art, but also because they exhibit some of the earliest real architecture in western Europe. It is a striking fact that we know little of the houses and villages the builders lived in; most of them were probably very flimsy and simple. Like the Egyptian pharaohs, the megalith builders lavished effort and skill on homes for the dead, not for the living. Among the Stone Age farmers who built most of the megaliths, there is little indication of social strata or of much wealth. With the arrival of metal technology and especially the exploitation of precious metals, there was a sharp increase in the occurrence of rich objects such as bracelets and maceheads. This has been seen as the rise of a warrior aristocracy whose wealth may have rested more heavily on stockbreeding than that of their predecessors; but raiding as well as rearing may have been an accepted activity.

The arrival in the archaeological record of a distinctive drinking vessel called the 'beaker' gives the first indications of such an aristocracy; various precious and metal objects have been found although most workers think that it was not the 'Beaker People' themselves who established metallurgy. The beakers are among the most attractively decorated ceramics of prehistoric times. They are often found in megaliths, particularly in Iberia and France, suggesting that Beaker 'chieftains', if such they were, had become integrated into the farming communities who adhered to the Megalithic religion. By the time of the fully developed Bronze Age, the megaliths had largely gone out of use except possibly in the Lot region in south-west France, and art was on the wane. It was not to see a revival before the impact of external influences; classical from the Mediterranean and Celtic from the European continent.

Desmond Collins

9

THE STONE AVENUES OF
CARNAC
late Neolithic to early Bronze Age,
2000–1500 BC
sandstone
Morbihan Department, Britanny

Carnac is the most spectacular of the Megalithic monuments in France, and occupies a similar position to that of Stonehenge in Britain, both in time and as the geographical centre of a great complex of Megalithic architecture. Some of the dozens of parallel avenues stretch for over a mile. They are generally oriented east to west and the stones, most of which are unshaped or barely modified, tend to be larger towards the west.

10

BATON DE COMMANDEMENT

Magdalenian 12,000–11,000 BC
engraved on reindeer antler
12 in (30·5 cm)
Musée des Antiquités Nationales,
Saint-Germain-en-Laye

This baton from Abri Mège near Teyjat
has two perforations, one round, the other
oval. The photograph is of a rolled out
plaster cast showing both sides so that the
delicate engravings are more clearly visible.
In the middle is a large galloping horse with
a smaller one behind; snake like creatures
meander around the other figures. Most
interesting are the little 'diablotins', half
human and half mountain goat, which
appear to be hopping about.

11 *bottom*

THE HUNTING ACCIDENT

Leptolithic, possibly Magdalenian,
c. 15,000 BC
painted in black
in the shaft of the Lascaux cave

The cave was discovered as recently as 1940.
The painting itself is puzzling. The bison
has a spear through it and appears to be
both dead and disembowelled; the man
may also be dead, but because of the crude
drawing it is difficult to be sure. Below him
is a totem stick or perhaps a spear thrower.
The rhinoceros is usually thought to be
trotting away from the scene, but it has
been suggested that he is part of a separate
scene.

12

THE VENUS OF LAUSSEL

c. 25,000 to 22,000 BC
probably de Noailles culture
limestone
h. 17·75 in (46 cm)
Musée d'Aquitaine, Bordeaux

This bas-relief was originally found carved on a slab which formed part of a rock shelter at the foot of the cliffs below the château of Laussel in the Beune valley. Even though not technically a statuette it clearly belongs with the 'venus' series; in side view the stomach is very protruding and the whole gives an excellent three-dimensional impression. The bison horn held in the right hand is reminiscent of the cornucopia of classical times.

13

SPEARED BISON, NIAUX

Leptolithic; probably Magdalenian,
c. 13,000 BC
painted with black manganese dioxide pigment
35 in (88·9 cm)
in the cave of Niaux near Tarascon, Ariège

This is one of several speared bison in the 'salon noir' of the Niaux cave, which was first recognised as prehistoric art in 1906 although it had been known as a cave long before. The 'salon noir' is some 700 yards from the entrance, reached through a spacious dry cave passage. For many workers the paintings of Niaux represent the climax of prehistoric art, late in the Magdalenian era.

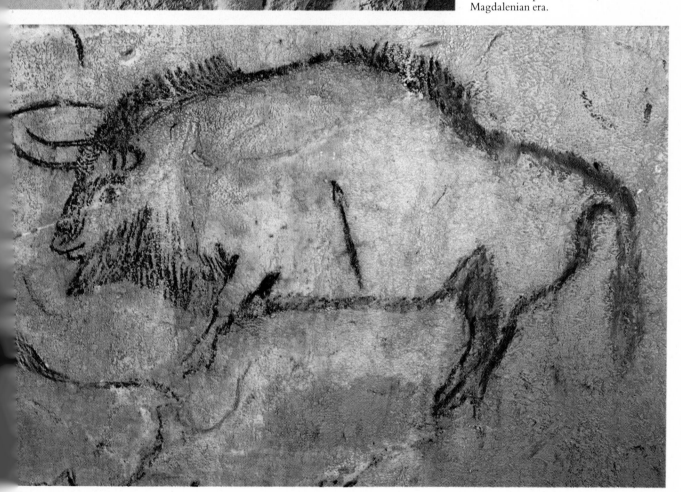

14

BULL AUROCHS

Leptolithic; possibly about 15,000 BC
painted in black manganese dioxide
156 in (380 cm)
in the axial gallery of Lascaux cave

A date of approximately 15,000 BC has been obtained from charcoal in an occupation area deep inside the cave, which probably relates to the Magdalenian culture. This occupation was some forty yards from the present entrance by which the cave was discovered in 1940 by four boys, and seems to be one of the few examples of early man living further in a cave than the daylight penetrates. A lamp was found here, indicating that it was by burning oil or fat that he was able to work in the caves.

Modern Marseilles retains few traces of her classical origins. It was however some years before 600 B.C., after their flight from Persian domination, that the citizens of the Greek city Phocaea landed on the site near the mouth of the Rhône and founded Greek Massilia. The most notable survivals are the beautiful coins with the head of Artemis, the goddess of hunting, on one side and a lion on the other which were minted in the city. There are also a number of stone representations of the goddess which depict her as a patroness of fertility rather than of chastity–a typical eastern Greek shift of emphasis. Although a theatre and part of the city wall were discovered, they have not been preserved and it is the massive walls of the trading post at Sainte-Blaise a few miles away, which remind us that the elegant outdoor lives of the Greeks, with their theatres, temples and market places, could only be achieved if their armies (of conscript citizens) were vigilant and the defences of their cities strong.

Unlike the colonies in Greece and Sicily, whose peace was mainly threatened by other Greeks, Marseilles was faced by the formidable number of native tribes in her hinterland, who doubtless welcomed the luxury goods provided by this 'Hong Kong' of the ancient world but at any time might have to resent her presence. These peoples, known collectively as Celts, had come into existence as a result of the inter-marriage of nomads from the Eurasian steppe with local women. They adopted a settled way of life in hill forts with earth or stone ramparts, containing a cluster of wattle or drystone huts. Nevertheless they preserved from their former way of life the custom of decorating themselves and their armour. Their art remained portable, and since they were a primitive community dependent on flocks and herds and subsistance agriculture, only the ruling classes could afford more than a few brooches and trinkets, though this privileged minority indulged itself with very elaborate and often imported luxuries.

Finds of wine jars (amphorae) and Greek painted pottery from hill forts situated on both sides of the river Rhône and in central France provided evidence of expensive drinking habits amongst these chieftains. When they died, their tombs were simple but often contained objects of astonishing value like the magnificent cauldron from eastern Greece or Etruscan Italy, ornamented with griffin heads and standing on a fine tripod found at Sainte-Colombe-sur-Seine. The most famous of these 'chieftain burials' was at Vix, where the body of a young princess was found lying upon a bier made of a dismantled cart, ancestor to the modern gypsies' caravan. Upon her head was a gold diadem while scattered around her were silver cups, Athenian black-figure cups, wine flagons and the largest bronze wine-mixing bowl (krater) to have survived from ancient times.

Celtic France

Social revolution swept away these sixth-century chieftains, and a new aristocracy representing a larger element in each tribe took their place. Tombs became poorer and there were fewer imported objects. On the other hand, a truly original Celtic art began to emerge as classical elements such as the palmette combined with traditional native patterns. The result was a decorative, abstract style, which exploited the curved line with great brilliance and was very suitable for both weapons and ornaments. This is the visual expression of the boasting and self-dramatisation that ran through every aspect of Celtic life. Looking at the delicately engraved and finely balanced sword scabbard from Cernon-sur-Coole (Museum of Châlons-sur-Marne) or admiring the S-curves on the openwork chariot fittings from La Bouvandau and Cuperly (Saint-German), one should visualise a fierce warrior standing in his two-horse chariot charging down

15
HELMET FROM AMFREVILLE
fourth century BC
bronze covered with gold foil and with enamel inlay
6·5 in (16 cm)
Louvre, Paris

This helmet was found in an old channel of the river Seine and may have been an offering to the deity of the river after a successful battle. It is an excellent example of abstract Celtic decoration; the Celts excelled in the art of metalwork and smiths were highly valued in the community. A helmet of such beauty would have distinguished a powerful warrior from the ordinary men in the tribe.

16
HUMAN FIGURE
FROM ROQUEPERTEUSE

third century BC
limestone
h. 39·5 in (100 cm)
Musée Archéologique, Marseilles

This statue probably represents a god as it
was found in a native shrine; its dignified
bearing and dress convey a feeling of
power. Although the stiff, hierarchic
stance contrasts with the humanism of
contemporary works in the Greek world,
the artist has clearly been influenced by the
Greeks of Massilia in his delicate modelling
of the anatomy and also in his provision of
a stone plinth for the statue.

upon his enemies dazzling them with the brilliance of his arms and the
wealth of gold or coral inlay upon his shield and helmet. The victor would **15**
strip his dead rival of all his fine weapons and ornaments, decapitate him
and carry his head back to his hill fort as a trophy. The encampment would
be lit by firelight, emphasising the richness of the gold neckbands or
torques worn by all noble freemen as a sign of status. There are fine
examples of these from Fenouillet and some even richer pieces from
Lasgraisses in the Musée Paul Dupuy, Toulouse. However most of
this Celtic treasure has disappeared, much of it in ancient times when it
was melted down and refashioned by the Romans and the peoples who
succeeded them.

The remains of a recently excavated stone temple or shrine at Roque- **16**
pertuse suggest the savage rituals of Celtic religion. Here sit two squatting
gods modelled in a dignified Greek fashion but wearing native dress and
neck torques symbolising power. Also from this site comes a strange
double arch, upon which a vulture-like bird crouches as guardian of the
severed human heads displayed in niches (Musée Archéologique, Marseilles).
At another such shrine, Entremont, there are both niches and symbolic
representations of severed heads in stone, as well as a pyramid of four
superimposed heads (Musée Granet, Aix-en-Provence). The spirit of this
compelling yet repulsive faith is most clearly manifested in the limestone
statue of a reptilian, man-eating monster found at Noves and now in the **17**
Musée Lapidaire at Avignon. Sadly, Greek Massilia had little effect on the
aspirations of the Celts and it was only with the advent of Roman power
in the second and first centuries B.C. that the territory of modern France,
which the Romans (using their own word for the Celts–Galli) called
Gallia (Gaul), was precipitated into the civilised world.

The Roman conquest

Southern France was conquered by Rome in the late second century B.C.
Indeed it is still called Provence, a reminder of the fact that it was a Roman
province when the wilder lands to the north–'Hairy Gaul' (or Gallia
Comata) were still unsubdued. Some seventy years later, however, Julius
Caesar's brilliant victories finally brought these areas under Roman
control, and 'Gaul was divided into three parts': Aquitania in the west,
Lugdunensis in the centre and east, Belgica in the north. The old Province,
now called Narbonensis, made up a fourth part. Caesar's commentaries
pay tribute to the reckless bravery of opponents like Vercingetorix of the
Arverni tribe, but one must not sentimentalise the conflict as one between
Roman 'storm troopers' and gallant 'free Gauls'. The Gauls never ceased
to be barbarians and particularly warlike ones, while the Romans brought
peace. The achievements of Celtic art–shields and swords–are far
removed from the comfortable and civilised life epitomised by the little
silver cup from Alesia with its naturalistic decoration of myrtle sprays. **24**

Roman civilization had a didactic quality, and in the first century after
the conquest a two-sided propaganda policy was adopted towards the
natives. On the one hand, victory monuments impressed on them the
might of the Roman legions, while, on the other, alluring public amenities
in the newly founded cities demonstrated the advantages of Roman peace.
The centre of this indoctrination process was southern Gaul, the old
Provincia of Narbonensis, where many retired soldiers were settled by
Julius Caesar and Augustus.

At Orange stands a famous triple arch on which are represented battle
scenes between Gauls and Romans. If one makes allowance for artistic
licence, which idealises the combatants and dramatises their gestures, one
can see why the legions won. The Roman is disciplined, a professional at

his job (though that may be dealing death to his opponents) and even in this desperate hour the Celtic host is merely a conglomeration of individuals fighting for personal honour. The decoration of the arch shows a liveliness and attention to detail that suggests the first-hand knowledge of a native artist composing a lesson in stone to remind future ages of the fate of those who opposed Rome.

25, 27 The impact is all the greater if we study the reliefs of captives on the arches of Saint-Rémy (Glanum) and Carpentras, particularly the latter. The fate of the prisoners depicted here was not pleasant. At worst, they would grace the triumph of the victorious general in Rome after which they were strangled, while the best they could expect was slavery in some distant province either as gladiators, where most would doubtless have a quick end, or as labourers in the mines or on great estates, where death would be greeted as a release from perpetual toil.

We miss some of these implications in the more formal classical monuments such as the representation of the captives in the museum at Saint-Bertrand-de-Comminges, or the cenotaph to Gaius and Lucius

28 Caesar at Saint-Rémy with its mythological battle scenes. Here, victory is seen as something heroic in which the great gods of Rome have a share. Above Monaco at La Turbie stands a circular structure surrounded by the simple columns of the Doric order. It commemorates Augustus's victory over the Alpine tribes and was designed to be seen from afar spreading its message of invincible power, which was not to be seriously challenged for two and a half centuries.

The veteran colonies established in the late first century B.C. (including Vienne, Nîmes, Arles, Orange, Fréjus and Lyons) served as models for the urbanisation of the rest of Gaul. Roman civilisation, no less than Greek, depended on the establishment of city communities rather than on a rural peasantry, which merely provided raw materials and a cheap reservoir of labour. Each town was self-governing with annual magistrates (decurions), joint mayors of the council (ordo), which consisted of a hundred men elected from among the wealthier citizens. Under their auspices fine public buildings were erected which still impress us today. These surviving theatres, amphitheatres, temples and aqueducts reflect the commercial success of the ancient settlements and the business acumen of the retired soldiers and their descendants who lived in them.

Temples and theatres

There are two complete classical temples in Gaul: the Maison Carrée at Nîmes, dedicated by Augustus's son-in-law Agrippa in 16 B.C. (and rededicated by his grandsons Gaius and Lucius in A.D. 1–2) and that at

26 Vienne constructed between 27 B.C. and A.D. 14 as a temple of Rome and Augustus and later reconsecrated to include Augustus's wife Livia after her death (in A.D. 29) and subsequent deification in 42. Both these buildings have an official character far removed from the private devotions of the common man as is shown by their formal dedicatory inscriptions. As for the constructions themselves, apart from the central shrine (or cella), which housed an image or images of a god and the temple plate and implements used in purifying and sacrificing the animal, they were little more than an imposing façade of columns like the great temples of Greece before them.

Although the remains in Gaul do not compare with those at Leptis Magna and Sabratha in Libya, enough survives to build up a picture of a Roman theatre in France by drawing on a number of them for elements of design. The back wall of the stage building (scaena) at Orange stands to a height of 120 feet and is 338 feet wide. It was fronted by the backdrop of

23 marble columns of which vestiges survive here and at Arles, and orna-

17

MAN-EATING MONSTER
FROM NOVES
probably pre-conquest
Coudoux limestone
h. 3 ft 9 in (112 cm)
Musée Lapidaire, Avignon

This statue gives expression to the nightmare terrors of the Celtic subconscious, and clearly shows the savage aspect of a religion which frequently called for human sacrifice as appeasement to the terrible deities. Its pose recalls the Entremont figures and the severed heads are familiar features in Celtic art. The inventiveness of the artist in producing an almost human arm from the creature's chin contrasts strongly with the humanistic traditions of the classical world.

mented with statues. Turning to Vienne we can still see the marble frieze of wild animals that decorated the stage (pulpitum) and the splendid auditorium which had a pit (orchestra) paved in violet breccia. Here important people sat; Vienne has eight seats of honour made of rose breccia and white marble (similar rich ornamentation can be seen at Lyons). Behind were tiers of seats (cavea), which held some ten thousand spectators, a very large number of people, perhaps a quarter of the population of the town. Since most theatres were terraced into the hillside, it was necessary to provide access to the seating from the upper tiers and at Vaison-la-Romaine much of the colonnade that ran around the top of the cavea still exists. The decoration would be completed by numerous statues and altars to Apollo, god of the arts, so that one might well imagine that the predominant motives in erecting these palaces of culture were artistic and religious. In fact they were conceived in a spirit of bitter inter-city rivalry, whose causes are often hard to discover. Tacitus tells us how Vienne and Lyons tried to pay off old scores against one another in the civil war of A.D. 69, but generally the Pax Romana meant that the only course each city could take was to emulate and outshine its neighbours by the splendour of its public buildings.

At both Vienne and Lyons there is a small theatre or odeon originally richly furnished and roofed which was probably used for concerts and recitals. As the use of a Greek name suggests, they are an indication of the minority tastes of men who came from abroad or were attracted to the cultivated life in the older provinces of the empire. Most citizens in Gaul had different tastes. In the north many of the theatres (les Arènes at Paris, for example) assumed the function of amphitheatres or bear pits where music and drama could only have provided an accompaniment to spectacles of the greatest brutality and sadism. In the south of Gaul, amphitheatres are twice the size of the theatres, and those of Nîmes and
23 Arles are considered to be among the best-preserved in the Roman world.

The Gallo-Romans

The Roman colonies of southern France remained more wealthy and sophisticated than the new towns of the north, which replaced old tribal hill forts. These, however, did not lag too far behind and throughout Gaul artists benefited from Roman administration, which led to the construction and embellishment of public buildings in the cities as well as private houses and religious shrines in both town and country. A key role in this spread of building activity was played by Lyons, which was more than merely a colony since it was also the meeting place of representatives from the tribes of Gaul. From 12 B.C., they came annually to pledge their loyalty to the Roman state and to discuss grievances at the altar of Rome and Augustus. The altar was a very beautiful structure, probably something like the Ara Pacis in Rome; coins suggest that it had a richly ornamented screen around it. Statues of winged victories stood at the corners.
19 One can judge what these were like from a little bronze figurine in the Musée des Beaux Arts, Lyons, which reflects a full-size masterpiece as fine as anything produced in the late first century B.C. The effect of the meeting place on the delegates was to increase their respect for Roman religion, art and dress: indeed they came as Aedui or Senones (to name two tribes) but left feeling like Romans. These sentiments were encouraged, especially by good emperors like Claudius, who saw that the best hope for the empire was to give its inhabitants dignity and pride in their status. In his wisdom he knew that the remnants of the old tribal nobility and the rising new aristocracy of the commercial classes were avid to emulate Roman manners and dress. These Gallo-Romans built

18

TOMBSTONE OF THE SCULPTOR AMABILIS
second to third century AD
limestone
h. 38·5 in (98 cm)
Musée Archéologique, Bordeaux

This is one of the few representations of an artist from Roman France. He sits dressed in his working clothes, holding the tools of his trade; a chisel in his left hand and a mason's mallet in his right, as though he were himself carving the pilasters that flank the relief. The inscription tells us that the tombstone was erected at the behest of the artist's brother Amandus. The names of both Amabilis and Amandus suggest that the family may have come originally from the east. When the towns were ravaged by Germanic tribesmen, the citizens uprooted even the sacred monuments to help build defences, and this tombstone was, like many others, re-used as a building stone in the city wall erected after the invasions of the third century AD.

19
WINGED VICTORY
probably second or first century BC
bronze
h. 9 in (23 cm)
Musée de la Civilisation
Gallo-Romaine, Lyons

This is a contemporary model of one of the
statues which flanked the altar of Rome and
Augustus at Lyons. The altar was erected
in 12 BC as a focus for provincial loyalty to
the empire. This in part took an aesthetic
form as both the altar itself and the monuments and sculpture that accompanied it
were in the late Hellenistic style which
Rome had made her own. Celtic art is here
decisively abandoned in favour of the
classical art of the Mediterranean. The
statuette itself may have been merely an
ornament, perhaps a fitting from a candel-
abrum or some other item of furniture,
without religious significance.

administrative centres, gateways, bridges and public baths as well as
theatres, amphitheatres, aqueducts and temples. Even their private houses
were constructed in the same style as those of Italy.

A traveller would have approached the town along a fine metalled
road (probably constructed in the late first century B.C. by Agrippa who
built the Maison Carrée), passing through a countryside which was as
prosperous then as it is now. Houses ranged from humble crofts to great
palaces or villas, such as those at Montmaurin (covering $44\frac{1}{2}$ acres) or
Chiragan near Martres-Tolosanes which were centres of great estates. The
lord of Chiragan, for such indeed he was, had a portrait gallery of fifty-
four busts of both imperial and family figures, and seeing them today in
the Musée Saint-Raymond, Toulouse, one can see how important the
ancestor was to the Roman. His personality was perpetuated in the death
mask or marble bust that graced his tomb, memorial or ultimately the
dwelling of his descendant. When a Roman died his tomb was dedicated
to the shades of the ancestors whom he now joined. Apart from these
busts, a villa owner would decorate his rooms with frescos and mosaic
floors; there was also a bath suite—all features found in the town houses
which the self-supporting country estate attempted to resemble. The
finest vessels were of silver like those which have been found at Graincourt-lès-Havrincourt and are now in the Louvre.

The aqueducts, water pipelines borne upon arches or earth embank-
ments, ran for as much as seventy miles in some cases. In the south
around Fréjus there are some fine remains and the famous bridge across the **34**
river Gard, thirty miles from Nîmes, carries an aqueduct. Bridges spanned
the rivers and were usually utilitarian in design though they sometimes
carried ornamental gateways. The Pont Flavien near Saint-Chamas and
the bridge at Saintes of which only a gate survives were built by priests of
Rome and Augustus, who had sat in the assembly at Lyons and were
inspired to create beautiful and useful structures for their communities.

Near the town one would have passed row after row of tombs ranging
from simple stones to great towers. A large number of tombstones survive,
many of them executed by artisans for artisans, who wished to be com-
memorated as they were in life, either at work or at play. Thus at Rheims
there is the clogmaker seated on his short bench. At Dijon there is a
representation of a wine shop with a high counter and other types of shop
are depicted on tombstones at Rouen, Metz and Grand, to take a few
examples. One of the best is a relief from Cabrieres-d'Aygues, now in the
Musée Lapidaire, Avignon, showing a river barge being towed along the
river Durance. Sometimes we find the tombstone of an artist, like that of
the sculptor Amabilis of Bordeaux, though we shall never know what he **18**
made in that great and important city.

The town gates at Autun were built at the same time as the walls in the **20**
first century A.D. Both the Porte Saint-André and the Porte d'Arroux
suggest the classical simplicity and order of that golden age. Elsewhere
gates were built as triumphal arches without walls. The Porte de Mars at
Rheims and the Porte Noire, Besançon, reflect a more pompous attitude
and a pride that disappeared during the terrible years of the barbarian
invasions less than a century after they were built.

Inside the town, the most important place was the great square or
forum with the town hall (or basilica) on one side and a classical temple
dedicated to the great god of the Roman state, Jupiter Greatest and Best,
on the other. Although the ground plans are often known, in most places
the forum remained the centre of the town even after the Middle Ages
and has since been lost below buildings. But in Narbonne, Arles, Bavai

20

PORTE ST ANDRE

late first century BC to early first century AD
Autun

This was the east gate of the Roman city of Augustodun, capital of the Aedui, founded to replace the ancient hill fort of Bibracte. Its simple plan with two central passageways for vehicles and one on each side for pedestrians, and its restrained decoration, are reminiscent of other early gateways such as the Porte d'Auguste at Nîmes. The pilasters of the upper storey inspired the twelfth-century builders who imitated them in the choir and nave of the great Romanesque cathedral of Autun.

21

HIPPOLYTUS AND PHAEDRA

detail of a sarcophagus
third century AD
marble
41 × 92·5 in (105 × 235 cm)
Musée Lapidaire, Arles

The classical myth of the rejection of the love of Phaedra by Hippolytus is interpreted here as the triumph of purity over vice. The dying hero is shown on the left-hand face of the sarcophagus in order to emphasise the necessity for the good to undergo suffering. Moral values and life after death assumed great importance for pagans as well as Christians in the uncertain times of the late third and early fourth centuries.

and Rheims the underground storehouses that lay beneath their fora still exist, for in a large town basic provisions had to be conserved against crop failure and hard winters. At Grand the basilica survives with a floor composed of square panels of mosaic, a long-wearing surface designed to stand up to the tread of many feet. One basilica is mentioned in literature– that erected at Nîmes by the Emperor Hadrian in honour of his adopted mother, Plotina, and thus a rare example of imperial patronage in Gaul.

Next or near to the forum were the baths, which played an important part in Roman life. Most people would go there daily to bathe, exercise and transact business, for it was the only convenient public meeting-place in the town away from the bustle of the forum and the street corner. The greatest surviving example of a cold room (frigidarium) is the Thermes de Cluny in the heart of Paris standing to the height of forty-eight feet. The so-called Palace of Constantine at Arles is a hot room (caldarium) so splendid that in later times it was thought to be an imperial palace. Unfortunately we see these buildings without their mosaics and statues and with the marble veneer stripped from their walls. Sometimes vestiges remain: the *Minerva of Poitiers*, a deliberate copy of archaic sixth-century   **29** work, was found in the hot room of a bath.

The last class of public building to note is the Romano-Celtic temple, which is quite different from the stately classical type already examined. The Romanised Gauls still hankered after the old religion and although they were prepared to give their own gods a Roman guise and to erect temples, they still performed distinctive rites and built religious buildings whose prototypes lay in the north. These had a square or occasionally a circular shrine, with a surrounding colonnade for processions and the occasional display of the temple plate to the public who waited in the sacred enclosure. Often these temples were very large. The square Tower of Janus at Autun is eighty feet high and the circular Tower of Vesunna at Perigueux is ninety feet high.

One can learn a little of the cults practised in places like these from sculptured reliefs found in them or elsewhere. Those preserved at Paris in the Musée de Cluny, originally formed part of a monumental column erected to Jupiter in honour of the Emperor Tiberius by the Corporation of Boatmen at Paris (Nautae Parisiaci) early in the first century. They show not only Roman gods–Jupiter, Vulcan and Minerva–but also native deities, for example Esus. Ancient gods recur frequently; often only names are known to us and their significance is lost. But one aspect of Romano-Celtic religion comes truly alive: the healing cults with their temples and fountains for the friendly nymphs who lived at the sources of rivers and by running water often many miles from a town. Here the faithful sick came to pray and, when they were cured, they left offerings of little wooden or stone figures, crude but direct in meaning. In some places, such as at the source of the Seine, fine works of art have been found, for instance the bronze of the goddess Sequana, while at Besançon   **32** and Nîmes, impressive classical buildings were constructed and dedicated to the local deities. This is not surprising when one considers that the Arverni paid forty million sesterces for a statue of Mercury by the famous Greek sculptor Zenodorus and that the treasure of Berthouville now in the Louvre was given to a local temple of Mercury by Romanised Gauls. In both cases Mercury was a native god, perhaps Esus or some other being whose name is lost, but whom the Roman conquerors recognised as one of their own deities.

The private houses of the countryside have been mentioned. In the town the artisans had their workshop houses while the wealthy lived in dwellings similar to those that still exist around the Mediterranean today. Around the central open space (atrium) rooms radiated in all directions, paved with mosaics and with a considerable array of cupboards, couches, tables and sculptures scattered around. Today one can see only the mosaic floors, but these almost certainly reflect the style of the walls. The House of the Ibex at Saint-Rémy has the simple carpet-like floor of the late republic, and its walls would also have been simple; the representation of the Drunkenness of Bacchus at Lyons, on the other hand, is drawn from a painting as is the celebrated circus scene in the same city. Almost all the **33** mosaics and sculpture that survive were executed by firms of travelling **35** craftsmen with copy books rather like our books of wallpaper. At Lillebonne there is a mosaic showing Apollo, Daphne and hunting scenes signed by the head, or at least the leading craftsman, of one such firm, Titus Senius Felix of Puteoli in Italy and his African apprentice, Amor.

Early Christians

Little has been said of the years after the mid-third century because the barbarians who sacked the cities in the third century were very thorough. Although local emperors set themselves up in Gaul during the third century to deal with the menace, the structure of Roman civilisation was shattered in a few years. Attention became focused on religion. Foreign cults including those of Mithras, Isis, the Magna Mater (Cybele) and Orpheus vied with the eventually all-conquering faith of Christianity. Comparing earlier tombstones with the Arles coffin showing the Greek hero Hippolytus rejecting the fleshly temptations, which are all that **21** Phaedra can offer him, one can see how the art of this period, like that of our own day, was haunted by the shadows of fear, impermanence and death. Just as the art of the twentieth century has fragmented and transfigured the settled order of the nineteenth, so the fourth century broke with earlier periods. Christian sarcophagi take up the story. There are elements of the 'comic strip' in these coffins which are understandable **22** when we realise that they stood in great open cemeteries like those of Les Aliscamps near Arles and were designed for the edification of all. Classical culture was confined to the few, but Christianity promised salvation even to the illiterate.

The churches of the early Christian communities of Gaul have largely disappeared, although even today St Martin, an early saint, is revered in remote villages where the first Christian places of worship existed in the later fourth century. The baptistries at Aix, Fréjus and Riez still stand, though they have lost much of their decoration. These stately columns and arcades have lasted for a thousand and a half years to remind us that Christianity was a legacy of Rome and that the church was to be the greatest patron of the arts for many hundreds of years.

Roman Gaul itself, however, ended in the fifth century with the arrival of Visigoths and Franks. The mass of people would not have noticed; politics would have had little effect on the peasant or the bands of landless men (bagaudae) who infested the countryside. For the aristocracy it was different; Sidonius Apollinaris, the warrior bishop of Clermont, the chief city of the Arverni, continued the fight until 475 when the authorities of the declining Western Empire ceded the Auvergne to the Visigoths. Upon the same ground that Vercingetorix defied Caesar and voiced his implacable hatred of Rome, the bishop threw out his own denunciations of a Rome which had betrayed him to the barbarian. Ironically, the story of Roman Gaul – now France (land of the Franks) – ends in the same place as it began.

Martin Henig

22

THE PETER SARCOPHAGUS
fourth to fifth century AD
21·5 × 87·5 in (55 × 222 cm)
crypt of St Maximin, Var

In this sarcophagus, probably from a southern Gaulish workshop, the aim of the artist is to tell a story rather than to satisfy the eye. In this case Christ is telling Peter that he will betray him, and the repetition of the cock in the next scene emphasises the fact that the sarcophagus would have stood in an open cemetery as a pictorial 'poor man's bible'. The deep grooves made with a bow-drill produce the black shadows which give the relief its restless character; here classical canons of taste have been abandoned in favour of medieval spirituality.

23

THEATRE AND AMPHITHEATRE

Arles

Roman theatres were places of entertainment rather than serious drama, and the fashion was for variety shows and pantomimes which made lavish use of scenic effects and required an opulent setting. Like many of the more important Roman theatres built in the time of Augustus, this one was originally richly furnished with statues. Unlike those at Lyons and Orange, the auditorium is not terraced into the hillside but is supported on arcades. The second-century amphitheatre, a utilitarian structure dedicated to slaughter, is the largest in Gaul, and could hold 26,000 spectators.

24

CUP FROM ALESIA

first century BC
silver, h. 4·4 in (11 cm)
Musée des Antiquités Nationales,
Saint-Germain-en-Laye

The cup is in the late Hellenistic style and was undoubtedly made by a Greek artist; the naturalistic decoration showing sprays of myrtle presents a contrast with native metalwork of this date. It probably belonged to a Roman officer in Caesar's army, who lost it while besieging the native hillfort. This popular type of subject was often imitated in pottery.

25 *below*

CAPTIVE GAULS

relief on arch, first century AD
courtyard of the Palais de Justice, Carpentras

In Roman art, prisoners representing the tribe defeated in battle were often shown chained to a tree, as in this relief. It is likely that a Gaulish sculptor worked here as the figures are boldly outlined as though the techniques of the craft were unfamiliar, and the folds in the garments are presented as abstract patterns in the manner of Celtic art. The sympathy which the artist displays in his anguished portrayal of the right-hand prisoner's face would have been shared by many Romans who contrasted the innocence of the savage with the corruption of city life.

26

ROMAN TEMPLE

early first century AD
Vienne

The temple has a façade with six columns and five free-standing columns on each side of the central shrine or cella. The last bay consists of two pilasters united by a wall. It was constructed between 27 BC and AD 14 as a temple of Rome and Augustus and afterwards reconsecrated to include Livia after her death in AD 29 and subsequent deification. This shows that it was intended to symbolise the presence of Rome in Gaul rather than to appeal to the religious instincts of the people.

27, 28

ARCH AND MAUSOLEUM

*c. 40 BC and first century BC respectively
near Saint-Rémy, Provence*

The arch is the northern entrance to the
Roman city of Glanum; it also commemorates Roman victories in Gaul. Reliefs of
bound prisoners still survive on each side
and there are winged victories in the
spandrels. Outside the gate, as befits a
memorial to the dead, is the mausoleum of
the grandsons of Augustus, Gaius and
Lucius Caesar, with battle scenes around
the plinth conceived in a mythological
style borrowed from Pergamum in Asia
Minor. The architectural design also shows
Greek influence.

29

THE MINERVA OF POITIERS

*first or second century AD
marble, h. 60 in (152 cm)
Musée des Beaux Arts, Poitiers*

This statue, which probably stood in a
private suite of baths, is a deliberate copy
of an archaic work made in the sixth
century BC. The forward gaze, enigmatic
smile and trailing hair are all foreign to the
conventional art of the period, reflecting
the personal taste of one citizen of Poitiers,
but the Romans were a conservative
people and similar statues are known from
this period.

30 *below and overleaf*

THE VIX KRATER

*c. 520 BC
bronze, h. 64 in (164 cm)
Musée Archéologique, Châtillon-sur-Seine*

In antiquity wine was always diluted with
water, so large mixing bowls were
necessary. This krater from a burial at Vix
must have arrived at the hill fort of Mont
Lassois, by way of trade or as a diplomatic
gift from Massilia. It was almost certainly
made in a Greek city of southern Italy,
perhaps at Tarentum, a colony of Sparta.
Although no other bronze vessel of this
quality survives from this period, Hero-
dotus tells of a similar krater which the
Spartans sent to Croesus in Lydia and
which was stolen by the men of Samos.

32

THE GODDESS SEQUANA

second century AD
bronze
h. 12 in (30 cm)
Musée Archéologique, Dijon

This statue, found at the source of the river Seine, combines the classical style with the Celtic and is typical of much of the best art of Roman Gaul. The goddess was venerated as a patroness of healing at the Seine sanctuary. The vessel has a prow in the form of a duck's head relating to the native belief in the power of birds as servants and messengers of the gods. Swans had been long regarded in Europe as sacred to the sun, while in Celtic times waterfowl were associated with the forces of healing.

31 *below*

DETAIL FROM THE VIX KRATER (30)

The frieze of foot soldiers (hoplites) and men in chariots was designed to appeal to the Celtic love of sportsmanship and warfare, and the ornate handles to the barbarian's taste for decoration.

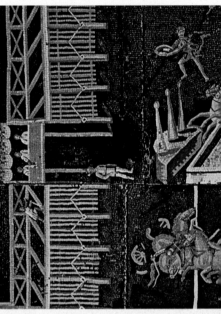

33
CIRCUS MOSAIC
second century AD
52 × 126 in (132 × 319 cm)
Musée de la Civilisation Gallo-Romaine,
Lyons

This mosaic found at Lyons is very similar
to others in Spain, Tunisia and Italy, and
like them was taken from a pattern book
which included subjects from paintings as
well as carpet designs. The absence of base
lines and the diagrammatic form of representation shows a drift away from formal
Classicism to the more symbolic art of
later times.

34
PONT DU GARD
c. 19 BC
Nîmes

Among the most famous examples of
Roman engineering, this was one of the
buildings erected in Roman Gaul by order
of Augustus's stepson Agrippa. It forms
part of the Nîmes aqueduct which carries
water to the city from springs thirty miles
away. At the point where it crosses the
river Gard it ceases to be a mere pipeline in
stone, and assumes the characteristic form
of superimposed arches, in this case
arranged in three tiers of six, eleven and
thirty-five. It epitomises the Roman genius
for surmounting difficulties of terrain in
the simplest and most elegant manner.

35
STATUE OF APOLLO
possibly second century AD, gilded bronze
h. 76·75 in (194 cm), Louvre, Paris

This statue from Lillebonne which copies
a Greek work of the fourth century and
stands slightly over life-size is remarkable
testimony to the existence of truly classical
taste even in the extreme north-west of
Gaul. Large-scale bronzes from antiquity
survive so rarely that it would be of
considerable interest even if found in the
Mediterranean area. Although the treatment of the anatomy and the facial features
is not entirely satisfactory, it is very close
indeed to its ancient model, and was
probably made by a Greek working
somewhere in the Mediterranean.

As the power of the Roman Empire declined, so the garrisons of her colonies were reduced by soldiers recalled to defend the city of Rome itself, allowing 'barbarians' to cross the Rhine and settle in the area of the Gallo-Roman empire now known as France. The Burgundians came from just across the Rhine to occupy the territories bordering the Saône and the Rhône; the Visigoths from eastern Germany overran Aquitaine; the Alamans moved into Alsace and the Franks settled in the northern part around the Ile-de-France. On the whole, the invaders seem to have met with little real resistance from the Gallo-Romans and settled down to live side by side with them, deeming it an honour to marry a Roman lady of patrician blood and gradually absorbing their culture and their language. Even today the French language is clearly Latin based. After the final collapse of the empire in 476, Clovis, as leader of the Franks, soon became the dominant figure in Gaul and was first of the Merovingian kings. Despite very distinct regional variations of culture the boundaries of medieval France (the country of the Franks) were established at this time. In many ways the Merovingian rulers were as barbaric as their forbears and their personal and political behaviour left much to be desired, yet surprisingly it was the unity of the church that held the community together. In 496 Clovis married a Christian and was baptised into the faith; for him religion remained a powerful influence, as he lived in fear of eternal damnation. The church prospered through the support of its benefactors and active monasticism under the Benedictine rule spread across the country. St Columbanus, an Irish missionary, founded the monasteries of Luxeuil in the Vosges; at St Martin at Tours, Clovis attended ceremonies.

Little architecture of the period has survived, although the contemporary bishop Gregory of Tours described some churches in the form of early Christian basilicas and a reconstruction of the fifth-century church of St Martin at Tours has been conjectured. At Poitiers the eighth-century baptistery seems to be a rebuilding of a sixth-century design and at Grenoble and Jouarre (near Meaux) Merovingian crypts survive. The most distinctive remains from the time of the warrior kings are regalia found in tombs. From Tournai, the tomb of Childeric, a fifth-century Frank and father of Clovis, yielded a treasure of sword fittings and jewellery that are now in the Bibliothèque Nationale in Paris. Similarly the tomb of Arnegundis, a princess who died c. 565 and was buried at St Denis, contained excellent examples of enamelled brooches and rings which are now in Paris at the Musée de Cluny. Not far east of Paris, the crypt of Jouarre houses a series of splendid sarcophagi decorated with characteristic designs.

An examination of the few surviving Merovingian works of art shows that the people of the time were little influenced by the elaborate Late Roman style, and the simplicity of decoration is far removed from the magnificent manuscripts of the English and Irish monks which must be nearly contemporary and yet outshine any Frankish monuments both in artistic achievement and religious feeling.

Charlemagne

When Charles, later known as Charlemagne, succeeded his father, the Frankish leader Pepin, a new era dawned for Europe. During his long reign he established an empire modelled on Roman lines that was to affect the whole of western Europe. It was an essentially Christian empire and at the suggestion of the pope Charlemagne was officially crowned by him in St Peter's, Rome, on Christmas Day 800. The virtual control of Europe was only won by hard fighting, and yet by the end of his reign the

Christian France and the Monastic Churches

500-1144

36
RELIQUARY
BUST OF ST BAUDIME
twelfth century
gilded copper on oak
h. 29 in (73 cm)
Church of St Nectaire en Haut, Puy de Dome

St Baudime was an early missionary sent from Rome to Gaul about AD 250. The reliquary bust, once studded with precious stones, is a typical example of twelfth-century metalwork. One hand raised in benediction, the figure is made to stare straight ahead, the hair arranged in a circlet of formalised curls and the beard marked by geometric striations.

37
CRYPT AT JOUARRE
seventh century
near Meaux

The crypt of Notre Dame at Jouarre is the best-preserved architectural monument of Merovingian France. The coffins are those of the Abbess Theodochilde who died there in 662 and of her brother Angilbert. Theodochilde's coffin is ornamented with flat scallop shells whilst Angilbert's has an elaborate scene of Christ with the Apostles.

Carolingian empire stretched from Aquitaine in south-western France to the river Vistula in Poland. In these exceptional circumstances a European style of art was developed that forms the basis of the art of the Middle Ages. Charlemagne has been idealised and his character romanticised by both contemporary and later historians, but exaggeration does not conceal the fact that he was a quite remarkable man. He gathered men of learning at his court in Aachen and then sent them forth to set up monastic and episcopal schools with the avowed purpose of restoring old manuscripts, of copying ancient texts and of infusing culture with new life. Alterations and damage conceal from us today the true glory of Carolingian art, but some buildings still survive in France to bear witness to that first golden age.

The abbey of St Denis near Paris had been the royal burial place of the Merovingian kings. When it was rebuilt Charlemagne was present at the consecration in 775. Only fragments of wall survive at the east end of the present St Denis, and yet it was obviously an important foundation with elaborate furnishings such as the altar frontal which is recorded in the painting *The Mass of St Giles* in the National Gallery, London. Theodulf, who was a much respected figure in the imperial court, built the little oratory which was attached to his villa at Germigny-des-Près. Despite extensive restoration the chapel is extant proof of a centrally planned building decorated with mosaics in the Byzantine manner.

The monastic reforms and foundations of Charlemagne were based on the rule of St Benedict, instigated at Monte Cassino in Italy and drawn up in a codex by St Benedict of Aniane (Burgundy) in 817. Typical of the great new monasteries was the abbey of Centula (St Riquier) near Corbie. Detailed contemporary descriptions and a drawing made before the eleventh-century rebuilding enable us to gain some idea of the complex. The work was carried out by Angilbert, a favourite in the court of Charlemagne, and was heavily endowed with gifts of money and objects imported from Italy by the emperor himself. The church was distinguished by two transepts each crowned with a great central tower and projecting arms. The design of Angilbert's church was obviously successful for it was taken up again at Rheims and its influence spread to Germany. It is sad that not a single stone of Centula is recognisable today. Carolingian masonry does remain visible at Beauvais in Notre Dame de la Basse Oeuvre, where a simple façade suggests that the church was steeply roofed and adorned with a great cross in the gable.

Carolingian manuscripts

The very nature of illuminated manuscripts which are small and can be stored in the comparative safety of libraries, each illustration protected from fading by being shut away from the light between stiff covers, means that a number of books have survived to give a good idea of painting in the Carolingian period. At Aachen itself Charlemagne had his own scriptorium and yet at Rheims and at Tours manuscript illumination flourished equally successfully. The Godescalc Gospels in the Bibliothèque Nationale in Paris were commissioned by Charlemagne for his visit to Rome at Easter in 781. This manuscript is lavishly produced in letters of gold on purple vellum suggesting a direct imitation of the most elegant books of the Byzantine emperors. The school at Rheims was directed by Archbishop Ebbo who had been a librarian in the imperial court, and it produced a number of manuscripts illustrated in a very distinctive style. For future generations, the Utrecht Psalter was the most important for it was taken to Canterbury and copied by Anglo-Saxon artists, but the Gospel Book of Archbishop Ebbo, now the most treasured possession of the Bibliothèque de la Ville at Epernay, is one of the principal glories of Carolingian painting. It was made directly for the archbishop before 823 and contains laudatory verses to his name. The title page of each gospel is preceded by a full-page illustration of the evangelist writing at his desk set in a landscape background. Instead of the calm atmosphere created in court school manuscripts, the figures here are drawn with rapid, lively strokes of the pen that give an impression of frenzied movement and a burning intensity. Again, in contrast to the court school, the illustrations are not highly coloured but simply washed in a predominance of blues and greys, allowing the calligraphic lines to make their full impact.

Among the most important figures at the imperial court was Alcuin of York, who had been summoned by Charlemagne to help with the revival of learning. At Aachen, he completely reorganised the scholastic environment and in 796 he retired to St Martin at Tours where he spent the last eight years of his life as abbot. There he was the guiding spirit behind the establishment of the Caroline script, a round, childlike, but very legible form, and he was also responsible for a revision of the vulgate text. Under Alcuin there flourished a very active scriptorium with

53 artists who created the Tours school of illumination. The most typical products of this school consisted of large illuminated bibles like the Bible of Count Vivian. Count Vivian was a lay abbot of Tours some years after Alcuin's death, and he appears to have commissioned the bible as a gift for Charles the Bald, for the book is also known as the First Bible of Charles the Bald. The illuminations are far more richly coloured than in the Rheims books, and much gold is used, although this may have been because it was to be an imperial gift. The biblical illustrations seem to be based on a much earlier model and it is likely that Alcuin may have endowed the monastery of Tours with a bible of early Christian origin.

Second only to manuscript illumination, the Carolingian artists were masters of ivory carving and small-scale metalwork. Some of the ninth-century gospel books in the Bibliothèque Nationale are still bound between their exquisitely carved ivory covers and the so-called Talisman

, 51 of Charlemagne is typical of the enamelled jewellery of the period.

The transition to Romanesque

The imperial territories of Charlemagne were too vast and extended to be maintained intact by any of his followers and they were divided into three parts for his grandsons in 843. By the Treaty of Verdun Charles the Bald received Neustria, that part of France lying west of the Rhône, while his brother Louis the German was given the eastern part of the empire and Lothair won the areas on the banks of the Meuse and the Rhine still known as Lorraine (Lotharingia). By the end of the ninth century, these three had already broken down into even smaller kingdoms and national

38 characteristics had begun to re-emerge, changing the Carolingian style.

During Charlemagne's reign, counts, marquises and dukes continued to protect their property against Norman and Saracen invaders, each forming the head of a complete hierarchy of serfs and vavasours, each answerable to their suzerain in war, and for tax and local government. The entourage of a feudal lord was bound to him by a strict sense of loyalty and often an independent farmer would offer his lands to a lord who would protect him in exchange for service. In name at least these feudal overseers were the forbears of the elegant courtiers who became so important in France during the thirteenth and fourteenth centuries, but in comparison these were mere warriors whose principal task was to protect their terrain. It seems that for many, a castle was a simply constructed wooden tower

38
CRYPT OF
ST MARTIN DU CANIGOU
1001–1026
This small church built high in the Pyrenees is a notable example of early Romanesque architecture. The crypt with transverse tunnel runs the full length of the church and forms a platform for the upper part. The monastery was built under the auspices of the abbot Sclua and later restorations have been carried out with great sympathy and understanding.

39

39

SOUTH TRANSEPT OF
THE ABBEY CHURCH OF
CLUNY

1088–1120

To the monks of Cluny, the abbey church
of St Hugh represented the heavenly city
of Jerusalem. The bold massing of towers
was most impressive with twin towers over
the narthex and a cluster of four spires at
the crossing, soaring upwards. One tower
survives on the south transept, the only
part of the fabric to avoid devastation in
the early nineteenth century. Some of the
capitals from the apse remain in the Musée
Ochier and among the most famous are
carved allegories of Gregorian chant or
plainsong that will have rung through the
magnificent building night and day.

40

PLAINSONG

c. 1095
Capital from the Abbey church of Cluny

raised on an artificial mound of earth for fortification, although the ruins
of a stone keep at Langeais suggest that the wealthy few had more
formidable protection.

During the eleventh century another important development was the
birth of the towns which grew up around fortified market places. The
various traders banded together to protect each other, forming confraternities and guilds, which made their own rules for the town dwellers
but in general accepted the feudal order. In contrast to the great wealth
of ecclesiastical architecture that has survived, very little secular art
remains, having been swept aside by modernisation. Yet the importance
of towns like Chartres and Dijon on the trade routes across France must
date from this era.

Cluny and the Benedictine order

In 926 a man named Odo became the second abbot of Cluny, and by sheer
force of personality he began a tradition of reform that was to influence
the whole of France. During the ninth century, the Benedictine rule had
lost much of the strict asceticism envisaged by St Benedict himself, the
numbers of monks had been swollen by the admission of sons of petty
lords who saw monasticism merely as an alternative to owning land, and
the spirit was lost. Abbot Odo sought a return to more idealistic devotion
and required continual services day and night to the greater glory of God.

It is only by understanding the intense religious devotion of the
monastic community that one may appreciate the true glory of
Romanesque art. In architecture, their aim was to build large and magnificent churches to celebrate the liturgy and to house their relics; in painting and sculpture, they were happy to sacrifice truth to nature for a
wider, more dramatic impact that might be achieved through stylisation.

The loss of the abbey church at Cluny is perhaps one of the most tragic
and most senseless in all France. The church stood intact until the early
nineteenth century when a road was made through the centre of the
nave and the rest of the fabric was taken down for building materials.
Only the south transept and the sculptured fragments in the Musée 39,
Ochier remain to suggest the grandeur that once was Cluny's. The
changes made in the building at Cluny typify the demands of a growing
monastic community. The first monks had gathered in a small Frankish
villa in 910, but within a generation a larger church was begun by Mayeul
and dedicated in 981. St Hugh of Semur became abbot in 1049, and was
to rule the ever-expanding order of Cluny for sixty years. In 1088, he
laid the foundations of yet another church at Cluny that was to form a
focus for the devotion of the whole order. St Hugh's church had double
aisles either side of the nave and two transepts each containing subsidiary
chapels. The great complex at the east end had five chapels radiating
around the ambulatory and the high altar set in the main apse. Above the
main altar, the great apse was filled with a fresco of Christ in Glory, whose
grave dignity is reflected in the surviving frescos at Berzé la Ville nearby. 49
The eleven bays of the nave were covered with a pointed barrel vault and
the whole church was dedicated by Pope Innocent II in 1130. The success
of Cluny was immediate, and the design was reproduced in a smaller
form at Paray-le-Monial, at La Charité-sur-Loire, and at Beaune. Cluny 4
was the most extensive and elaborate of all Romanesque schemes and
local influences can be seen. The Saracens had long harassed the region,
and their art seems to be suggested in the pointed arches and cusped
decoration of the arcades and the decorative parts of the great doorway;
amphitheatres and gateways of the Roman period, such as the Porte
d'Arroux at Autun, survived in Burgundy, and a direct borrowing

may be seen in the classical fluted pilasters remaining in the south transept at Cluny and used to such effect in the cathedral of Autun. At Autun, the **42** nave arcade is decorated with a series of magnificent capitals carved in **43** conjunction with the great tympanum over the west doorway. This shows the *Last Judgment* carved by Gislebertus and is a masterpiece of Romanesque sculpture. The figures vary in size according to their importance and each is displayed in an exaggerated posture. Autun's *Last Judgment* is related stylistically to the majestic vision of the Ascension in the narthex **58** (porch) of La Madeleine at Vézelay.

Vézelay is closely connected with the cult of relics, for until the eleventh century when it was put about that the church possessed the precious bones of St Mary Magdalen, the church had remained a little-known dependence. From then on, the abbey became famous. Thousands came for the feast of the Magdalen and, endowed by the many gifts of the pilgrims both in money and in kind, the monastic community prospered. The new church was dedicated in 1104 and was substantially completed by 1132. The choir of the present church is later, but in a church like this the monks would have used the chancel, while the pilgrims were confined to the nave. In order to accommodate as many as possible the nave was long and wide, and more people could see the altar through the open doorways from the narthex which adds another three bays to the length of the church. Above the doorways opening onto the aisles from this narthex at either side of the central portal with the Ascension are scenes **58** from the Nativity and of the last days of Christ on earth. A host of biblical stories and Christian fables decorate the exquisite capitals of the nave, providing the pilgrim with a 'poor man's bible' to read and understand.

The old abbey of Fleury or St Benoît-sur-Loire has an equally august history, for bones believed to be those of St Benedict were brought to Fleury after the desolation of his foundation at Monte Cassino in 685. With the growing popularity of relics, St Benoît-sur-Loire flourished in the same way as Vézelay, and to this day a remarkable church in the mature Romanesque style survives. At St Benoît the great porch or narthex at the west end is not enclosed like Vézelay but arcaded with massive piers and magnificent carved capitals. The choir and choir aisles are covered with a barrel vault and a flight of steps leads to the sanctuary of the main apse set above the crypt. Again, an ambulatory encircles the high altar at ground level permitting entrance to the radiating chapels and small chapels set on the chord of the apse.

Often fire caught hold of timber roofs and caused untold damage to the rest of the fabric; thus the main problem facing the builders of the period was the creation of permanent stone vaulting. Naturally the altar was the most important part of the church, not only as the table on which the Eucharist was celebrated, but also as a repository for the precious relics. Thus, when the architects made their first hesitant steps towards stone vaulting, the chancel was the first wide space to be spanned. The narrower aisles and compartments of the narthex at St Benoît, for instance, could be groin-vaulted, that is, with a vault produced by intersecting barrel vaults at right angles to each other. Unfortunately the great weight of groin vaults could not be supported over a large span. St Benoît has a plain barrel vault in the chancel, but obviously the builders were prepared to risk the hazard of fire in the nave, for the vaults there are of the Gothic period and were put up only after a fire had gutted the nave in the later twelfth century. Evidence of burning can still be seen on the walls of that part. To some extent, the problems of vaulting dictate the whole architectural style of Romanesque buildings with those massive **59**

41

THE PRIORY CHURCH OF
PARAY-LE-MONIAL

east end
begun 1109

The building of the church at Paray-le-Monial was started under the direction of Hugh, abbot of Cluny, and gives an impression on a small scale of how the abbey church of Cluny must have looked. This view shows the octagonal central tower and the beautiful east end, with its apsidal chapels radiating from the choir, showing strong influence of Auvergnat architecture.

walls needed to support barrel vaults, and it was not until the possibilities of the rib vault had been fully explored that the transition to the lighter Gothic style was effected.

The pilgrimage churches

St Benoît-sur-Loire and La Madeleine at Vézelay were shrines of devotion in themselves, yet they also lie on or near the roads that lead to Santiago de Compostela. The shrine of St James at Compostela drew pilgrims from all over Europe and a twelfth-century manuscript, the Liber S Jacobi, is a guidebook for the faithful with the different routes across France listed to provide an itinerary. From the south, one would pass through Saint-Gilles-du-Gard and Toulouse or Le Puy, Conques and Moissac, or one would travel along roads leading west from Vézelay, or south from Paris. Hospices and monasteries were established along the way to care for the pilgrim, and no doubt the journey represented for him an unforgettable experience of religious devotion and brotherly fellowship. Each route across France had at least one shrine of outstanding importance. From Paris the road passed through St Martin at Tours; from Vézelay through St Martial at Limoges; from Le Puy through Conques; from Arles through Toulouse. It is a symbol of the international character of the pilgrimage to Santiago that each great church had a very similar architectural form and was related stylistically to Santiago itself. The plan of the great pilgrimage churches usually provided for a long nave with two aisles either side where the crowds could gather more easily, a wide-aisled transept with additional altars and an ambulatory with three or five radiating chapels around the high altar. Each was roofed with barrel vaults throughout. Two of the major monuments on the pilgrimage routes remain substantially intact to give an idea of their scope and
63   ambition. At Toulouse, the church of St Sernin stands for a great moment in Benedictine civilization. Building began c. 1077 and in 1096 Pope Urban II passed through Toulouse on a pilgrimage pausing to dedicate the high altar in the presence of fifteen French and Spanish bishops. A carved stone slab which now stands in the crossing is believed to be the front of that high altar, and is stylistically related to the plaques set into the wall of the ambulatory around the altar. The Porte Miégeville at St Sernin was carved during the first or second decade of the twelfth century with a powerful composition of the Ascension in which two angels bear aloft a monumental figure of Christ, watched by the awestruck apostles. The sculptor had a particular stylistic autograph of double-cut folds in the draperies that can be traced from Santiago through southern France to Emilia in Italy, and even as far as Hungary. This style did not necessarily originate in Toulouse, indeed, it seems to be based on early Christian prototypes and yet the hallmark of these draperies is to be found
55, 56 on many other sculptures in south-western France, notably at Moissac, Souillac, and Conques.

    Little is known about the movement of trained sculptors but they obviously travelled from one building site to another carrying pattern books with them. They seem to have derived their compositions from illuminated manuscripts, for the *Christ in Judgment* at Moissac is inspired by the French copy of a Spanish Apocalypse known as the
54   Apocalypse of St Sever, now in the Bibliothèque Nationale, a manuscript which was also used as the model for the visionary paintings on the ceiling of the church of St Savin at Gartempe. Similarly, the great figure of
56   Jeremiah and the rampant lions on the doorjamb at Moissac and the Isaiah at Souillac can only be understood in the light of the elongated figures that fill the decorated initials of a manuscript like the Bible of St Martial

42

NAVE OF AUTUN CATHEDRAL

c. 1120–1132

Founded by Bishop Etienne de Bagé, Autun is one of the best preserved examples of Burgundian Romanesque architecture. Although it is an episcopal foundation its architecture is closely connected with the monastic church founded by St Hugh at Cluny. The sculptors workshop at Autun was headed by Master Gislebertus who carved the outstanding tympanum of the *Last Judgment* before 1135. His influence may be detected in the magnificent series of historiated capitals that ornament the architectural pilasters.

43

THE DEVIL TEMPTING CHRIST

detail from a nave capital, Autun Cathedral

c. 1130

from Limoges now in the Bibliothèque Nationale. Originally all the sculptured decoration of churches was highly coloured and the connection between the two media of illumination and stone sculpture would have been much more obvious. At Conques a porch-like projection over the tympanum on the west front has protected the sculpture from the worst of the weather and traces of colouring are still to be seen. Because it was a less important shrine than Toulouse, the church at Conques is smaller with only five bays to the nave and single aisles, three radiating chapels instead of five. At the crossing, the belfry tower is supported on a

44 system of squinches in which there are carved angels. To this day, the church of Ste Foy at Conques remains isolated on the rugged slopes of a depopulated valley, and its impact is as startling and dramatic as it must have been in olden times. It was built to house the precious relics of the dedicatory saint, and the chapter still possesses the small reliquary statue of Ste Foy which was made *c.* 980, and was the principal attraction for the pilgrims. The statue is a hierarchical seated image with arms outstretched and the gaze fixed ahead. The golden work is studded with jewels and cameos that were votive offerings from the faithful.

Similar reliquary statues have been preserved elsewhere in France,
36 among them St Baudime at the church of St Nectaire in the Auvergne and St Césaire at Maurs.

Regional schools

Although the Santiago pilgrimage did much to unify French Romanesque architecture and sculpture, it never completely overcame the inherent regional characteristics of the style. For instance, many churches south and west of the Loire are roofed with a series of domes that give a highly distinctive silhouette. Among these the finest examples are the cathedrals of Cahors and Perigueux, and the abbey of Fontevrault, which was for a time the royal pantheon of the Plantagenets and contained their tombs. Apart from its domed roof and aisleless nave, Angoulême Cathedral also has a characteristic Charentais west front ornamented with a riot of sculpture interpreting the vision of the second coming of Christ spread across the whole façade which is crowned by tiled beehive-shaped turrets. This formula is found throughout Poitou with fine examples at
60 Saint-Jouin-de-Marnes and Notre Dame la Grande at Poitiers. In direct contrast, the churches of Provence have almost classical façades with porticos of columns carrying a flat entablature and enclosing single statues. Most famous of these are the abbey of Saint-Gilles-du-Gard and the former cathedral of St Trophime at Arles. In Arles, the nearby Musée Lapidaire furnishes the historian with ample proof of the sculptors' debt to the classical tradition, for the Roman sarcophagi there have many of the Provençal Romanesque idiosyncrasies including the use of drill holes to undercut drapery folds and to elaborate the foliage decoration. The portico of St Trophime is complemented by one of the finest cloisters in France, beautiful carving and elegant stonework enhancing varied design.

Politically and ethnically, the duchy of Normandy stood apart from the rest of France during the period under discussion. The Normans or Northmen came from Norway or Denmark to rule at Caen, Bayeux and Rouen. Once securely settled, the Normans undertook to build a state, levying taxes and administering their financial affairs with skill. Learned clerics like the Lombard Lanfranc, who was later appointed archbishop of Canterbury by William the Conqueror, came to the Norman abbey of Bec and set up a scriptorium of international importance.

Duke William was personally involved with the three major architectural enterprises of the eleventh century. The abbey church of Jumièges

44
ABBEY CHURCH OF STE FOY
c. 1052–1130
Conques

The pilgrimage centre of Conques is unique in that both the precious relic that was the object of devotion and the eleventh-century abbey church have remained together. The nave is not long but the barrel vault is raised high above the comparatively narrow aisle. The double doorway of the west front is surmounted by a tympanum containing a representation of the Last Judgment, interpreted in everyday language and easily understood by pilgrims; traces of the painting can still be seen on the sculpted figures.

which is now in ruins has a pair of twin towers at the west end and an alternating system of bays in the nave which was immediately taken up by Edward the Confessor for his new abbey at Westminster. In Caen, William and his wife Matilda built the Abbaye aux Hommes (St Etienne) and the Abbaye aux Dames (La Trinité) as expiation of their marriage made outside the canons of the church and these rank among the most advanced structures of their day. The great themes suggested by these churches were taken up with vigour by the Norman bishops in England, but in contrast the twelfth-century churches on Norman soil are modest in scale and ambition. Close links with England even before the Conquest meant that the Anglo-Saxon style of illumination had influenced many scriptoria in the north of France and the gospels written for the abbey of St Bertin at Saint-Omer, which are now at Boulogne in the Bibliothèque Municipale, have that rapid calligraphic technique and feeling for movement and expression also found in manuscripts of the Winchester school. After the Conquest, the English influence unexpectedly faded and new ideas gave rise to a harder, quite individual style at the abbey of Mont-St-Michel. The great architectural complex clinging to the rock of Mont-St-Michel is held dear in the hearts of all Frenchmen. At first it was a centre of pilgrimage and its foundation was greatly enriched by pious gifts. The abbey church at the very top of the rock was begun during the eleventh century and the successive patronage of Norman rulers and French kings is reflected in the different parts of abbey buildings. For instance, the magnificent 'hanging' cloister was built at the time of St Louis and many of the domestic offices were enlarged after the creation of the chivalrous order of St Michel by Louis XI in 1469.

The Cistercian order

The Cistercian order was founded in Burgundy by monks from the priory of Molesme. Dissatisfied with lax customs prevailing in their monastery, they obtained land in a forest belonging to Raymond, Vicomte de Beaune, and by symbolically changing their monkish habits from black to white, they founded the order of Cîteaux on the feast of St Benedict 1098. The order attracted the most austere asceticism and was led at first by an Englishman, St Stephen Harding who came from Sherborne in Dorset. With him he brought manuscript illuminators who were responsible for the large, four-volumed Bible of St Stephen Harding which is decorated with elaborate historiated initials and coloured illustrations. No great artistic changes were to become evident in the earliest years, but when Bernard of Clairvaux joined the order in 1114 a dramatic transformation occurred. Born a member of a landed Burgundian family, St Bernard had a fanatical, if narrow, outlook and an immensely strong character that greatly helped the growth of the Cistercian order. Each house was strictly governed by prescribed rules laid down by St Bernard himself, and these were so detailed that even a uniformity of architecture became necessary. He had a horror of any but the plainest style of building; in 1124, all sculptural embellishment was forbidden by decree and later stone belfries and stained glass were banished from Cistercian abbeys. Fontenay is the oldest existing example of a church built according to the precepts of St Bernard. Still standing in a wooded glade, the building invites the starkest comparison with a church like Autun. The interior is lit only by windows in the façade, the crossing and the sanctuary, for the nave and elevation has no clerestory, only a simple arcade supporting the pointed barrel vault. Instead of the typical Burgundian semicircular apse with ambulatory and radiating chapels, the sanctuary and transepts are terminated with a flat eastern wall pierced with six lights. The capitals of

64
45

62

61

46

45
CHURCH OF ST ETIENNE (ABBAYE AUX HOMMES)
begun 1068
Caen

Duke William of Normandy personally commissioned the building of the church, and despite the addition of the Gothic choir around 1200, it is one of the finest monuments of French Norman architecture. The thick walls, the continuous passages at all levels of the elevation and the sense of grand design were adopted time and again by English architects. The elegant west front crowned by twin towers provides the prototype for the development of Gothic façades in the Ile de France.

46
ABBEY CHURCH OF FONTENAY
1139–1147

Founded by St Bernard in 1118 as a small Cistercian colony, the original retreat was soon too small for the increasing numbers of monks who flocked to the monastery under the direction of Godefroy de la Roche. The present buildings were built to accommodate these numbers and embody the stark simplicity of St Bernard's ideals. Such purity of conception did not outlive St Bernard himself for any length of time and by 1185 Cistercian churches were coming into line with the developments of normal French Gothic forms.

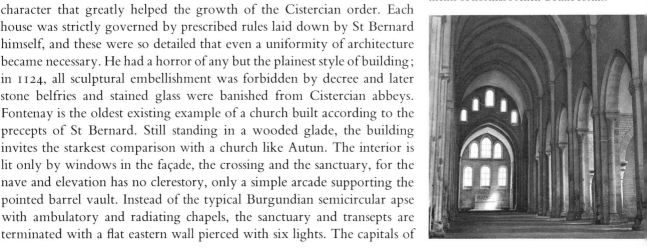

47

THE ARK OF THE COVENANT

799–818
Theodulf's oratory, Germigny des Prés

This apse mosaic is one of the few to survive from the time of Charlemagne. The theme of the Ark of the Covenant is unusual and, as in the architecture of the oratory itself, strong eastern influences are suggested by the Byzantine treatment of the face and hair.

48

CHILDERIC'S SWORD FITTINGS

c. 482
Cabinet des Medailles,
Bibliothèque Nationale, Paris

The tomb of Childeric was discovered at Tournai in the seventeenth century and the contents, which included coins, a signet ring and fittings from the hilt of a sword are among the most complete treasures from a Merovingian tomb. The sword was richly ornamented with gold and with cloisonné enamel inlaid with garnets making a decorative geometric design.

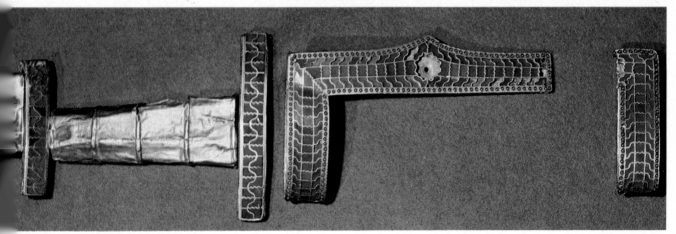

49
CHRIST IN MAJESTY

c. 1100
fresco in the apse, Berzé la Ville

Berzé la Ville is a small foundation
dependent on the abbey of Cluny and its
frescos provide the historian with the best
impression of what wall painting at Cluny
itself was like. Despite the small size of the
chapel the Christ is handled with great
monumentality and suggests knowledge
of Byzantine paintings, possibly via Italy.

50
RELIQUARY OF PEPIN OF AQUITAINE

817–38
repoussé metalwork
7·25 × 7·5 × 3·5 in (18·5 × 18·6 × 8·8 cm)
treasury of Ste Foy at Conques

The reliquary casket was a votive offering
to the abbey of Ste Foy from Pepin of
Aquitaine in the ninth century. It is
delicately worked in a repoussé technique,
that is, beaten through from the back, and
further ornamented with filigree, precious
stones and enamelled plaques. This detail
shows the two eagles from the sloping lid of
the casket, which is shaped like a house or
tomb with a handle at each end.

51

CHARLEMAGNE'S TALISMAN

ninth century
2·5 × 2·75 × 1·5 in (0·65 × 0·73 × 0·38 cm)
treasury of the Cathedral of Rheims

The talisman is supposed to have been found in Charlemagne's tomb when it was opened in 1166. The tiny relic of the True Cross is set in a blue ground and enclosed by a jewel-studded band of fine filigree. The delicate setting of the stones and the excellence of the filigree are typical of the high standards attained by the jewellers of the Carolingian era.

52

ST JOHN

from the Godescalc Evangelistary
781–83
Bibliothèque Nationale, Paris (MS Lat. 1203)

The title page of the Gospel according to St John is a full page illustration of the evangelist at his desk. The Gospels were probably made at Charlemagne's court school in Aachen and the illuminations are early examples of the court style which was to reach an even higher standard in later works.

53

THE EMPEROR LOTHAIR

849–51
Bibliothèque Nationale, Paris (MS Lat. 266)

The Gospel Book is prefaced by a portrait
of the donor, Emperor Lothair, who ruled
from 840 until 855. The illustration is a
fine example of work from the scriptorium
that flourished at Tours. The rich colouring and the lavish use of gold in borders
and highlights emphasises the imperial
nature of the commission.

54

BEATUS' APOCALYPSE OF
ST SEVER

1028–72
Bibliothèque Nationale, Paris
(MS Lat. 8878 f 145)

The text of the manuscript is taken from
the commentaries on the Revelations of
St John the Divine by a Spanish monk,
Beatus of Liebana, composed in 784.
There are several copies illuminated with
bold visionary scenes and a dazzling
richness of colour. The St Sever
Apocalypse dates from the time of Abbot
Gregor, and seems to have influenced
much of the splendid twelfth-century
sculpture in south-western France.

the arcade, like those in the adjoining cloister, are either completely plain or cut with volutes so that, according to St Bernard, the faithful may not be distracted from their worship. In 1134, St Bernard issued his famous *Consuetudines* decrying all forms of pictorial representation of religious subjects. His bible, now in the Bibliothèque Municipale at Troyes, has no kind of narrative illustration, although it is a masterpiece of elegant restraint with exquisite script and finely painted initials.

Abbot Suger

St Bernard's austere teachings were by no means universally accepted by the Benedictine order outside the Cistercian movement, and elaborate sculptural programmes, lavishly illustrated manuscripts, and delicately wrought objets d'art remained in fashion. Indeed, after St Bernard's death, even the Cistercians permitted ornament little by little to return to their churches. One of his principal opponents was Suger, abbot of St Denis, who saw art as a direct link between man and the divine order of things. 'Art guides the souls with the help of material things to the immaterial,' he declared. Born of humble parentage, Suger entered the monastic community of St Denis near Paris as a young man, there he chanced to meet the king's son, the future Louis VI, who was to elect him chancellor and advisor to the royal house. In 1122, Suger became abbot and was able to embark on his lifelong ambition to restore the abbey church of St Denis to something of the glory it had enjoyed in Carolingian times. Having brought together the best architects, sculptors, glassworkers and masons he could find, he spared no expense on materials which included stone from Pontoise, especially hewn timber, marble from Italy, and as much precious metal as he could obtain. In order that services might not be disrupted, Suger began by rebuilding the old Carolingian narthex in an up-to-date manner with three portals and twin towers over the aisles. In fact, the various elements are purely Romanesque, and yet the overall design was to become the standard pattern for early Gothic churches in the north of France.

Unfortunately, the sculpture on the portals was drastically restored during the nineteenth century, but an examination of the minor sculpture on the jambs and in the voussoirs reveals the hands of a sensitive and advanced group of artists. Today, the column figures have been replaced by patterned columns and those original statues are only known in drawings by Montfaucon. Certainly Suger devised the complicated iconographic theme of the precursors for the portal in the same way as he had outlined programmes for his workshop of Lotharingian goldsmiths.

Next, Suger began the greater task of rebuilding the church itself and in the year 1144 the choir was consecrated in the presence of King Louis VII, his queen Eleanor of Aquitaine and the principal aristocracy and clergy of the day. This consecration of the choir, then adorned with the most magnificent furnishings of gold and jewels, marked the fulfilment of Suger's ambition both as a devout churchman and as a member of the

55 state. Now the choir seems cold and empty and yet the basic conception remains. Unlike a Romanesque chevet, which consists of several parts (apse, ambulatory and radiating chapels), Suger's architect drew the choir into a unified whole, so that the chapel divisions are defined only by a single pillar giving visual access onto the nave and are as high as the main arcade of the apse. After Suger's death reconstruction of the old abbey was delayed until the thirteenth century when Pierre de Montreuil, working under the direct patronage of St Louis, was called on to build transepts and nave in the current style.

Sabrina Mitchell

55

CHOIR OF ST DENIS

c. 1140
Paris

The upper part of the choir of the abbey church was modified to comply with the overall design of the thirteenth century rebuilding by Pierre de Montreuil, but a view through the columns of the ambulatory shows how Abbot Suger intended to merge the various elements of the design. The fine volute and crocket capitals mark a complete break with the Romanesque tradition of historiated capitals.

56, 57 *right and bottom right*

ST PIERRE, MOISSAC

The cloister of the abbey church of St Pierre, *below right*, was rebuilt with red-brick pointed arches in the Gothic period but its principle glory lies in the series of capitals carved at the time of Abbot Asnquetil (1085–1115). The rows of alternating single and double columns are capped with the finest foliate interlace, each capital surmounted by a broad abacus and sculpted with biblical and legendary scenes, or decorative devices. The ranges of columns are interspersed with piers decorated in shallow relief, these carved in a more voluminous, sober vein. The southern doorway of the church is enhanced by a central doorjamb decorated with elongated rampant lions and the figures of St Paul and Jeremiah (**56**). Swathed in sinuous, almost transparent draperies, these tall attenuated figures have heads of extreme sensitivity, carved with expression and grace.

58

THE ASCENSION

c. 1125–30
La Madeleine, Vézelay

On the tympanum of the doorway leading to the main aisle the theme of the Ascension is combined with Christ's Mission to the Apostles. The scenes on the lintel are less explicit, with monstrous creatures interspersed with everyday figures. The voussoirs are filled with decorative rosettes on the outer register and the signs of the zodiac and labours of the months on the inner. This complex iconographic programme may be the design of the theologian Peter the Venerable.

59

NARTHEX OF ST PHILIBERT

c.960–1120
Tournus

Although the nave of the church is characterised by mighty drum pillars rising up to the roof, the narthex is divided into two storeys. In the lower level the same drum pillars support a system of transverse arches and groin vaults. On the exterior of the church an ornamentation of corbel tables and pilaster strips suggests that the architecture of Tournus originates from northern Italy and the first Romanesque style. The monastery was founded originally in 875 when monks from Noirmoutiers, fleeing from the Normans, arrived with the relics of St Philibert.

60

NOTRE DAME LA GRANDE

c.1130–45
Poitiers

The façade of Notre Dame is typical of Poiterin west fronts with the profile masking the building behind it. The doorway, which is enclosed by squat columns has neither lintel nor tympanum but decoration is profuse on other parts of the façade. The richness of the ornamentation seems to reflect oriental influences which may have been brought to Poitiers as a result of the Crusades.

61

CLOISTER OF MONT ST MICHEL

thirteenth century

Apart from a man-made causeway the island of the Mont St Michel is isolated from the mainland at high tide. The rock, some two hundred and fifty feet high, is crowned by the famous abbey whose relics have attracted pilgrims since the eighth century, *opposite*. Although the church nave and transept date from the Romanesque period the main parts of the abbey were built during the thirteenth century and are arranged on three different levels, each level being divided into two parts. One feature is this magnificent hanging cloister, graced with two hundred and twenty columns of polished granite and delicately carved friezes.

62 *top right*

MONT ST MICHEL

mainly twelfth to fifteenth centuries

63

ABBEY CHURCH OF ST SERNIN

c. 1077–1119
Toulouse

This abbey church is the largest and most complete example of a pilgrimage church in France. The nave of eleven bays is flanked by double aisles, and aisles run on all sides of the transepts. Apart from the high altar there are nine apses for additional chapels. The painted columns inside may offend the twentieth-century eye but are a reminder that all medieval churches were richly painted in warm colours.

64

THE BAYEUX TAPESTRY

first half of the twelfth century
linen embroidered with wool
Bayeux Museum

The long tapestry illustrating William the
Conqueror's invasion of England is thought
to have been commissioned by Odo,
Bishop of Bayeux. Right up until the
French Revolution it was used to adorn
the nave of Bayeux Cathedral. The
continuous narrative is explained with
bold captions; this detail shows Harold
crowned and enthroned at Westminster
flanked by two nobles to the left, and the
Archbishop of Canterbury on the right.

HENRICVS·III·GALLIARVM·POLONIARVMQVE·REX·HANC·DEIPARÆ
VIRGINI·NAVICVLAM·VT·RES·GALLICA·DIVTVRNIS·IACTATA
SEDITIONVM·FLVCTIBVS·OPE·DIVINA·TANDEM·CONFERRETVR
IN·TRANQVILLVM·MORE·MAIORVM·INAVGVRATVS·POSVIT·ANNO·CIƆIƆLXXIIII

St Denis marks both the beginning and the end of an episode in French art. For the Benedictines it was the culmination of religious ideals and was one of the last great monastic enterprises in architecture. During the second half of the twelfth century, the leading artistic programmes moved from the hands of the cloistered monk to the more worldly urbanity of diocesan bishops. The intensive building that took place in the Ile-de-France during that time was due in part to growing security of the Capetian dynasty. In gratitude for ecclesiastical support to which the dynasty owed its existence, the king endowed many foundations where new work was undertaken. Suger's achievement at St Denis must have stood as a great example to other bishops many of whom would have been present at the consecration 55 itself. Technically, the choir of St Denis was brilliant, due in the main to the complete understanding of the rib vault which gave the architect so much more freedom of design.

Not once was St Denis copied exactly, but its influence may be seen in a whole series of larger churches spread across northern France, in the cathedrals of Noyon, Sens, Senlis, Soissons, and Laon, in the abbey church of St Remi at Rheims, and at Nantes. Simon Bishop of Noyon is known to have been present at the consecration of St Denis in 1144 and his cathedral is an excellent, fairly complete example of the new style. Here the choir wall rises above the delicate arcade of columns to a wide tribune over the aisles and is flooded with light from the large clerestory windows between the ribs of the vault. The fourth element in the elevation, a blind triforium arcade, became a characteristic of these early Gothic , 66 churches and is to be found again at Laon and Soissons. Laon Cathedral, situated high on the hill and dominating the town, is perhaps more imposing than Noyon. Nowhere else can the aims and achievements of this twelfth-century Gothic style be seen in such unity. The prospect of the nave emphasises the still horizontal feeling of the design, with each level firmly defined by a string course and the longitudinal axis strengthened visually by banding on the attached colonnettes. The most striking feature of these early Gothic churches is the apparent solidity of the elevation up to clerestory level. Tribunes are used to form an aisle above the ground level aisles simply to absorb some of the thrust of the main vault. Later, at Paris and Chartres, the development of exterior flying buttresses was to offer the architect a new dimension in his search for spacious light effects. Outside, the silhouette of Laon with its five magnificent towers is also typical of the transition from Romanesque to Gothic, for the massing of towers was used at Cluny, in the Rhineland, and 89 particularly at nearby Tournai. But the dramatic shape of Laon with massive stone oxen placed on the western towers foreshadows the more delicate traceried façades of the thirteenth century.

The changes in architecture during the second half of the twelfth century are largely due to the ever-increasing technical expertise of the architects and masons. Desire to create the most magnificent building possible was not a new phenomenon; this ambition could hardly have been stronger in the monks of Vézelay or Cluny, but with a growing understanding of geometry and science the twelfth-century builders had more skill at their fingertips. At the same time, however, a definite change was taking place in the figurative arts. To some extent, the emergence of the new style was due to fresh contact with the eastern Empire either through the Norman connections with Byzantine Sicily, or direct links with Constantinople. The crusade preached by Suger in 1146 brought artists into contact with more naturalistic forms, and a book such as the Souvigny Bible now in the Bibliothèque Nationale has scenes permeated

Church, King and Court in the Gothic Age
1144-1500

65
NEF OF ST URSULA
late fifteenth century
gold, silver, enamelled copper
18 × 11 × 6·5 in (46 × 28 × 16·5 cm)
Cathedral treasury, Rheims
A nef was the principal ornament on the dining table of a medieval courtier. Often made of silver or another precious metal, it was designed to hold the napkin and knife and fork. This nef, shaped like a ship, once belonged to Anne of Brittany but was later given to the cathedral of Rheims as a reliquary of St Ursula.

with a new sense of form and composition. In the manuscripts of the mid-twelfth century made in and around Paris, the importance of metalwork from the valley of the river Meuse must be stressed. Suger certainly employed Mosan artists like Godefroid de Claire to work on the metal furnishings of his abbey and many of the small bronze statuettes made by him and his followers have naturalistic expression, movement and drapery.

77 A psalter made for the Danish queen of Philip Augustus known as the Ingeborg Psalter has paintings which have taken on the metallic quality of its prototypes and the draperies have swinging horizontal folds of a 'classical'
69 format that recur in some of the stone figures at Rheims.

The cathedrals of Chartres and Rheims

The classic forms of Gothic art are embodied in the majestic cathedral of Chartres. There, architecture, stained glass and sculpture stand together in perfect harmony. From olden times, Chartres had been an important shrine attracting pilgrims to see relics of the tunic of the Virgin. Already rich in gifts from the faithful, Bishop Fulbert built the Portail Royal at the
67 west end of the cathedral soon after Suger's west front, and to some extent the two doorways are related. At Chartres the column figures
88 remain; tall kings and queens of Judah stand straight as the columns they partially replace, their drapery falling in tight, narrow folds, their gaze ahead. Above, the tympana are dominated by a monumental Christ in Majesty, but the exacting sightseer may observe a number of other themes worked out in voussoirs and a continuous narrative running across
68 the columns of the three portals. Yet again, fire was the cause for the major rebuilding at Chartres, which was started immediately after the main part was razed to the ground in 1194. Instead of the normal procedure of building from the chancel towards the nave, work began from behind the Portail Royal and progressed eastwards with the choir only completed about 1220. Munificent gifts of money and labour were made
71 to the new fabric of the church and the stained glass windows record the benefits not only of kings and visiting bishops, but also of trade confraternities of the town. Freed from the problems of thrust from the nave walls by the invention of flying buttresses, at Chartres the architect was able to lighten the visual effect of the elevation. He did away with the tribune found in a church like Laon, and greatly enlarged the clerestory allowing two openings and a small rose window to each bay. The horizontal axis was eliminated by the vault supports to give an impression of soaring airy height immeasurably enhanced by the rich tonality of stained glass. The search for an effective vehicle to show off stained glass is clearly seen in a comparison between the rose window at the west end of the nave, a wheel of masonry pierced by rosettes, and the transept windows where the stonework is reduced to a skeletal support. The stylistic road travelled by
68 sculptors is also visible, for on the transept doorways, built and carved during the early years of the thirteenth century, the column figures are no longer hieratic, architectonic ornamentations, but stand more realistically, each beneath a canopy and having movement in their limbs and expression in their faces.

75, 83 The exactly contemporary cathedral of Bourges provides a radically different alternative to Chartres. It is much longer and has no transepts or crossing. The nave arcade is of immense height and is balanced by the ascending aisles on either side, so that a cross section gives an impression of a soaring, upward movement. In its way the solution at Bourges was as effective as Chartres, but it had fewer imitations, although its example was certainly responsible for the extreme delicacy of the choir of Le Mans and Coutances.

66
CATHEDRAL OF ST GERVAIS
AND ST PROTAIS
south transept
c.1175
Soissons

The south transept is the earliest part of Soissons Cathedral and the elevation is typical of twelfth-century Gothic architecture. It is divided into four storeys with the lighting contributing to the horizontal divisions which are very distinct. Another feature of Soissons is the use of an apsidal transept. Both these characteristics recur several times in northern France but they were an architectural experiment dispensed with by later architects.

67, 68
CATHEDRAL OF NOTRE DAME
CHARTRES
mainly built 1140–1160

The tall elegant towers of Chartres Cathedral form a prominent landmark in the flat plains around the city and must have been a welcome sight to the devout pilgrims who came to see the venerated tunic of the Virgin. Originally the Portail Royal was set back between the towers which were later moved to their present position. The building of the north tower was started after a fire which ravaged the town in 1134. The south tower was begun about 1144 and finished by 1160 although the west front was not completed until Jean Texier crowned the north tower with its lacy pinnacle in the early sixteenth century. The west front towers and crypt were the only parts of Bishop Fulbert's church to escape the second fire of 1194. The transept portals (68) are contemporary with the rebuilding of the cathedral after the fire. Each transept has an entrance of three doorways and these were further elaborated by the addition of porches in the mid-thirteenth century. Each portal has a comprehensive iconographic scheme, that of the south transept dominated by the *Last Judgment* in the principal tympanum.

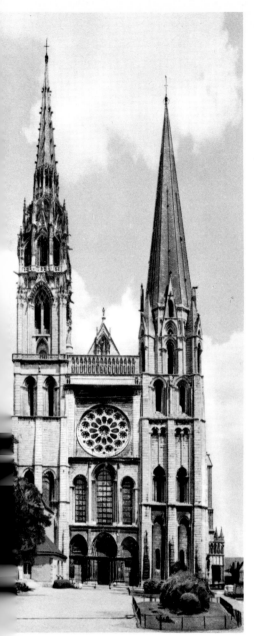

The cathedral of Notre Dame at Rheims was no less a pilgrimage church than Chartres. When fire damaged the Carolingian work in 1211, rebuilding was begun by the architect Jean d'Orbais. In general the design follows the formula of Chartres, but at Rheims the windows of the clerestory have traceried divisions allowing an even greater area of glass. The architect Villard d'Honnecourt seems to have visited Rheims during building, and his drawings of the chevet chapels and the choir façade are a unique contemporary record. Most architects must have used sketch- 70
books to note down ideas and projects, but only this one has survived. From it one learns that Villard travelled widely from Cambrai to Chartres, Lausanne and even as far as Hungary. Purely from the evidence of his sketchbook it has been suggested that he was the architect of the collegiate church of St Quentin. Apart from his architectural drawings, there are also fanciful designs and drawings of figures in those peculiar parallel draperies seen in Mosan metalwork, the Ingeborg Psalter, and the figures of the Visitation at Rheims. At Rheims the names of the successive master 69
masons were recorded in a labyrinth that once ornamented the pavement in the nave. To these men, Jean d'Orbais, Jean le Loup, Gaucher de Reims 82
and Bernard de Soissons, belong one of the most monumental cycles of figure sculpture in Gothic art. Five hundred and fifty column figures adorn the portals of the north transept and the west front—a façade in which stained glass replaces the traditional carved tympanum, providing yet another contrast between the monumental figures, the lacy pinnacles and the soaring towers.

St Louis

From 1226–1270 King Louis IX ruled France giving Paris a new stature in the eyes of all Europe. His piety and fairness of judgment gained him an international reputation and in 1297 a canonisation. As early as the twelfth century Paris was a celebrated teaching centre; by the mid-thirteenth century the university of Paris was renowned as the fount of logic and catholic thought. Students and scholars from all over the continent flocked to Paris to learn and discuss scholarly matters. Knights returning from crusades against the infidel introduced eastern theory and science. The role of the monastic scriptorium was transferred to commercial guilds founded to produce books for private ownership. Instead of the large ceremonial books of the eleventh and twelfth centuries, psalters became fashionable and eventually these gave way to smaller books of hours for private prayer, although the former were popular in the thirteenth century. The artistic milieu of the Paris of St Louis may be represented in those works carried out at the king's personal wishes. At his instigation, the architect Pierre de Montreuil completed the work begun by Abbot Suger in St Denis and also built out the transepts of Notre 74
Dame in Paris. Originally, the plan of this church (a long nave with a continuous aisle running round the chevet) had been the model for Sens and Bourges. Compared with Rheims or Amiens, Montreuil's transept projections have rather flat façades which are lit by very large rose windows filled with delicate tracery, tracery which is also used to decorate the stone-work itself. At St Denis and Notre Dame, Pierre de Montreuil's work was limited by the existing fabric, but in the Ste Chapelle he was able to give 72
full rein to his ideas. In 1239, St Louis bought the relic of the crown of thorns from the emperor of Constantinople, and he had the Ste Chapelle built to enshrine his new acquisition as well as his other treasured posses-sions. Compared to the great cathedrals, the royal chapel is tiny and was completed in a few years; it is the epitome of mid-thirteenth-century Parisian architecture. It was constructed on two levels so that the lesser

69
THE VISITATION
before 1250
central west portal, cathedral of Notre Dame,
Rheims

The sculpture on the various doorways at Rheims presents a synthesis of styles current before 1250 in northern France. Among the artists working there the so called Visitation Master displays an indisputable classical influence. His figures are standing in classical counter-poise and are draped in heavy swinging folds of cloth in contrast to the work of the more refined Annunciation Master on the same doorway. The drawing of the ambulatory windows is from the sketchbook of the travelling architect Villard d'Honnecourt.

70
AMBULATORY WINDOWS
from a sketchbook of Villard d'Honnecourt
thirteenth century
Bibliothèque Nationale, Paris

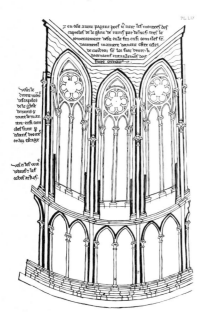

members of the royal house might worship in the lower chapel while St Louis retained the upper chapel as a personal oratory in which he could pray alone. This upper chapel has often been likened to a precious reliquary itself, for the long aisleless chapel gleams like a jewel from the light of the great stained glass windows that glows from more than three-quarters of the wall. The glass is arranged in medallions telling a host of biblical stories, and every part of the building is ornamented with decorative patterns and gilding.

Sometime between 1253 and his death in 1270, St Louis had a psalter written for him and illustrated in the royal guild. It has seventy-eight full-page illustrations of scenes from the Old Testament which are set against an architectural background, precise copies of details in the Ste Chapelle. Painted in rich colours, the figures are placed on a ground of shimmering gold that seems to bathe them in glorious sunlight. They are extremely elegant in design with small heads and tall, thin bodies moving with an easy grace. This manuscript is, above all, an 'edition de luxe' adjudged worthy of the great king.

The typology of the 'bible moralisée' was a product of the Dominican scholar, Hugues de St Cher. It contains stories from the bible juxtaposed with fables of moral significance and a famous copy is the Bible Moralisée of St Louis (now divided into three parts, one of which belongs to the Bibliothèque Nationale in Paris). In this the illustrations are arranged like medallions of stained glass transposed onto parchment with the intervening strips of text replacing the stone mullions of the windows. The analogy is further enhanced by the deep luminosity of the colouring and the strong outlines reminding one of the leads. Occasionally the quality of the interpretation varies, but the artists must be excused as the whole book contained over five-thousand medallions.

Much of the fine work made in gold and other precious metals has long since fallen prey to fortune hunters and marauders, but the so-called Crown of St Louis represents the current style with its delicately carved **73** angels and rich jewelling. The tomb of Louis's son, made *c.* 1260 and now standing in St Denis, shows a distinct relaxation of the earlier, rigid, impersonal effigy, and some attempt at portraiture is suggested by the long face and high forehead of the prince. Around the sides of the tomb a procession of mourners are stylistically reminiscent of the contemporary Psalter of St Louis.

After the death of St Louis, Paris remained the principal centre of manuscript illumination. Towards the end of the thirteenth century, the illuminator emerged as a distinct artistic personality. More than one reference was made to a Master Honoré of the rue Boutebrie in Paris and his name was recorded in the account books of the king. On the basis of a signed manuscript Master Honoré is attributed with the royal Breviary of Philip the Fair now in the Bibliothèque Nationale. The one full page **98** illustration with scenes from the life of David marks the culmination of trends embarked upon during the earlier part of the century. The episodes are full of life and movement with the bodies clearly defined beneath the draperies. Patterned backgrounds remain, but in the lower scene hills scattered with trees are introduced to suggest a naturalistic setting.

The effect of the Albigensian crusade

In order to see monumental Gothic architecture after 1250, it is necessary to turn to the south, to places where the bishops had close connections with the crown or to lands won in the struggles between the king and the feudal princes.

The principal change in the artistic community of the south and west

71

CHARLEMAGNE GIVING ORDERS
FOR BUILDING
THE CHURCH OF ST JAMES

early thirteenth century
stained glass
Chartres cathedral

The stained glass at Chartres is among the most beautiful in France. The central medallion of the 'Charlemagne' window illustrates the legend of the emperor giving orders for a church to be built in honour of St James who had assisted him in conquering the town of Pamplona. The royal house of France, knights and nobles are all known to have donated windows while the guilds of craftsmen and merchants are often represented in windows presented by them.

72 *right*

LA SAINTE CHAPELLE

1234–1248
Pierre de Montreuil and others, Paris

73 *far right*

CROWN OF ST LOUIS
c. 1260
diameter 8·25 in (21 cm)
Louvre, Paris

In 1239 St Louis bought the relic of the crown of thorns from the emperor of Constantinople, and the Ste Chapelle (**72**) was built to house the precious relic. St Louis reserved this upper chapel as his own personal oratory. The sumptuous effect derives from the excellent structural proportions and the rich colouring that radiates through the stained glass windows; the arcading is also enamelled and gilded giving an overall impression of a jewelled casket. The reliquary crown (**73**) was offered to the Dominican convent of Liège by St Louis around 1260. The eight plaques which traditionally contain relics of the Passion are interspersed with delicately worked statuettes of angels in silver-gilt. The handling of the angels suggests the closest links with St Louis' court school, for they compare closely with manuscripts like the Psalter of St Louis and with the larger angels in the Ste Chapelle.

74 *bottom left*
NOTRE DAME
mainly built during twelfth and thirteenth centuries
Paris

The cathedral of Notre Dame is magnificently situated, looking over the Seine from the Ile de la Cité. The present building was begun by Maurice de Sully in 1163 and was substantially complete by the time of St Louis. Pierre de Montreuil built the transepts lit by the rose windows with their delicate tracery. Stylistically it compares with Laon and Chartres as a classic example of early Gothic architecture.

75
CATHEDRAL OF ST ETIENNE
1195 – c. 1270/80
Bourges

The cathedral of Bourges was begun by St Guillaume in 1195. The architectural design is based on a triangular cross section with the two aisles on either side ascending in height towards the lofty proportions of the nave. The impression of soaring, upward movement is enhanced by the tall main arcade and the narrow triforium (plate **83**).

76

VIRGIN AND CHILD

1339
silver gilt and enamel
h. 27 in (69 cm)
Louvre, Paris

This exquisitely worked statuette of the
Virgin and Child was presented to the
Abbey of St Denis by Jeanne d'Evreux in
1339. The fleur de lis in the hand of the
Madonna may have once contained relics.
The figure is draped with sharply defined
folds of fabric and the sculptor has captured
the intimate, exclusive relationship
between mother and child.

77

THE AGONY IN THE GARDEN

from the Psalter of Queen Ingeborg
c. 1200–1205
Musée Condé, Chantilly (MS 1695)

The psalter was written and illustrated for
Queen Ingeborg, the Danish-born wife of
Philip Augustus. The illustrations are
richly coloured, fit for a royal commission,
and their hard metallic quality suggests that
the manuscript was produced in north-
eastern France, for it is stylistically connected with the metalwork that flourished in
the valley of the river Meuse.

came about as the result of the Albigensian crusades. Before the end of the twelfth century Toulouse, Aquitaine and Provence had been totally isolated from the royal house in Paris. The romantic literature and songs of the troubadours written in the Oc dialect (hence Languedoc) flourished at the courts of Aquitaine and Toulouse, but at the same time heretical teachings were put about and a general spirit of revolt against the church siezed the lords and common people. Eventually, in 1208, Pope Innocent III preached a crusade against the heretics which was led by Simon de Montfort who occupied Toulouse and who was, as the church's leader, responsible for cruel fighting and atrocities. Despite the religious incentives for the crusade, the outcome was in effect a military conquest of the north over the south. As the religious wars died away there was an influx of northern arts to the shores of the Mediterranean which extinguished the individual styles of Languedoc. The cathedrals of Narbonne and Rodez were built by an architect, Jean Deschamps, who was certainly conversant with the works of Pierre de Montreuil; Bayonne (begun after 1258) develops the theme of Soissons, and St Nazaire in the old walled city of Carcassonne is in fact a masterpiece in the northern style with **90** rose windows and blind tracery decoration on the wall surfaces. There are, however, a number of churches with specific characteristics that form an independent group within the Gothic idiom. Instead of the usual stone, many of these southern churches are built of brick. The cathedral of Albi **78** is a typical example and gives the impression of being a mighty fortress. The Dominican order was founded in Languedoc when St Dominic began preaching to the Albigensian heretics and papal recognition of the rule was granted in 1216.

Like Albi Cathedral, the Dominican Church of the Jacobins in Toulouse is built of brick and the exterior has that same effect of fortification. The lofty interior is divided into two aisles by a central file of columns, one side having been reserved for the monks, the other for the laity or university students, as this was the church of the university of Toulouse.

The papal court at Avignon

The south of France gained added importance during the fourteenth century from the installation of the papacy at Avignon. This period of papal rule at Avignon, known as the Babylonian Captivity, lasted from 1309 until 1377 with the popes being utterly subjected to the influence of the kings of France. In the history of the papacy this was an unhappy period, but Avignon and the arts of France greatly benefited from the exile. Avignon itself was completely transformed, with the modest bishop's palace being turned into the official papal residence filled with works of art. Under the guidance of Benedict XII, Pierre Obreri and **95** Pierre Poisson built the cathedral of Notre Dame des Doms and the papal apartments in the Tour des Anges. Outside, the papal palace looks like an impregnable fortress with crenellated battlements and protective shot towers, but within the vast complex appears more like a palace. A Sienese artist, Simone Martini, spent the last five years of his life working at Avignon in the service of the popes and he is known to have decorated the tympanum and gable of the west front of the cathedral. Only the underpainting of these frescos survives, but the monumentality of the master's touch remains. The frescoed decorations of the papal apartments are in a lighter vein showing men hunting with fine hounds, fishermen gathered with nets around a pond, falconers standing in the wooded glades; these are truly pastoral scenes that predate the achievements of the Limbourg **84, 85** brothers by more than half a century. Painting at Avignon at this time is particularly interesting as it shows the fusion of northern and southern

78

CATHEDRAL OF STE CECILE

begun 1282, completed in the sixteenth century Albi

The cathedral was originally built to serve as a citadel as well as a church by Bernard de Castanet, archbishop of Albi, who needed a strong defence against the heretics. Tall buttresses and narrow slits of windows heighten the fortress-like aspect of the building, which is built of pinkish brick and towers precipitously over the ancient city. The south porch, added in the sixteenth century, provides a complete contrast with its lacy pinnacles and flamboyant tracery designs.

79
STATUE OF CHARLES V
1375–1380
Louvre, Paris

The statue has the facial characteristics of king Charles V but was made as a statue of St Louis to decorate the portal of the Hospice des Quinze Vingts. As its name implies the hospital, founded in 1260 by St Louis, was built to accommodate three hundred blind people. The statue has all the realism and vitality of the best sculpture made in France at the time of Charles V. The companion piece, representing Marguerite de Provence, is a portrait of Jeanne de Bourbon.

80
VIRGIN AND CHILD
from the doorway of the Chartreuse de Champmol
c. 1400
school of Claus Sluter active 1385–1406
Musée des Beaux Arts, Dijon

The Virgin is one of a group of five statues from the entrance doorway to the charterhouse of Champmol which was founded in 1383 to be the family mausoleum of Philip the Bold. Unlike the statues from most French cathedral doorways these were designed as a separate feature and stand apart from their architectural setting. The strong, dynamic figure of the Virgin is forcefully characterised, her draperies swept up in a firm energetic hand.

ideals. Certainly the painting of the pastoral scenes is Sienese in style and compares closely with frescos by Ambrogio Lorenzetti in the Palazzo Pubblico, Siena, although the interpretation is more northern in flavour.

At about the same time Jean Pucelle, the artist of the Belleville Breviary, was working in Paris in a style in many ways directly dependent on the earlier Master Honoré. However, a new interest in nature is evident which is perfectly exemplified by his use of a simple tree which changes its foliage according to the seasons instead of the traditional scenes of the labours of the months. This delight in nature and an attempt to understand the Italian mastery of volumes and space suggests a new direction in the development of painting, comparable only to the Avignon frescos.

National instability and private wealth

Apart from the introduction of Italian elements into French painting, the middle years of the fourteenth century were a period of comparative stagnation for the arts. Two major factors, the Black Death and the Hundred Years War, confined the minds of men to the mere struggle for existence. The English armies sacked the countryside leaving a trail of devastated monastic lands; for funds to fight their enemies, the French king and his suzerains were forced to melt down gold and silver furnishings in the cathedral treasuries; churches fell down for want of men to maintain the fabric, and there was neither time nor inclination to erect new buildings. In this period of instability, there was little change in the current sculptural tradition and it is hard to believe that the beautiful statuette of the Virgin made for Jeanne d'Evreux in 1339 as a gift to the   **76** abbey of St Denis can be as much as a hundred years later than the apostle statues of the Ste Chapelle.

One of the reasons for France's early reversals in the Hundred Years War was the continued social structure of feudal society. Tradition claimed that the aristocracy and its entourage could only fight on horseback and when confronted with the infantry of Edward III at Crécy (1346) the French lost the battle partly because they had underestimated the strength of common foot soldiers and each knight in armour was intent on individual valour rather than collective discipline. These courtly knights lived in castles which became more and more splendid as the century passed. Inventories of the furnishings describe wooden chests, magnificent tapestries which provided both decoration and warmth for the great halls,   **100** large collections of gold and silver plate and ivory ornaments. The   **91** courtly elegance fashionable in the later fourteenth century is epitomised by the records and artistic commissions of the sons of King John the Good. His portrait in the Louvre, painted by Girart d'Orléans *c.* 1359, is the earliest French panel portrait known, the head being shown in profile but with realistic treatment of the nose and eyes. John the Good's eldest son became King Charles V in 1364 and ruled far more effectively than his father, managing to sweep the English from most parts of his kingdom. He was a highly intelligent man who gathered scholars and technicians about him. Among these were the poetess Christine de Pisan and the   **101** ballad writer Guillaume de Machault. At the palace of the Louvre, Charles V collected a magnificent library of books and his architect, Raymond du Temple, built a staircase decorated on the outside with statues of the royal family. The staircase itself is now lost, but an idea of the sculptural decoration may be gained from the statue of Charles V   **79** which is handled with impressive naturalism and sensitivity. In the *Parement de Narbonne* in the Musée de Cluny the donors, Charles V and his queen, are placed beneath an architectural canopy on either side of the Crucifixion. The whole altar frontal, on white silk, is painted in grisaille and was intended for use during Lent. The figures are tall and elegant and yet the attempt to display extreme dramatic emotion, particularly in the Entombment scene, suggests some knowledge of Sienese painting.

One of Charles V's brothers, Louis Duke of Anjou, commissioned a set of tapestries to decorate the chapel of his castle at Angers. Originally there were ninety panels of scenes from the Apocalypse and Angers still possesses sixty-nine of them. Each scene is set within a border resembling a window frame and the decorated borders are filled with flowers, insects and stars. The scenes must be based on manuscript illumination and rely on architectural elements to set the perspective for the episode.

The Burgundian court

Politically, Philip the Bold, Duke of Burgundy, was the most important of the brothers of Charles V. In 1361, the lands of Burgundy reverted to the French crown and were given by King John the Good to his son Philip, who later married Margaret, daughter of the count of Flanders. Through the trading cities of Bruges and Ghent, Burgundy became so strong and so rich that the course of French history at this period was largely dictated by the policy of successive dukes of Burgundy. Flemish sculptors, painters and goldsmiths flocked to Philip's court at Dijon,
80 among them Claus Sluter and Melchior Broederlam. The charterhouse of Champmol was founded in 1383 and the duke intended it to be his family mausoleum. For the chapel he commissioned his tomb from Jean de Marville and the Fleming Claus Sluter. Along the sides of the tomb, on which rests an alabaster effigy of the duke, little figures of mourners stand
81 in pairs. Each one is an individual even though the faces are often half hidden by the cowls of their cloaks. The heavy draperies certainly reflect the inspiration of Sluter, although he may have left much of the actual execution of the tomb to his nephew Claus de Werve. At the charterhouse of Champmol, Sluter's most monumental work is the surviving Puits de Moise. This well was commissioned to stand in the centre of a cloister with figures of the prophets holding scrolls surrounding the base of a calvary. Only the base and part of the figure of Christ remain. Each prophet is treated individually with realistic details (such as a pair of glasses) and accurate interpretation of facial types. Great solidity is given to bodies by means of thick, bulky draperies that enhance rather than conceal the form beneath. The torso of the Christ shows how well Sluter understood the human form and the head is treated with monumental pathos. From the Flemings Jacques de Baerze and Melchior Broederlam, Philip the Bold ordered a wooden altarpiece for his chapel. Jacques de Baerze carved exquisite saints and angels on the outside supposedly based on a wooden altarpiece Philip had seen in the Flemish abbey of Terne-monde. Within the wooden doors, Melchior Broederlam's *Nativity* is treated with realism far removed from the refined delicacy of contemporary Parisian painting.

The Duke of Berry

Philip the Bold's younger brother, John Duke of Berry, was also a great patron. A real connoisseur, he vied with his brother for the employment
83 of the very finest artists; he had a tomb prepared which he hoped would rival that in the charterhouse of Champmol and built magnificent castles throughout his duchy. He was also closely involved with the manuscripts which he commissioned, often having extra scenes painted into books of hours; and from the number of unfinished books from his library, it must be assumed that he sometimes lacked the patience to await their
85 completion. The most famous manuscript from the library of the Duke of
84 Berry is the *Très Riches Heures*. Illustrated by the Limbourg brothers

81
MOURNERS
detail from the tomb of John the Fearless
before 1435
after Claus Sluter active 1385–1406
Musée des Beaux Arts, Dijon

The tradition of placing mourners around the sides of a tomb goes back to the thirteenth century. This tomb of John Duke of Burgundy is one of the finest examples of this type. As in the tomb of his father, Philip the Bold, the mourners are sculpted in a monumental manner, their dignity and grief seeming to transcend the actual size of the figures.

c. 1409–1416, the calendar that prefaces the hours is shown in a semi-circle at the top of each of the twelve pages and is embellished with signs of the zodiac set against a stormy sky. The usual labours of the months are replaced by scenes of the duke going about his courtly pursuits. The page for December, for instance, shows a hunt with the hounds at the kill **84** before a wooded thicket. May has the patron out riding in his estate and January shows the noble duke entertaining his friends, a lavish feast set before them, wine flowing from golden ewers as the host bids his guests draw near. The most remarkable feature of this beautiful book is the advance made in the development of landscape painting. Great vistas stretch into the distance, castles and trees are drawn with loving care and the sky pales as it touches the horizon. The castles are so carefully painted that often they provide the historian with his only record of those that are lost; thus, Charles V's Louvre is known from one page, and on another page, the Duke of Berry's castle at Mehun-sur-Yevre is recorded. Of the castle of Mehun built on an island in the river Yevre, only the foundations remain, and yet the painting by the Limbourg brothers shows the entrance across the bridge, the castle chapel, towers capped with polygonal, traceried pinnacles, and the large, airy windows of the residential quarters. At Poitiers, parts of the duke's castle are still preserved and among other features, there is a magnificent fireplace, built by his architect Guy de Dammartin, embellished with a screen of glazed tracery and statues of Charles V and his queen, the duke and his wife Jeanne of Armagnac.

Between them, the four sons of John the Good monopolised the greater part of the artistic scene in France at the turn of the century, but in Paris the commercial guilds for manuscript illumination were still very active. Many knights and noblemen wanted books for their personal devotion. One such a man was the Maréchal de Boucicaut, a man steeped in the ideas of chivalry and one of the last crusaders. His book of hours, now in the Musée Jacquemart André in Paris, includes an illustration of St George and the Dragon, a subject dear to the heart of such a character.

Foreign influences

After 1420, the importance of Paris declined as a result of English occupation under the regency of the duke of Bedford, the madness of Charles VI **99** and terrible political strife. In 1439, there was grass growing in the streets of Paris. Throughout the country the ravages of a hundred years of war was taking its toll and many other cities were greatly depopulated. Poets and artists became obsessed with death, so that tombs which had once displayed an idealised effigy were now ornamented with grotesque corpses and tragic epitaphs. René Duke of Anjou, son of the Valois Duke Louis, was a man typical of the age. A devoutly religious philosopher, he could write fine poetry and his *Mortifiement de la Vaine Plaisance* is a Christian allegory on the futility of earthly life, written after the death of his first wife. Yet he still cherished the old chivalrous ideals of the fourteenth century, founding the Order of the Knights of St Maurice and writing a book of tournaments (in the Bibliothèque Nationale) which he may have illustrated himself.

With Paris no longer the artistic centre of France, provincial styles developed and with this provincialism art tended to become more bourgeois. The principal patrons of the fifteenth century were not the royal house nor the aristocratic courtiers, but rather civic communes, financiers and politicians. One of the most influential figures in the court of King Charles VII was the merchant Jacques Coeur. His house at **92** Bourges, dating from the 1440s, is a remarkable example of a medieval town house with numerous rooms facing the large courtyard which were

82

SYNAGOGUE

c. 1220–50
south transept, cathedral of Notre Dame,
Strasbourg

The double portal of the south transept at Strasbourg is flanked by the allegorical statues of the *Ecclesia Triumphant* and the *Synagogue*. With drooping head and eyes blindfold, *Synagogue* leans on a broken staff, her crown slipping from her head. The carving of these figures suggests close connections with Rheims and Rheims sculptors may have later travelled to Strasbourg.

83 CRYPT OF THE CATHEDRAL OF ST ETIENNE

c. 1200, Bourges

The present cathedral of Bourges was built during the arch-bishopric of Henry de Sully to replace an earlier church. He was obviously fully conversant with contemporary developments in architecture in the Ile de France. It was necessary to raise the level of the east end by means of a large crypt. The superstructure is supported on massive piers with attached columns, decorated with the characteristic crocket capitals and a comprehensive system of rib vaults. The effigy of John Duke of Berry is all that remains of an impressive tomb executed c. 1430 by Jean de Cambrai.

84 THE MONTH OF DECEMBER *detail*

from the Très Riches Heures of the Duke of Berry
Pol, Jean and Herman de Limbourg active early fifteenth century
Musée Condé, Chantilly (MS 65)

The book of hours made for the Duke of Berry is one of the most attractive treasures of medieval France. Each scene in the calendar has immediate appeal and conjures up a clear picture of courtly life in the middle ages. No less exquisite is the treatment of the biblical illustrations which are interspersed throughout the pages of the hours themselves. The scene of the kill is set against a background of the towers of Vincennes, which used to be a favourite castle of Charles V.

85

THE BUILDING OF THE TEMPLE

from Flavius Josephus: Antiquités Judaiques, c. 1470
Jean Fouquet c. 1420–1477
Bibliothèque Nationale, Paris (MS Fr. 247)

The manuscript once belonged to the Duke of Berry but the
original illustrations by the Limbourg brothers were completed
only after his death, by Jean Fouquet. Fouquet felt it unnecessary
to give the scenes a strictly historical setting and the biblical temple
is interpreted as a French Gothic building set in a medieval town.

reached by exterior staircases decorated with stone tracery and carved plaques, often embossed with hearts and the shells of St James, alluding to the owner's name.

85 The painter Jean Fouquet, who was born at Tours *c.* 1420, was the finest French artist of his day and many of his commissions were for Etienne Chevalier, another advisor to King Charles VII. In 1445–7, Fouquet travelled to Italy to paint a portrait of Pope Eugenius IV, and Italian painting left a permanent impression on his own. In the Hours of Etienne Chevalier the scenes are set before a mixture of Gothic and Italianate architecture, and reflections of the art of Fra Angelico can be seen in the stance of the figures and in the 'putti-like' angels. Etienne Chevalier was proud to own such a book and on almost every illustrated page his name is prominently displayed. The painting of Pope Eugenius is lost, but Fouquet has left admirable likenesses of Charles VII, of Etienne Chevalier, and the chancellor Juvenal des Ursins, each well characterised and suggesting a knowledge of Flemish portraiture on the part of Fouquet.

Just as the dukes of Burgundy continued to influence political affairs throughout the fifteenth century, so the successors of Philip the Bold continued to patronise Flemish artists. The 'peintre et varlet de chambre' of Philip the Good was Jan van Eyck, who travelled to Portugal for the duke to paint a portrait of Isabella during negotiations for their betrothal. For Philip the Good's chancellor, Nicolas Rolin, Van Eyck painted one of his major altarpieces– *The Rolin Madonna* (Louvre, Paris). Rolin also founded the Hôtel Dieu at Beaune as a hospital in 1443. Here, the main 'chambre des povres' is of immense length and originally the chapel at the end was enriched by Roger van der Weyden's majestic *Last Judgment* (still at Beaune) for all the patients to see.

With the advent of panel painting, the French rapidly became aware of
96 the greater artistic developments of Flanders and Italy. Thus, *The Avignon Pietà* was painted *c.* 1460 by a Frenchman and yet the flat relief format and the intense emotion on each face are unthinkable without the foreknowledge of a painting like Roger van der Weyden's *Deposition* now in Madrid. In architecture, however, the French masons remained loyal to their native traditions. Their only limitation was that by the end of the fourteenth century almost every structural permutation of soaring vaults and elaborate buttressing had been tried, so that these later architects would seem to be less adventurous than their forbears, being forced to
94 concentrate on virtuoso effects with decorative design and tracery. At St
86 Maclou in Rouen, begun *c.* 1432, the church has lost all semblance of a solid structure with the façade and the crossing tower reduced to a system of struts and flame-shaped forms (hence the term Flamboyant).
87 The same loss of structural sense may be seen in the Butter Tower of Rouen Cathedral, a tower built 1485–1507 from money received for indulgences to eat butter during Lent, and in the cathedral façade (1509–14) which, in direct contrast to a church like Rheims, masks the shape of the building behind in the manner of an English façade such as Exeter.

By the beginning of the sixteenth century, the Renaissance was to affect every facet of man's intellectual and artistic existence. The invention of printing burst upon the tranquil world of illuminated, handwritten books like some undreamed-of automation in our modern world, but even if such technical advance had not precipitated the decline of manuscript illumination, the questionings of the great Renaissance intellectuals would have sufficed to change the attitude of painters. In architecture, it was the triumph of rationalised, classical designers from Italy that brought the Middle Ages to a close. Sabrina Mitchell

86

ST MACLOU
fifteenth century
Rouen

The city of Rouen possesses two of the most extreme examples of Flamboyant architecture. This church is a fine example of the late, florid style of Gothic architecture, as is the Butter Tower of the cathedral *below*. The fragile-looking exterior is reduced to a pattern of struts and pinnacles soaring upwards which is enhanced by the tall nineteenth-century spire.

87

THE BUTTER TOWER
1485–1507
cathedral of Notre Dame, Rouen

The Butter Tower, built with money raised from indulgences to eat butter during Lent, was erected when the rest of the cathedral was substantially complete. It is a magnificent example of Flamboyant architecture, two hundred and fifty two feet high, crowned with pinnacles and richly articulated at every level.

88

COLUMN FIGURES ON THE PORTAIL ROYAL

c. 1150
cathedral of Notre Dame, Chartres

Like St Denis, the west front of Chartres Cathedral has one of the earliest sculptural programmes to include column figures. The thin parallel folds of the draperies and the elongation of the figures subject these kings and queens of Judah to a strictly architectural role and help to retain the overall unity of the portal.

89

TOWERS OF LAON CATHEDRAL

c. 1165–1205

The construction of the present cathedral of Laon was largely supervised by the bishop Gautier de Mortagne and continued after his death. The exterior is treated with bold massing of forms: deepset doorways and large window openings create effects of light and shade that throw the whole façade into high relief. The church is crowned by five towers (originally seven were planned), and in these the square shape is enlivened by exhedrae with cattle peering out. These cattle were put up in memory of the oxen who dragged the stone to the site of the cathedral.

90 CARCASSONNE, THE OLD CITY

Despite restorations by Viollet-le-Duc in the nineteenth century, Carcassonne remains one of the most completely fortified cities of the middle ages. The original walls date back to Merovingian times but the city was greatly enlarged when it became a stronghold of royal power in the south of France in the thirteenth century. The two walls include no less than forty-two towers to protect the fortress.

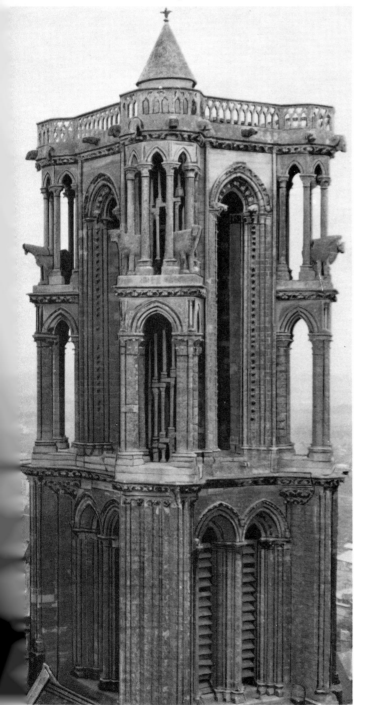

91 IVORY TRIPTYCH *central portion*

mid-14th century, probably by the Master of the Death of the Virgin h. 12·5 in (32 cm), Musée de Cluny, Paris

During the fourteenth century small scale ivories of both ecclesiastical and secular nature were produced in numerous quantities in France. Caskets and mirror backs were richly carved with scenes of chivalry and courtly life. Articles such as this triptych from the church of St Sulpice de Tarn would illustrate scenes from the life of Christ. The scenes on this central panel show the Crucifixion and the Virgin in Glory.

92, 93

HOUSE OF JACQUES COEUR

c. 1440
Bourges

Few medieval houses of any kind have
survived in France; it is thus all the more
fortunate that the house of the silversmith
Jacques Coeur should be such a magnificent
example. This view shows the central
court around which are built the four
wings of the mansion. Above the Gothic
porch was a statue of Coeur's patron
Charles VII and on each side, sculptured
in a false window, is the head of a servant
supposedly watching out for his master.
The coat of arms with hearts and shells
occurs frequently.

94

CHOIR SCREEN

1508–1517
Jean Gailde, active 1508–1517
La Madeleine, Troyes

The magnificent screen across the choir of
the church is a very late example of the
medieval carver's art. It is a virtuoso
masterpiece of hanging arches and
flamboyant designs built at a time when
Francis I was busy with Italianate commissions at Fontainebleau.

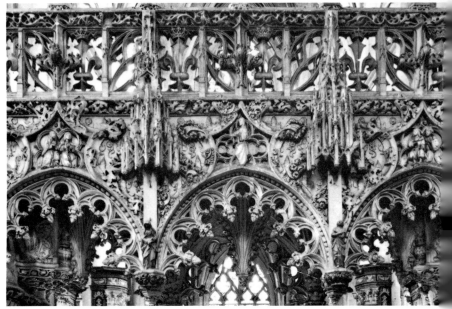

95
PALACE OF THE POPES

1336–1352
Avignon

Situated on the top of a hill, the magnificent palace and the cathedral of Notre Dame des Doms dominate the entire city of Avignon. During the fourteenth century when the Papacy was in exile, Avignon flourished as an artistic centre and attracted the finest artists to France. The early part of the palace, built for Benedict XII, was severely in keeping with his Cistercian austerity while the 'New Palace' built by Clement VI is lavishly decorated with magnificent frescos by Italian painters.

96
THE AVIGNON PIETA

c. 1455
oil on panel
63·75 × 86 in (162 × 218 cm)
Louvre, Paris

This magnificent representation of the Pietà from the charterhouse of Villeneuve les Avignon is one of the most moving and noble of all French medieval paintings. The figures gather around the central dead Christ; each one is carefully and individually modelled. The donor stands out on the left as a real person differing from the idealised religious figures.

97
HUNTING SCENE
from the Book of Hunting MS Français 616 f 85 v
c. 1405–10
Gaston Phebus d. 1391
Bibliothèque Nationale, Paris

The text of this treatise on hunting was written by the Comte de Foix (Gaston Phebus). Each illustration shows a different facet of the hunt. Here the decorative element supersedes a desire for realism with gaily caparisoned horses, delicately drawn stag and hounds set before a patterned background of rosettes. Contrast these with the contemporary hunting scenes in the *Très Riches Heures* of the Duke of Berry (plate **84**).

98
THE ANOINTING OF DAVID: DAVID AND GOLIATH
detail from the Breviary of Philip the Fair
Master Honoré active late thirteenth century
Bibliothèque Nationale, Paris (MS Lat. 1023)

This breviary contains a number of historiated initials as well as a single full page illustration with scenes from the Life of David. Master Honoré has made the narrative easy to follow with the names of principal characters written below the figures as well as a variation in the sizes of each individual.

99
THE DEATH OF ST EDWARD
from the Breviary of the Duke of Bedford
MS Lat. 17294 f 432 v, 1425–35
Bibliothèque Nationale, Paris

John of Lancaster, Duke of Bedford was regent for the English crown in France. This lavishly decorated breviary is one of the illuminated manuscripts that he commissioned. Many of the pages have subsidiary scenes as well as the main subject and all spaces are filled with foliage.

100
LA DAME A LA LICORNE
c. 1500
tapestry
Musée de Cluny, Paris

This is one of a set of six tapestries from the Château de Boussac now arranged in a special room in the Musée de Cluny. Despite their late date the conception of the scenes remains entirely medieval with tall elegant figures and fanciful beasts set against exquisitely delicate foliage and flowers.

101
THE TROJAN WAR
from the Epistle from Othea to Hector
MS Français 606 f 40, c. 1400–02
illustrated under the direction of Christine de Pisan, Bibliothèque Nationale, Paris

Like many of her compatriots, the Italian poetess Christine de Pisan was drawn to Paris by its reputation as a cultural centre. The copy of the *Epistle from Othea to Hector* was made for the Valois Louis Duke of Orleans and is embellished with more than a hundred painted scenes. The romantic subject was most attractive to the courtly knights of the period.

In the years around 1500 the basic style in French architecture was still the Late Gothic, and architecture was still, as it had been throughout the Gothic period, the prime art. But in these years a hybrid style was to emerge in France, a somewhat uneasy compound of essentially Gothic structures and applied Renaissance decorative features imported, fully matured, from Italy. Some writers have refused to allow that this constitutes a new style in French art—for Walter Pater it was merely 'the finest and subtlest phase of the middle age itself'—but what is undeniable is that this peculiar artistic compromise was the first link in a chain of development which was to produce, within less than a quarter of a century, a distinct style which can confidently be called the French Renaissance style.

That France, the homeland of the Gothic, had not in the course of the fifteenth century evolved a Renaissance style of her own was not from a lack of awareness of Renaissance ideas: as far back as the late 14th century John Duke of Berry had created at his court at Bourges a Humanist environment as enlightened as any to be found in Italy at that time—the kind of soil from which a French Renaissance could perhaps ultimately have grown. Nor was it from a want of contact with Renaissance artifacts, for during the second half of the century minor works of art were imported from Italy in ever-increasing numbers. Already in the 1470s Francesco Laurana, working at the court of René of Anjou in Provence, had built the first Renaissance structure in France, the chapel of St Lazare in the old cathedral of Marseilles, and as far north as Le Mans the tomb of René's brother Charles of Maine had been made by a Florentine artist. But the cultural climate of Bourges evaporated completely on the duke's death in 1416; and René's court, which also died with him in 1480, had no impact on central France. The kings of France of the middle years of the fifteenth century, Charles VII and Louis XI, were too occupied with the unification of French territories under their crown to give much thought to the arts at all, much less to cultural developments outside the borders of France.

The medieval guilds still held France in the grip of the Gothic. Whereas in Germany the Renaissance style was to a large extent introduced by German artists who had travelled, a French artist like Jean Fouquet, painter to Louis XI, who had worked in Rome and who returned to place his figures in Italianate settings, was exceptional. The French Renaissance style was to be in the first instance the creation of French patrons and of Italian artists working to their requirements. It was informed as much by the specific needs and limitations of the patrons as by the skills of the Italian artists themselves and the degree of resistance of the French artists with whom they were to collaborate. What was needed was, first, for those who were in a position to become the patrons of a new style—the rich and powerful bourgeois class of ministers of the crown, financiers and merchants who had come to the fore in the middle years of the century—to be made fully aware of the new Italian culture and secondly a nucleus of Italian artists resident in France.

The Italian influence

These two requirements were fulfilled in the course of Charles VIII's Italian campaign of 1494–96. The campaign was designed to assert his claim to the throne of Naples; this prize, although he won it, he failed to hold, but a real and lasting prize was the enthusiasm engendered in himself and those who accompanied him by all that they saw in their journey throughout the length of Italy. Although unable to appreciate finer points of style, they were overwhelmed by the beauty and richness

Princely Patrons and the French Renaissance
1500–1600

102

KING FRANCIS I OF FRANCE

c. 1525
oil on panel
Jean Clouet active 1509 died 1540/41
37·75 × 29 in (96 × 74 cm)
Louvre, Paris

A Fleming by origin, Jean Clouet, known as 'Janet', first appears in French royal accounts in 1516. He succeeded Bourdichon as court painter to Francis I in 1523, and retained the position until his death, when he was succeeded by his son François. His chief function at the court was to provide officially approved drawings which served as prototypes for all court portraiture, and in this painting, which is almost certainly attributable to his own hand, the head is directly based on his chalk drawing of the king preserved in the Louvre. In 1540, just before he died, this image of the king was superseded by another drawing which he made of him at a more advanced age. The painting demonstrates that while in other fields of painting the king acquired Italian taste, he retained a totally Northern conception of the portrait as image.

85

73

of their surroundings. A typical reaction was that of Bishop Briçonnet, son of the king's financial adviser, who wrote to the queen from Naples: 'Madame, I would that you might have seen this city, and the fair things which are therein, for it is an earthly paradise.'

In 1495 Charles sent home from Naples a group of twenty-two Italian artists and artisans 'pour oeuvrer de leur métier à l'usage et mode d'Italie'. The wording is significant here, for it was more an Italian fashion than a specifically Renaissance style which Charles and his courtiers wished to import, and it is doubtful whether they had any appreciation of the classical basis of the new style. The choice of artists is interesting: most highly salaried was a sculptor, Guido Mazzoni, whose naturalistic style owed much to northern Late Gothic; next came an architect, Fra Giovanni Giocondo, followed by a garden designer, Dom Pacello da Mercoliano. The remainder, at lower salaries, were minor decorative artists and craftsmen.

These artists were installed at Amboise, but little trace of their work there has survived the subsequent demolitions and rebuildings. The earliest example of Italian art in France attributable to one of them is to be found in the two purely Italian pilasters dated 1496 which flank the typical Late Gothic Easter sepulchre in the abbey church at Solesmes.

Charles VIII died in 1498, and his tomb, based on a traditional French pattern, was ordered by his successor Louis XII from Guido Mazzoni. Louis himself was not a vastly ambitious patron: his tastes were on the whole simple and bourgeois and his chief virtue as a monarch was a sensible and cautious attitude to royal spending. But Louis also had a claim to realise in Italy, the duchy of Milan, and it was during his reign that the French established themselves on Italian soil, occupying both Milan and Genoa. This was the beginning of a deep French involvement in the affairs of Italy, which, punctuated by successive campaigns, was to last until the Peace of Cateau-Cambrésis in 1559, and was to be a vital factor in the development of the French Renaissance.

As ruler of Milan and Genoa Louis made surprisingly slight use of his resources. In Milan he appointed Leonardo da Vinci to be his painter and architect, and attempted unsuccessfully to remove Leonardo's *Last Supper* from its wall. It was possibly he who brought to France from Milan the *Madonna of the Rocks* now in the Louvre. In Genoa he ordered from Girolamo Viscardi the first of a series of works to be commissioned from there by Frenchmen, the tomb of his ancestors the dukes of Orleans, in St Denis.

All this was modest in comparison with the ambitious undertakings of his courtiers. The wing which he added to his château at Blois is conservative in comparison with the Hôtel d'Alluye which his treasurer Florimond Robertet built in the town, and pales almost to insignificance beside Robertet's great Renaissance palace at Bury. It was in the courtyard at the Hôtel d'Alluye that the first work by Michelangelo to reach France was installed, the lost bronze *David*.

It was to be expected that French churchmen, with their special contact with Rome, would be prominent in the introduction of the Renaissance style, and indeed Cardinal Georges d'Amboise, archbishop of Rouen and Louis's chief minister, was the most important patron of the reign. His great palace of Gaillon, near Rouen, was begun in 1501 in a traditional Gothic style, but he employed several of the Amboise Italians there together with other Italians whom he attracted to France himself, like the painter Andrea Solario and the sculptor Antonio Giusti, and from 1508 the building was continued in an Italianate style. Gaillon was largely

103
ST GEORGE
AND THE DRAGON
1508–09
Michel Colombe 1430/5, last recorded 1512
marble
Louvre, Paris

The relief was made for Cardinal Georges d'Amboise, archbishop of Rouen, for the chapel (now demolished) of his château of Gaillon, where it stood above the altar. The frame was carved by the Genoese artist Jerome Pacherot, one of the twenty-two Italians brought to Amboise by Charles VIII. Colombe, whose workshop was at Tours, was the leading French sculptor of his time, and usually worked in a Late Gothic idiom. Here he adapted his style to conform with the prevailing Lombard Renaissance style at Gaillon, and seems to have based the overall conception of his relief on similar panels by the Genoese family of the Gaggini.

CHATEAU DE CHENONCEAUX
1515–1580

The square keep incorporating the entrance (shown here on the left) was built between 1515 and 1522 for Thomas Bohier, Général des Finances of Normandy. The château was confiscated by Francis I in 1535, and was given in 1547 by Henry II to Diane de Poitiers, who in 1556 commissioned Philibert de l'Orme to build onto it the bridge across the river Cher which was completed in 1559, the year of Henry's death. In the following year the château was confiscated by Catherine de 'Medici who in about 1576 entrusted Jean Bullant with the construction of the galleries on the bridge, completed about 1580.

105 CHEST
c. 1525–35, oak, Louvre, Paris

The chest was once part of the original furnishings of the chateau of Azay-le-Rideau, built in 1518–27 for the financier Gilles Berthelot. Although Italians were employed at Azay, it is almost certainly the work of a French craftsman. The light and graceful arabesque pattern incorporating medallions and grotesques is typical of the early Francis I style of decoration and corresponds with the decorative carving on the building itself.

destroyed in the Revolution, but some of the more important parts, such as the Renaissance entrance gate of 1508, remain on the site in a mutilated condition, and many details are preserved in the courtyard of the Ecole des Beaux Arts. In 1506 the cardinal commissioned the great fountain for the main courtyard from the sculptors Antonio della Porta and Pace Gaggini in Genoa, and when the French sculptor Michel Colombe carved the relief of St George, now in the Louvre, for the altarpiece of the chapel, **103** he adopted a style heavily influenced by contemporary Genoese sculpture.

A Genoese element predominates in another great undertaking initiated by a Norman churchman–the redecoration of the abbey church at Fécamp by Abbot Antoine Bohier. Bohier visited Genoa in 1507 and commissioned the high altar and its surrounding sculpture from the same Pace Gaggini who had provided the fountain for Gaillon and Girolamo Viscardi who had made the Orléans tomb for the king. Other parts of the scheme, such as the screens around the choir, were carried out by Italians working on the site but most of the work was entrusted to French artists working in the Italian style. The importance of Fécamp, where the work probably continued until 1519, was that it provided an opportunity for Frenchmen to learn the new techniques of decoration. When the tomb-chest, also by Pace Gaggini, of Bohier's friend Raoul de Lannoy, the French governor of Genoa, was installed after his death in the church at Folleville, the surround was almost certainly carved by Frenchmen trained at Fécamp.

Antoine Bohier was exceptional in his time in promoting an important ecclesiastical project in the Renaissance style: in general the style is associated at this period with secular buildings, above all with châteaux. His brother Thomas Bohier, Général des Finances of Normandy, in the early years of the following reign was to be the builder of the entrance block of the château of Chenonceaux (1515–22). Thomas was related through his **104** wife (the sister of the Bishop Briçonnet who had written so enthusiastically to the queen from Naples) to the banker Gilles Berthelot, who in 1518–27 built for himself the beautiful château of Azay-le-Rideau.

These charming châteaux, built within the first few years of the reign of Francis I, with their regular plans and sophisticated decoration embody a whole new stage of advance on the rambling and ponderous Gaillon. They represent the epitome of the early 'style François Premier', and tend to eclipse the early efforts in building of the young king himself.

Francis I

Francis, when he began in 1515 (the first year of his reign) his new **102** Italianate wing at Blois, was indeed only a patron among patrons. In the **121** same year he reasserted the claim of the French crown to the duchy of Milan with his brilliant victory at Melegnano. Now an Italian prince, he began gradually to establish himself as a princely patron on the Italian model, competing, as his predecessors had not done, for the services of the very finest artists alive. Building on the firm political basis established by his predecessors, he gradually drew the whole of the power and wealth of his vast kingdom into his own hands and was able to become a patron possessed of resources such as few Italian princes had enjoyed. Not only did he eventually eclipse all competitors in France, but he emerged as one of the greatest patrons of art in Europe.

His ambitions began to be apparent quite early. In 1517 he invited Leonardo to come from Milan and installed him at the Manoir de Cloux at Amboise, but it was already too late: Leonardo was old, partially paralysed and unable to paint during the bare two years which he still had to live. The only lasting result of his visit was that Francis acquired for his

107
127 already growing collection the *St John the Baptist* and the *Virgin and Child with St Anne* of the Louvre and possibly also the *Mona Lisa*. The arrival in 1518 of Andrea del Sarto should have been more propitious, but he
106 was to stay for just over a year, contributing his *Charity* to the king's collection. Raphael never allowed himself to be persuaded to come to France, but his *St Michael* had been in the possession of Francis from early in his reign as had the painting which is known today as the *Holy Family*
108 *of Francis I*. The king was later to acquire Raphael's portrait of Joanna of Aragon and the *Belle Jardinière*. All these are now in the Louvre.

French painting was very little affected by these additions to the royal collection. Whereas in architecture, sculpture and the decorative arts the example of the Italians was comparatively soon assimilated and distilled to produce a new French style in which Frenchmen took the lead, for most of the sixteenth century the primacy in painting in France was to be held by Italian painters. The art of court portraiture, under the
102 leadership of the Fleming Jean Clouet and, later, his son François was in effect a separate branch of art in which a basically northern style predominated.

After Francis's return in 1526 from his first great reverse in Italy at the Battle of Pavia and his captivity in Madrid, political events in Italy provided an opportunity for enriching his collection of Italian art which he was quick to seize. 1527 was the year of the sack of Rome and the restoration of the republic in Florence. For three years his agent Giambattista della Palla despoiled Florence for him, buying works of art cheaply from the abandoned great houses of the city. Among the haul from this source were sculptures by Bandinelli and Tribolo, paintings by Fra Bartolommeo and Pontormo, and, most important of all, Michelangelo's lost marble *Hercules*.

What was more important was that Francis now embarked on what
119 might be fairly described as an orgy of building. Chambord, begun fairly modestly in 1519 as a hunting lodge and now completed on an ambitious scale to a design by Domenico da Cortona, remained isolated in the old royal centre of the valley of the Loire. Francis had decided on his return to base the court on Paris, and it was on his new châteaux in the Ile-de-France that his interest was now chiefly centred. St Germain and Challuau, both by Pierre Chambiges, were the first to be built there, followed in 1528 by the Château de Madrid (wholly destroyed) in the Bois de Boulogne, and Fontainebleau.

The Château de Madrid, built to a basically traditional design by French architects, with overall decoration in glazed terra-cotta by Girolamo della Robbia, marks the highest development of the fussy, highly decorated style of the first phase of the French Renaissance. The new building at Fontainebleau, initially designed by the Frenchman Gilles le Breton, was by contrast classically simple and restrained. Although much of this original construction has not survived the many rebuildings
110 the Porte Dorée, intended for the main entrance to the château, still stands as Le Breton built it, recognisably in the French tradition but with a totally new severity.

Fontainebleau

With the beginning of work at Fontainebleau a new phase in the history of the French Renaissance opens. Fontainebleau was to become the king's favourite seat, and the main centre of artistic activity in France until well into the seventeenth century. It was here that the new court style of the school of Fontainebleau was forged in the decoration of the interior of the building.

106

CHARITY *detail*

1518
Andrea del Sarto 1486–1531
oil
73 × 54 in (185 × 137 cm)
Louvre, Paris

In 1515/16 Francis I received from his Florentine agent a painting by Andrea del Sarto (now lost) which pleased him so much that he ordered more work from the artist. Andrea decided to go to France in person, and was installed at the French court by May of 1518. We are told by Vasari that he painted many pictures in France for the king, but this is the only one to have survived. In the summer of 1519 Andrea was persuaded to revisit Florence by a letter from his wife, and never returned to France.

107
THE VIRGIN AND CHILD AND ST ANNE
c. 1508–10
Leonardo da Vinci 1452–1519
oil on wood
69 × 51 in (170 × 129 cm)
Louvre, Paris

On 10th October, 1517 Cardinal Louis of Aragon, according to an account by his secretary, visited Leonardo at the Manoir de Cloux at Amboise and was shown three paintings by the artist. This painting was one of them, the second was the *St John the Baptist*, also now in the Louvre, and the third was a portrait of a lady, sometimes identified with the Mona Lisa, though probably incorrectly. The panel was painted with the help of assistants in Milan, and was taken uncompleted to France by Leonardo in late 1516. At his death in 1519, it was bequeathed by him to his assistant Francesco Melzi.

108
THE HOLY FAMILY OF FRANCIS I *detail*
1518
Raphael (Raffaello Sanzio) 1483–1520
oil on canvas
81·5 × 55 in (207 × 140 cm)
Louvre, Paris

This is one of four paintings by Raphael owned by Francis I. Together with the great *St Michael*, also in the Louvre, it was commissioned from the artist by Lorenzo de'Medici, Duke of Urbino, in 1517 on behalf of his uncle Pope Leo X for presentation to Francis. Painted between March and May of 1518 by Raphael with the assistance of Guilio Romano, it was personally delivered to Francis at Fontainebleau by Lorenzo in June 1518. It remained there, where it was restored by Primaticcio between 1537 and 1540, until it was removed to Versailles under Louis XIV.

78

DIANA THE HUNTRESS

c. 1550
Luca Penni d. 1556
oil
75·5 × 52·5 in (192 × 133 cm)
Louvre, Paris

This is a portrait of Diane de Poitiers in her favourite personification as the Goddess Diana, and is one of the most famous examples of the Diana symbolism which pervades French art of this time. Penni, a pupil of Raphael, was in France from 1537 and worked at Fontainebleau as assistant to Rosso on the decoration of the Galerie Francois Ier. In about 1550 he settled in Paris, where the picture was probably painted to the order of Diane, perhaps for her château of Anet. It was inspired by the Roman statue of the goddess, now in the Louvre, which was owned by Diane de Poitiers. Penni was also the designer of the famous set of tapestries of the *Story of Diana* formerly at Anet.

110

PORTE DOREE

1528–40
Gilles le Breton
Palace of Fontainebleau

The contract for rebuilding parts of the old château of Fontainebleau was concluded on the 28th April 1528 between Francis's controller of buildings and the master mason Gilles le Breton, of whom nothing else is known. One of the first parts to be built was this gateway giving access to the Cour Ovale, the courtyard of the old castle, which was intended to form the principal entrance to the new palace. Most of Le Breton's work at Fontainebleau has been altered or replaced, but the gateway still stands exactly as he built it, as can be seen from a representation of it in one of Rosso's frescos.

Of the Italian artists who came to France before 1530, the major ones had been there for too short a time to make an impression, and the ones who stayed to make their careers there were minor figures who merely reflected the current styles of their native schools and attempted to adapt them to a French environment. The arrival in 1530 of a major artist, displaced by the sack of Rome, who was to make at Fontainebleau a unique contribution to European art, is symptomatic of Francis's emergence as a patron on a truly international scale.

This artist was Rosso Fiorentino; his major work was the decoration of the Galerie François Premier at Fontainebleau on which he was engaged 117 from 1533 to 1540, the year of his death. In this he had the collaboration of a second major Italian artist, Francesco Primaticcio, who arrived in 1532, having learned at Mantua under Giulio Romano the technique of decoration in painting and stucco which he and Rosso were to develop at Fontainebleau. After Rosso's death Primaticcio was placed in charge of all the decorative work at Fontainebleau under the special protection of the king's mistress, the Duchesse d'Etampes, for whom he decorated between 1541 and 1543 the room known as the Chambre de la Duchesse 118 d'Etampes.

These are the chief seminal works of the Fontainebleau style, but the contribution of a third major Italian artist was also of vital importance. Benvenuto Cellini, who had visited France briefly in 1537, came again in 1540 to stay for five years bringing with him the great saltcellar, which he had begun in Italy for Cardinal Ippolito d'Este and was to complete for the king. It was in France that he was to make his first large-scale sculpture, *The Nymph of Fontainebleau*, the influence of which is visible 126 throughout French art of the next generation.

Cellini's great salt, now in Vienna, is a lone survival of the silver-ware of Francis I. The fate of French royal silver has always been subject to economic crisis, and the salt itself only just escaped being melted down in 1566. That it survives today is due to the fact that Charles IX, on the occasion of his marriage in 1570 to Elizabeth of Austria, presented it to the Archduke Ferdinand. Few examples of the decorative arts remain from 116 Francis's reign. The furniture of the period, although it reflected Italian influence in its decoration, remained largely traditional in form, and was quickly superseded by the more sophisticated types of the reign of Henry 129 II. The fine chest from Azay-le-Rideau is a rare example. Native French 105 pottery remained comparatively crude and medieval in form; one major development was the establishment of Italian potters at Lyons, from about 1512, who produced maiolica in the Italian style, but it was only during the second half of the century that the art of pottery began to flourish in France.

Another Italian attracted to Francis's court in these years was the architect Sebastiano Serlio, who in 1541 was placed in charge of building at Fontainebleau. Only one of his buildings survives, the château of Ancy-le-Franc. Of the influential palace he built at Fontainebleau for Ippolito d'Este only the gateway remains. His main importance lies in his illustrated treatise, published in France, which was used by French architects as a prime source for the Italian High Renaissance style.

The style of Henry II

As a result of these developments under Francis I, France was now in tune with the High Renaissance in Italy, and the way was open for the French Renaissance to move into its mature period after the accession of Henry II in 1547. Henry's own reign was short – he was to die in a jousting accident in 1559 – but the so-called 'Style Henri II' can fairly be said to have lasted until the murder in 1589 of his third son, Henry III, the last of the Valois kings. Henry himself was, unlike his father, neither a great nor imaginative patron, just as he was not a great or forceful monarch, but the artistic effort of France continued to be centred on the court, if not personally on the king, and there were great patrons to be found in Henry's immediate circle: his mistress Diane de Poitiers, his queen **109** Catherine de' Medici, and, among his advisers, the Constable Anne de **131** Montmorency and the powerful Guise family. During his reign the arts in France reached an extraordinary level of sophistication in every field.

Henry's own efforts were largely directed towards carrying on projects initiated by his father. Fontainebleau continued to be his favourite residence, and here he completed the Salle de Bal (also called Galerie Henri II) begun in 1540, and the vast Galerie d'Ulysse begun in 1541, which was demolished in the eighteenth century. Both of these rooms were frescoed during his reign by Primaticcio, who from 1552 had the help of the third important painter of the first school of Fontainebleau, **128** Niccolò dell'Abbate.

An undertaking in which Henry took a special interest was the rebuilding of the Louvre, which Francis in the year before his death had entrusted to the architect Pierre Lescot. Lescot built the two wings which form the south-west angle of the present Cour Carré, and the façade on **112** the western side of the court, completed in the mid-1550s, with reliefs by the most important French sculptor of this period, Jean Goujon, is of a sophistication undreamed of under Francis I.

An abrupt change in the hierarchy of court artists occurred on Henry's accession: in general Italians were demoted and Frenchmen came to the fore. Lescot survived with his authority unimpaired but Primaticcio and Serlio both lost their positions at Fontainebleau to the architect Philibert de l'Orme, who was to be superintendent of the king's buildings with the sole exception of the Louvre throughout Henry's reign. De l'Orme may be seen as the lieutenant of Diane de Poitiers, who became dictator in the arts as she was in the court. Undoubtedly the greatest and most original French architect of the period, he had studied in Italy, where he met the Cardinal Jean du Bellay. Du Bellay became his first patron when in 1540 he commissioned him to build the château of St Maur-lès-Fossés, and it was he who introduced him to Diane de Poitiers. She in turn induced Henry, while still dauphin, to make him his personal architect. His first royal commissions were for the monument to Francis I at St Denis and for the beautiful monument to the heart of Francis I, the sculptor for both of which was Pierre Bontemps, an artist with a special talent for the decorative who had trained under Primaticcio at Fontainebleau.

The fact that these monuments were entrusted to Frenchmen is significant: throughout Henry's reign the lead in sculpture and architecture was taken by Frenchmen who had absorbed the Italian Mannerist style and were intent on forging a new style with a definite French accent. In De l'Orme's own masterpiece, the great palace of Anet which he built for **11** Diane de Poitiers, we can feel for the first time that the French have really made the Renaissance their own, for it is at once entirely of the Renaissance and entirely French in character. It is a bold building, and Diane was a **1** bold patron: as early as 1540 the tomb which she built in Rouen Cathedral to the memory of her husband, the Grand Senechal Louis de Brézé, had been highly unconventional, a complete departure from the established norm of Franco-Italian tomb. Here she was in all probability one of the **1** earliest patrons of the sculptor Jean Goujon.

III
THE THREE GRACES
detail from the monument of the heart of Henry II
1560–63
Germain Pilon c. 1535–90
marble
h. 4 ft 11 in (150 cm)
Louvre, Paris

The monument was commissioned by Catherine de'Medici in the year following the death of Henry II, and was installed in 1563 in the church of the Célestins in Paris. The ensemble was the joint work of several members of the workshop of Primaticcio, who may have been the overall designer. The plinth and the original bronze urn (the present one is a modern wooden replacement) were executed by Domenico del Barbiere after models by Jean Picard, but the figures of the three Graces are the work of Pilon.

112

COUR CARRE OF THE LOUVRE

western side begun 1546
Pierre Lescot c. 1515 – 78 with sculptural
decoration by Jean Goujon died c. 1568

In 1527 Francis I announced his intention of living in the Louvre Palace and had the medieval keep demolished preparatory to rebuilding. No building began, however, until 1546 when he entrusted Pierre Lescot with the erection of this new wing on the foundations of the western side of the old keep. It was originally built only two storeys high, but, after Lescot had built another, three storeys high, on the south side of the court, an extra floor was added by him, which was decorated with relief sculpture by Jean Goujon, a regular collaborator with Lescot. The layout of the court was planned by Lescot before Henry's death, but under half was built by him.

113

**ENTRANCE GATEWAY,
CHATEAU D'ANET**

1552
Philibert de l'Orme 1500/15 – 1570

The construction of the château of Anet for Diane de Poitiers was begun at some time before 1547, when we know that De l'Orme was called in as architect. This vast palace was largely pulled down during the Revolution, but parts of De l'Orme's building remain, including the chapel and this entrance gate which has survived intact. It is the finest example of the architect's highly personal mature style. Originally it incorporated Cellini's *Nymph of Fontainebleau*, now replaced by a cast.

Private patrons

Another early patron of Jean Goujon, and a perceptive patron of French artists in general, was the Constable Anne de Montmorency, who **131** employed him in the early 1540s at his principal residence, the château of Ecouen near Paris. Montmorency became Constable of France in 1538, and it was probably in that year that he began building Ecouen. The north wing, built in the 1550s, was the first important commission to be given to the architect Jean Bullant, De l'Orme's great rival, who was also employed by the constable at his other seats of Chantilly and Fère-en-Tardenois. Under Bullant's monumental porch on the left-hand side of the court at Ecouen stood at one time the two most important works in the constable's collection, the *Slaves* of Michelangelo now in the Louvre. **125** For the decoration of the Salle du Connétable at Ecouen Montmorency apparently had recourse to members of Rosso's team from Fontainebleau, for the frescos there, executed in 1540 immediately after the completion of the Galerie François Premier, are imbued with Rosso's style. Shortly before his death in 1540 Rosso painted for him the *Pietà* now in the Louvre, and his taste in painting is further attested by the beautiful book of hours preserved at Chantilly to which Niccolò dell'Abbate contributed.

Montmorency was very influential in the flowering of French decorative arts which occurred at this time. The first patron of Bernard Palissy, the great French potter, he commissioned from him as early as 1556 the fantastic grotto of coloured earthenware which Palissy describes in his book. He was also the principal encourager of one of the earliest French potters to work in the style and technique of Italian maiolica, Masseot Abaquesne of Rouen, who supplied splendid tiled pavements for Ecouen. Montmorency was also one of the chief patrons of the factory at Saint-Porchaire which produced the unique and rare inlaid pottery known as 'Henri II ware'. In the art of stained glass in which France was pre-eminent, he commissioned in 1542 for Ecouen the finest known examples of this period, the grisaille windows with scenes from the story of Psyche preserved at Chantilly.

The only other private patrons who came near to rivalling Montmorency were the two brothers of the Guise family, François Duke of Guise and Charles Cardinal of Lorraine who showed by contrast a penchant for Italian artists such as Domenico del Barbiere, who executed the tomb of their father Claude de Guise at Joinville in 1551–52. Both Domenico and Primaticcio were employed by the cardinal at the great château at Meudon which he started in 1554. In 1555 Primaticcio designed for the duke the decorative scheme for the chapel at the Hôtel de Guise in Paris which was executed by Niccolò dell'Abbate.

The troubled years

After the death of Henry II in 1559, the monarchy's grip on the country began to slacken: under two young and weak kings the already latent religious strife began to split France asunder. The massacre of Wassy in 1562 touched off the first of eight civil wars, the Wars of Religion, which were to succeed each other until the end of the century. During this time of chronic crisis the life of the court continued superficially unchanged: **115** Charles IX prudently fortified Fontainebleau, while within he commissioned Primaticcio to build the Aile de la Belle Cheminée. But the peak of achievement was over. Charles's own colossal project, the château of Charleval, almost neurotic in its grandiosity, was scarcely begun before it was abandoned. The work of Antoine Caron, painter to Charles IX and Henry III, reflects the state of perpetual anxiety in which the court lived and the violence outside the gates.

This troubled scene was dominated by Henry's formidable widow Catherine de' Medici, who ruled the country as regent during the minority of Charles. Throughout these years she embarked, almost frantically it seems, on one ambitious building scheme after another. An Italian herself, she rearranged the hierarchy of royal artists so as to bring Italians into prominence again, dismissing the all-powerful De l'Orme, and appointing in his stead as superintendent of buildings Primaticcio, who now emerged as an architect.

The great rotunda which Primaticcio began for Catherine at St Denis in 1560 is remarkable for its pure Italian High Renaissance classicism. It was designed as a kind of pantheon for the kings of the Valois dynasty;
123 in it the tomb of Henry II and Catherine herself would be surrounded by the tombs of the other Valois kings. The grandiose conception of the rotunda is as characteristic of the time as was its eventual fate. Built by fits and starts, scarcely begun by Primaticcio's death in 1570, and continued intermittently through the following decade, it was finally abandoned unfinished in 1585 to be demolished in 1719. The tomb of Henry and Catherine, which was to have stood in the centre, was practically completed and can be seen today erected in the abbey church of St Denis.

Catherine in her desire for great new buildings did however give De l'Orme new employment as architect of her huge new palace of the Tuileries in Paris begun in 1564 (destroyed under the Commune in 1871). After the death of both Primaticcio and De l'Orme in 1570 she appointed as her architect Jean Bullant, the designer of Ecouen. In her service he was fated often to finish the work of other men: for her he continued the building of Primaticcio's Valois chapel, built the gallery on De l'Orme's
104 bridge at Chenonceaux, added a wing to his Tuileries, and enlarged his château of St Maur.

The sculptor Jean Goujon, a Huguenot, was to fall foul of the religious strife in France. From 1562, the year of Wassy, his name no longer appears in royal accounts. It seems that he left France in 1563 for Italy, to die there some years later. But the same years produced another great French sculptor, Germain Pilon. Pilon's early work was executed to the designs of Primaticcio—he was responsible for most of the sculpture on the monu-
111, 123 ment to Henry II as well as the figures known as the *Three Graces* for the monument to the heart of Henry—but he was to develop into as French a
114 sculptor as De l'Orme had been an architect. In the *Virgin* which he carved in the 1580s for one of the apses of the Valois chapel he re-establish-ed a link with the French Late Gothic style.

Pilon was mostly employed on work for Catherine, but some of his finest work was done in the 1580s for a private patron, the chancellor René de Birague. Birague entrusted Pilon with the sculpture for the chapel which he built to house the tombs of his wife, Valentine Balbiani, and himself in the church of St Catherine du Val-des-Ecoliers in Paris. The chapel was destroyed in the Revolution, but much of Pilon's sculpture is preserved in the Louvre: the figure of Valentine Balbiani, and her harrowing cadaver in relief, the kneeling bronze figure of the chancellor, and the bronze relief of the Deposition are among the most moving works of art of their age.

Pilon was to die in 1590, the year after the end of the Valois dynasty. A product initially of the school of Fontainebleau, but marked as much by the strife of the last years of the Valois, he had moved beyond the environment which had produced him and his last work hovers on the edge of the Baroque.

Anthony Radcliffe

114
THE VIRGIN OF PITY
1586
Germain Pilon c. 1535 – 90
h. 5 ft 10 in (178 cm)
Louvre, Paris

This figure affords a valuable insight into Pilon's method of working since it is the full-sized clay model for his marble *Virgin* now in the church of St Paul–St Louis, Paris. Like his *Risen Christ* of 1583 in the same church, the *Virgin* was originally destined for Catherine de'Medici's chapel of the Valois kings at St Denis, but the building was never sufficiently completed to receive it. The model, which is the most moving example of Pilon's later style, differs considerably from the marble, showing more obviously his return to Late Gothic sources.

115
SHIELD OF KING CHARLES IX OF FRANCE
c. 1570
enamelled gold
26·75 × 19·25 in (68 × 49 cm)
Louvre, Paris

The shield, with a similarly decorated morion (helmet), also in the Louvre, forms part of a set of parade armour made for Charles IX, whose monogram, a crowned letter K, appears on the rim. The richness of this armour is unparalleled: both morion and shield are made of solid gold with embossed and engraved decoration en-riched with translucent enamelling. While the enamelling must be French, the shield itself seems to be the work of a German artist working in the Louvre armouries. The artist is not yet identified, but other work of his, including armour made for Henry II, can be recognised. In the centre of the shield is an elaborate battle scene, surrounded by a strapwork pattern con-taining trophies, cannon and bound captives. Formerly part of the crown treasure, the armour was bought by the French state in 1793 at the sale of the collection of the duke of Choiseul-Praslin.

116

COVERED VASE

c. 1540–50
possibly by Giulio Taverna, active c. 1540
rock crystal with enamelled mounts
h. 15·5 in (39 cm)
Louvre, Paris

This sumptuous vase came to the Louvre from the old French royal collections, in which it can be traced back as far as Louis XIV. The two scenes engraved on either side of it showing the stories of Judith and Susanna are closely related to crystal plaques signed by the Milanese artist Giulio Taverna. Taverna is known to have been active in the years around 1540, and it may conceivably have once formed part of the collection of Italian art objects of Francis I.

Fontainebleau. Rosso began work on the Galerie François Premier three years after his arrival in France, and it appears to have been not quite complete at his death in 1540. This is the most important surviving piece of the Fontainebleau of Francis I. The extent to which Primaticcio, who arrived in France in 1532, may have been involved in it is difficult to determine – he was working on the decoration of the Chambre de la Reine at the same time. The gallery, altered and entirely repainted in the nineteenth century, has recently been restored to its original condition. The woodwork is a close nineteenth-century copy of the original panelling by Francis's chief Italian cabinet maker Scibec de Carpi. The decoration of the Chambre de la Duchesse d'Etampes *right* was the first major work by Primaticcio at Fontainebleau after the death of Rosso Fiorentino. A staircase was installed during the reign of Louis XIV, and the present ceiling made in the nineteenth century under Louis Philippe, and the frescos repainted at the same time. The superb stucco surrounds are, however, quite intact. As examples of Primaticcio's fully emancipated style they contrast strongly with those of Rosso in the gallery.

117 GALERIE FRANÇOIS PREMIER

c. 1533–40, fresco and stucco decoration by Rosso Fiorentino (Giovanni Battista Rosso) 1494–1540

118 *right* CHAMBRE DE LA DUCHESSE D'ETAMPES

fresco and stucco, 1541–43 Francesco Primaticcio 1504/5–1570

119

CHATEAU DE CHAMBORD

detail of roof
1519 to after 1550; the roof 1537
Domenico da Cortona and others

In 1519 Francis I commissioned Domenico da Cortona to build a comparatively modest château at Chambord to be used as a hunting lodge. The keep of the present building represents Domenico's original plan. Work seems to have been interrupted by the Italian campaign of 1524–26 during which the king was captured at the Battle of Pavia, but it was carried on again on a more ambitious scale after his return, and Domenico's original plan was now considerably modified. By 1537 the roof of the keep was in the course of construction, and the wings of the château were not completed until some time after Francis's death. The roof is the most extraordinary feature of the building, in form a fantasy in the spirit of the Late Gothic, but decorated with Italian detail of absolute purity.

120
THE ERMINE

emblem of Anne of Brittany, detail from a chimneypiece, Blois

The distinctive emblems of the royal household recur throughout their châteaux as decorative details. The porcupine of Louis XII, the ermine of Anne of Brittany his second wife and the salamander of Francis I (*see previous page*).

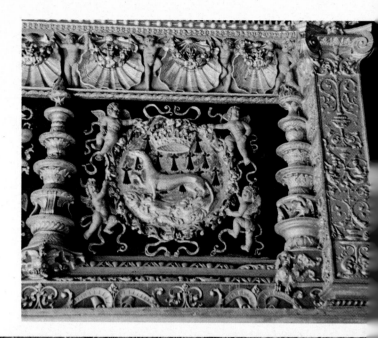

121
FRANCIS I WING

1515–24
château of Blois

Francis began building operations at Blois soon after his accession in 1515, and work continued there almost without interruption until 1524 when this great wing was completed. It was largely built on the foundations of the medieval castle, and retains a medieval layout, but the decorative detail is in a Renaissance style which represents an advance on the decoration of the earlier wing of Louis XII. The great staircase on the court was heavily restored in the nineteenth century, but the restoration is fairly accurate. It is one of the most remarkable examples of the mixture of Gothic structure and Renaissance detail which is characteristic of the early years of Francis I.

122 THE DEATH OF ORION

c. 1550–55, tapestry, château d'Anet

The tapestry forms part of a set representing the story of Diana. This is one of four pieces of the set which are preserved at Anet. One further piece is in Rouen and two more in the Metropolitan Museum in New York. Although their origin is not documented, it seems certain that they were woven to the order of Diane de Poitiers for her château of Anet, and it is most likely that they were made in the royal tapestry workshop at Fontainebleau. There is no foundation for the suggestion that they were designed by Diane's architect Philibert de l'Orme but the mastery of design exhibited by the set is quite extraordinary.

123

TOMB OF HENRY II AND CATHERINE DE'MEDICI

1563–70
Francesco Primaticcio 1504/5 – 1570 and members of his workshop
marble and bronze
abbey church of St Denis, near Paris

The tomb was commissioned from Primaticcio by Catherine to stand in the centre of his great rotunda, the chapel of the Valois kings at St Denis begun in 1560. The sculpture is all by Germain Pilon, with the exception of the two bronze corner-figures of virtues (not visible here) at the other end of the tomb which were the work of Ponce Jacquio, who made the model for the whole of the tomb. The tomb was erected in the rotunda during the reign of Henry IV, dismantled under the Revolution, and re-erected on its present site in 1867.

124

TOMB OF LOUIS XII AND ANNE OF BRITTANY

1513–31
Antonio Giusti 1479–1519 and Giovanni Giusti 1485–1549
marble
abbey church of St Denis, near Paris

Commissioned by Francis I on his accession in 1515, the tomb is mainly the work of the younger Giusti brother Giovanni, but several other hands, both French and Italian are discernible in the sculpture. The general design, which was to set the pattern for subsequent French royal tombs, is derived from the tomb of Gian Galeazzo Visconti at Pavia by Gian Cristoforo Romano (1493–97), but it also incorporates traditional French features, such as the praying figures on the top. The latter, and the effigies lying inside the tomb are the work of Frenchmen. The Giusti were Florentines who settled in Tours in about 1504, and the figures attributable to them, the apostles and virtues, are in a markedly Florentine style.

125

THE REBELLIOUS SLAVE

1513, marble
Michelangelo Buonarrotti 1475–1564
h. 7 ft (215 cm)
Louvre, Paris

This and the so-called 'Dying Slave' (plate **194**) are the two earliest and most finished of the six slaves which Michelangelo made for the tomb of Pope Julius II. They were not in the event used for the tomb, and were given by Michelangelo to Roberto Strozzi, who in 1546 presented them to Francis I. His successor Henry II gave them in turn to the constable Anne de Montmorency, who set them up in the courtyard of his château of Ecouen. Later in the possession of Richelieu at his château they were finally bought by the French state in 1794.

126

THE NYMPH OF FONTAINEBLEAU

1543–44, bronze
Benvenuto Cellini 1500–1571
6 ft 8·5 in × 13 ft 5 in (205 × 409 cm)
Louvre, Paris

This relief was commissioned by Francis I as a lunette for the Porte Dorée which was at that time the principal entrance to the palace of Fontainebleau. It was never erected there, because Cellini left France before completing the two pilaster-figures of satyrs which were to have supported it. Two spandrel reliefs with figures of victories which Cellini made to go above the lunette survived until the last century, when they disappeared. The work was given by Henry II to Diane de Poitiers and built into Philibert de l'Orme's gateway to Diane's château of Anet (plate **113**), where it is today replaced by a cast.

127 *opposite*

MONA LISA

1503, oil on panel
Leonardo da Vinci 1452–1519
30·25 × 21 in (77 × 53 cm)
Louvre, Paris

The painting is a portrait of Lisa Gherardini, wife of Francesco del Giocondo, and was painted in Florence in 1503, when Leonardo was working on the cartoon for the *Battle of Anghiari*. It has often been identified with a painting which was seen by Cardinal Louis of Aragon on a visit to Leonardo's studio at Amboise in 1517, but this is extremely doubtful. How the painting in fact came to France is unknown, but it was certainly in the collection of Francis I, and its influence can be seen in later portraits of the School of Fontainebleau.

128 *right*

THE RAPE OF PROSERPINE *detail*

1558–60, Niccolo dell' Abbate c. 1512–71
76.75 × 85 in (195 × 216 cm), Louvre, Paris

Niccolo dell'Abbate arrived in France in 1552, and joined Primaticcio in the decoration of the great galleries at Fontainebleau. This painting can be dated to around 1560, at which time Niccolo was engaged on the decoration of the Salle de Bal. It was almost certainly painted for Fontainebleau, as was the landscape with the story of Eurydice and Aristaeus, of the same date (now in London). The artist's principal contribution to French painting was the Mannerist landscape. He worked for the duke of Guise and for the constable de Montmorency at Ecouen as well as for the king.

129
CUPBOARD

c. 1585, French provincial, oak
6 ft 10 in × 5 ft 1 in (2·08 × 1·55 m)
Musée des Arts Décoratifs, Paris

The cupboard, which may have been made in the reign of
Henry III, is of the sophisticated type developed during the
second half of the sixteenth century. This style of furniture is
traditionally ascribed to the 'Burgundian School' and associated
with the Dijon architect Hugues Sambin, who published an
important work on architectural decoration in 1572. However
it in fact stems originally from the furniture designs published
by Jacques Androuet Ducerceau in 1550. The cupboard is
probably an excellent provincial version of the court furniture
of a few years earlier.

130
THE DIANA OF ANET

c. 1550–54, marble
unknown French sculptor
h. 5 ft 1 in (1·55 m)
Louvre, Paris

This celebrated statue was recorded in 1554 at Diane de
Poitiers' château of Anet, where it surmounted the great
fountain in the principal courtyard. It has been ascribed at
various times to Jean Goujon, to the young Germain Pilon,
and even to Cellini, but it has finally to be admitted that the
sculptor is unidentifiable. He must however have been, like
Pilon, a Frenchman trained in the workshop of Primaticcio,
and we may assume that the statue was carried out and installed
under the close personal supervision of Philibert de l'Orme,
Diane's architect at Anet.

131

ANNE DE MONTMORENCY,
CONSTABLE OF FRANCE

1556, enamel on copper
Léonard Limosin active 1532 died 1575/7
28·5 × 22 in (72 × 56 cm)
Louvre, Paris

Léonard Limosin was the outstanding member of the Limoges
school of enamellists of his period. His earliest works date from
the 1530s and he was in the service of Francis I at Fontainebleau
by 1544. He continued to work there for Henry II and he also
executed commissions for the Guise family as well as the
constable de Montmorency. His portraits in enamel are of
outstanding quality, and this one, signed and dated 1556 is
generally considered to be his masterpiece. The decorative
surround shows the influence of the School of Fontainebleau.
The portrait was commissioned by the constable and remained
in the Montmorency family's possession until the Revolution.

91

Towards the end of the sixteenth century France had not only been impoverished economically by the effects of thirty years of civil and religious wars but had also been drained of most of its creative spirit. The efforts of Henry IV (1589–1610) and his first minister Sully to revive the arts were only partially successful, for the nobles were more interested in gaming and drinking than aesthetic pleasures and only secular building received a fresh impetus. Henry IV's most revolutionary contributions were his public schemes for the city of Paris. Two of these, consisting of a series of small houses standardised in design and grouped round an open square, still exist today at the Place Dauphine on the Ile de la Cité and at the Place des Vosges. These formed part of his great central-planning schemes which established a tradition for town planning in Paris and which spread to other parts of France such as Charleville and Montauban.

New areas round these squares were opened up for development and for the rest of the century three districts became the most fashionable for the aristocracy to build their large free-standing hôtels. The Marais has
135 the Hôtels de Sully, Aubert de Fontenay, de Beauvais and Carnavalet; the area north of the Louvre has the Palais Royal and the Bibliothèque
134 Nationale, formerly Cardinal Mazarin's palace; and the Ile de Saint-
153 Louis has the Hôtels de Lauzun and Lambert. In the reign of Henry IV most of the country châteaux, such as Grosbois and Rosny, and town houses like the Hôtel de Mayenne in the Marais were built in the simple brick and stone façades of the Place des Vosges. During the regency for the young Louis XIII of Marie de' Medici, following Henry IV's assassination in 1610, a more Mannerist and fantastic type of decoration came into fashion and the surfaces of the façades, as at the Hôtel de Sully and the château of Brissac, near Angers, were broken up by a conglomeration of architectural units and elaborate ornamentation.

To encourage painting and the minor arts Henry IV established lodgings for artists and artisans in the ground floor of the Louvre Long Gallery, but due to the mediocre standard of the painters this had little success beyond providing enrichment for the royal palaces of the Louvre and Fontainebleau. Indeed for the first quarter of the century there was virtually no school of painting in France, and it was necessary to call in artists from abroad for the most important commissions. Thus the main state portraits of Henry IV and Marie de' Medici now in the Louvre were painted by the Flemish artist, Frans Pourbus the Younger, and the most famous decorative commission, the gallery of Marie de' Medici's new
152 palace at the Luxembourg, was given to Rubens. Pourbus's type of portrait became the basis for French portraiture in the middle of the century, but the Baroque style of Rubens's great series of large-scale paintings was so alien to the prevalent French taste for a decorative form of Mannerism that it exerted almost no influence at this time.

The only really important representative of French art during this period worked in both Nancy and Florence – the engraver and etcher,
57 Jacques Callot. In his series of *Beggars* and the *Miseries of War* he interpreted the world around him with acute originality and wit. Such was his ability that he became the first printmaker to acquire an international reputation.

The first reaction against the general decorative trend current in buildings, paintings and the minor arts took place in architecture. At the palace of the Luxembourg in Paris and at the Palais de Justice in Rennes Salomon de Brosse introduced a new monumental quality which was to lead to the classicism of the next generation. His buildings were no longer

Versailles and the Age of the Cardinals
1600–1700

132

SALON DE LA GUERRE
begun 1678
Versailles

This is one of three rooms, including the Galerie des Glaces, added on to the ceremonial suite by Jules Hardouin Mansart. The decoration, directed by Charles le Brun, is unusual in that it is mainly sculptural; the huge white plaster oval by Coysevox showing Louis XIV triumphing over his enemies is surrounded by gilt-bronze reliefs. The effect of splendour would have been even richer with the original furniture and costumes of the courtiers.

a conglomeration of individual parts but compact blocks composed of carefully balanced masses, enriched only by classical details.

Richelieu, Mazarin and private patrons

136 Under Cardinal Richelieu and Cardinal Mazarin, the powerful first ministers of Louis XIII (1610–43) and the youthful Louis XIV, France became established as a great power in Europe. During this period from 1630 to 1661 a totally new approach to the arts emerged. Many amateurs of art began to assemble great collections, the most famous of which were those of the two cardinals. Richelieu's collection contained not only
162, 133 paintings of contemporary artists like Nicolas Poussin and Philippe de Champaigne but also such famous Italian Renaissance masterpieces as Leonardo's *St Anne* and the series of paintings by Perugino, Mantegna and Lorenzo Costa from the collection formed by Isabella d'Este in her
134 'studiolo' at Mantua. Mazarin was an even more avid collector of every type of curio and treasure and his greatest acquisitions were the famous
151, 137 paintings of Raphael, Titian and Correggio that he bought from the sale of the collection of Charles I of England. On their deaths, the greatest of both the cardinals' collections, one by bequest and the other by purchase, passed into the royal collection which is now in the Louvre.

Efforts made to establish a court art were only partly successful. Apart from works commissioned by the crown and the first ministers, nearly every single work of importance during this period was produced for the new middle class. The meteoric increase in wealth and power of the bourgeoisie in France, which resulted indirectly from Richelieu's and Mazarin's political policies, was extremely important for the arts. These new patrons brought to their patronage far more enlightenment, sound judgment and taste than the aristocracy had previously shown. More than that, they gave to the artists scope and freedom to express their own individual artistic qualities, and this helped to foster a great revival of the arts in Paris during the middle of the century.

The new generation of artists was a brilliant one and, although the development of classicism and rationalism was the linking spirit throughout the period, the contribution of each artist was quite individual. The rise of the French classical spirit was not confined to the visual arts and a parallel development appeared in the philosophic and literary fields in the writings of Descartes, Pascal and Corneille.

The predominant taste for the decorative Mannerist style was finally dispelled during the last years of the 1620s by a broad new influx of Italian ideas. In architecture this new stimulus was first introduced by Jacques Lemercier, the official architect to Louis XIII and the great protégé of Richelieu, for whom he built two châteaux, the town of Richelieu and the Palais Cardinal (now the Palais Royal). Lemercier had spent at least seven years in Rome and his chief importance lies in his re-interpretation of the Roman domed churches with their grand columned porticoes at the churches of the Sorbonne and Val-de-Grâce.

The most important architects of this period were François Mansart and Louis Le Vau. Mansart was the great exponent of the French classical spirit in architecture for his buildings embodied the ideals of clarity, harmony and balance of form that had been the principles of ancient and High Renaissance artists. Taking up Salomon de Brosse's treatment of simple masses he conceived his buildings as three-dimensional blocks in which all parts of the architecture were related by carefully harmonised proportions. He brought the same high level of intellectual refinement to
158 all types of buildings, to his châteaux at Blois and Maisons, to his town houses of which the Carnavalet and de Guénégaud in the Marais survive,

133
PORTRAIT
OF AN UNKNOWN MAN
1650
Philippe de Champaigne 1602–74
oil on canvas, detail
36 × 28·5 in (91·4 × 72·4 cm)
Louvre, Paris

This grave and simple portrait, formerly believed to represent Arnauld d'Andilly, belongs to a group of half-length portraits by Champaigne, of lawyers, merchants and ecclesiasts which are the French equivalent of the 'bourgeois' portraiture then flourishing in Holland. The painter treats his subject with sensitive observation and great restraint of gesture, expression and colour.

134
CARDINAL MAZARIN
IN HIS GALLERY
1659
head only by Robert Nanteuil 1625–78
engraving
19 × 22·75 in (48·3 × 57·8 cm)
Bibliothèque Nationale, Paris

135
HOTEL DE SULLY
1624–29
Jean du Cerceau 1585–c.1650
Paris

The hôtel was built for a rich financier and bought soon after by Sully, Henry IV's chief minister. It is a typical example of the private houses built for wealthy patrons during Louis XIII's reign, and consists of three sides built round a court with a lower screen wall dividing it from the street. Its novelty is in the richly carved decoration which covers the three court façades.

Jules Mazarin was an Italian who became a famous French statesman and first minister during Louis XIV's minority. This portrait shows him in his other great role as patron of the arts. He added two splendid galleries to his palace, both of which survive in the Bibliothèque Nationale, to house his immense collection of paintings, portrait busts, antique statues, furniture, silver and objets d'art.

and to his churches of the Visitation and Val-de-Grâce. His lack of success with royal commissions was mainly due to his difficult temperament and to his uncompromising artistic conscience and it is to the credit of his wealthy middle-class patrons that their sensitivity and devotion to the abstract qualities of his art allowed Mansart the free hand he required.

Louis Le Vau was a more Baroque designer than Mansart. He lacked the latter's refinement and purity of detail and his success in obtaining the post of first architect to the king and large public commissions such as the Collège des Quatre Nations (now the Institut de France) depended on his ability to produce a striking general effect of grandeur and elegance on both the exterior and interior of his buildings. Two of his houses for private patrons, the Hôtels de Lauzun and Lambert on the Ile de Saint-Louis, still retain much of the original decoration. His masterpiece was the château of Vaux-le-Vicomte where he headed a team of painters, sculptors, decorators and gardeners with whom he created, in a typically Baroque combination of the arts, a setting of great splendour for the immensely rich financier, Nicolas Fouquet. Both the architecture and decoration were, however, restrained compared to their Italian counterparts; and it was this style, developed by Le Vau, of Baroque elements tempered by the French classical spirit that was taken up by Louis XIV in the second half of the century.

The same introduction of Italian idioms that had characterised the architecture appeared in painting. The first artist to bring back to France an Italian Baroque style was Simon Vouet whom Louis XIII recalled from Rome in 1627 to become first painter. Although he lacked the ability to establish a court art as such, Vouet's type of moderated Baroque style was immediately successful and he became the most popular and best-established painter till his death in 1649. His real significance in the development of French painting was not however in his numerous altarpieces such as *The Presentation* (Louvre), but in the decorative field, in tapestry design (Louvre and Musée des Gobelins) and in interior decoration. His attempts to link up the different parts of the painted decoration by a consistent illusionism throughout a room founded a tradition of decorative painting that dominated France for the rest of the century; and his type of large studio through which most of the principal artists passed – Eustache Le Sueur, François Perrier and Charles Le Brun – was the precursor of the Gobelins.

Both in Paris and in the provinces, however, the fundamental qualities that linked the great art of the mid-century were classical. The natural simplicity of the *Unknown Man* and *Two Nuns of Port-Royal* by Philippe de Champaigne, the humble peasant scenes in *The Forge* and *The Peasants at Supper* by Louis Le Nain and the candle-lit religious paintings of *Christ and St Joseph* and the Rennes *Nativity* by the Lorraine artist Georges de la Tour are all very different in their treatment. Nevertheless they share the same restraint of gesture, elimination of movement, subdued colour and simplified composition which gives them a sense of detachment, calm stillness and grave dignity that is purely classical in its approach. It was this approach rather than the representation of mythological scenes that was typically French.

Poussin and the classical influence

The two most important artists of the middle of the seventeenth century, Nicolas Poussin and Claude Lorraine, lived in Rome. Poussin's approach to painting was essentially intellectual; he meant his paintings to be read, that is to appeal to the mind rather than the eye. His early paintings such as *The Inspiration of the Poet* and *The Triumph of Flora* show spontaneity,

153

163

156

133
155

140

movement, poetry and glowing colours which he consciously eliminated in his later paintings. By means of rational processes he moulded his art into forms of perfect clarity whether religious paintings like *The Finding*
162 *of Moses*, mythological subjects or landscape scenes such as *The Arcadian Shepherds* and *Orpheus and Eurydice*. Poussin took his interpretation of classicism far further than other French painters, for he studied not only Roman marble reliefs but also the ideas and attitudes of the ancient world in his attempts to portray the classical ideal, and more than any other artist sums up all the qualities of French classicism.

Although he spent most of his working life in Rome, Poussin was held in the greatest esteem in France. In 1640 Richelieu, who already owned several of his paintings, finally persuaded him to return to Paris to direct the arts. The visit was not a success and only lasted eighteen months. The tangible evidence of Poussin's visit was the decoration of the much-admired Louvre Long Gallery (now destroyed) but the most fruitful result was the close friendship he made with a group of intellectual Parisian bourgeoisie. Not only were they his best patrons for the rest of his life but they also revolutionised his outlook. The paintings executed on his return to Rome are considered the purest expression of the French classical spirit; among these works painted for his new patrons are the *Self-Portrait* for Chantelou and the *Judgment of Solomon* and *Eliezer and Rebecca* for Pointel, all of which are now in the Louvre.

The effect of Poussin's visit to Paris was considerable; not only did he strengthen the classical bias that already existed in painting but he also exerted an immense influence on artistic theory during the reign of Louis XIV. The continuity of French interest in classicism during the seventeenth century was specifically national, for other European countries were developing towards Baroque and naturalistic trends.

Claude Lorraine, the other great expatriate working in Rome, never returned to France. Nevertheless his representation of a classical type of landscape and not a realistic one was typically French in its approach. The subjects of his landscapes were, like those of Poussin, often of mythological scenes. Claude, however, was less interested in the figures and buildings than in the changing effects of light. He filled his scenes of the Roman
164 countryside, *Seaport at Sunset* and *Ulysses restoring Chryseis to her Father*, with a soft luminous light that not only gave a continuous spatial unity to the composition but also created a poetic mood of beauty. His influence, which was brought back to France by French landscape painters visiting Rome, established landscape painting as a means of artistic expression in French art.

Sculpture did not share the same importance as painting and architecture. During the first quarter of the century it played a minor role but from
144 the third decade was used extensively for portraiture, such as Warin's
136 bust of Richelieu, and in church decoration, for example Michel Anguier's *Nativity* at St Roch and Jacques Sarrazin's tomb of Henri de Bourbon at Chantilly. Sculpted figures and ornaments became an important
158, 163 part of the interior decoration of private houses, as for example at the
153 châteaux of Maisons and Vaux-le-Vicomte and the Hôtel Lambert. Most sculptors studied in Rome and Italian influences appeared in their work with the same varying mixture of classical and Baroque elements that were found in painting and architecture.

The minor arts in France had even less significance during the first half of the century; foreign craftsmen and foreign products dominated the industry. Furniture retained the solid block-like shapes of the sixteenth century and was strongly influenced in design and decoration by Flemish

136
CARDINAL RICHELIEU
c. 1640
Jean Warin 1604–72
bronze
h. 28 in (71 cm)
Bibliothèque Mazarine, Paris

The bust of Armand-Jean du Plessis, Duke of Richelieu (1585–1642), first minister and principal advisor to Louis XIII, is one of six versions cast from a model made during the last years of his life. Richelieu was an enthusiastic collector and a great patron of both artists and writers. His protégés included Corneille, Lemercier, Poussin and Philippe de Champaigne.

137
ANTIOPE
c. 1521–22
Antonio Correggio 1494 (or 1489) – 1534
oil on canvas
75 × 49 in (190 × 124 cm)
Louvre, Paris

This painting was in the collection of the dukes of Mantua for a hundred years and was then purchased by Charles I of England. After Charles's sale in 1649 it passed through two famous Parisian collections, those of the banker Everhard Jabach and of Cardinal Mazarin, before being bought in 1661 by Louis XIV. This voluptuous yet tender scene shows the sleeping Antiope admired by Jupiter in the guise of a satyr.

97

138

**YOUNG WOMAN
AT HER TOILET**

c. 1520
Titian c. 1487/90–1576
oil on canvas
37.5 × 30 in (96 × 76 cm)
Louvre, Paris

Originally in the collection of the duke of
Mantua, this poetic but as yet unidentified
portrait by Titian was one of many famous
Italian paintings, including works by
Giorgione, Titian, Caravaggio and
Guido Reni, bought by the banker
Everhard Jabach at the sale of Charles I
of England. In 1671 Jabach sold this
painting to Louis XIV together with a
hundred other paintings and over five
thousand drawings.

In 1527 Francis I decided to convert the old medieval fortress of
the Louvre into a royal palace. But it was not until nearly 150 years
later that the last wing of the new Square Court, the east façade,
was built by a team of architects. Its most outstanding feature is
the tall coupled columns that animate its simple rectilinear masses.

Georges de la Tour is best known for his sensitive paintings of
sacred subjects which appear to reflect the religious revival in his
native Lorraine. His late style, of which this is an example, was
quite individual; he combined a dramatic use of light derived
from Caravaggio with an elimination of detail and movement
which gives his forms a monumental simplicity.

141

COMMODE

1708–9
André Charles Boulle 1642–1732
wood inlaid with copper and tortoiseshell
Bibliothèque Mazarine, Paris

This commode or chest-of-drawers with
its curved legs, elegant copper fittings and
delicate arabesque traceries on the drawers,
is a typical example of the kind of furniture
developed by Boulle for Louis XIV. It is
one of a pair made for the Trianon at
Versailles, one of several retreats built for
the king to escape from the publicity of
official court life.

142

POT-POURRI

made at Rouen, pottery, h. 10 in (25 cm)
Musée des Arts Décoratifs, Paris

This is a typical example of the simple shapes and 'lambrequin'
decoration evolved at the Rouen potteries which had a great
vogue from the last quarter of the century. The earlier
decoration of figured scenes imitating Italian and oriental
porcelain was abandoned and replaced by delicate patterns of
purely ornamental motifs which were silhouetted in blue and
polychrome colours.

143

LOUIS XIV BRACKET CLOCK

c. 1700
André Charles Boulle 1642–1732, Mynuel, active c. 1693–c. 1750
encased in wood inlaid with copper and tortoiseshell
private collection

The increased popularity of portable watches during the
seventeenth century led to a transformation in the use and
shape of clocks; the little portable table clocks were superseded
by much larger pedestal and bracket clocks which were placed
against the wall. Boulle gave a new elegance to their silhouette
and decoration.

and Italian pieces. The porcelain of Nevers, of which the Louvre has many examples, depended closely on Italian and Chinese models for its colouring, its figures and mythological and oriental scenes. The one applied art to show any originality was tapestry design. Tapestries had always been popular in France, but at the beginning of the seventeenth century production was monopolised by Flanders. Vouet's return to Paris in 1627 gave a new impetus to this decorative art in France; his large figure compositions of Old Testament and mythological scenes with their light, gay colours and richly inventive borders were particularly suited to this medium.

Colbert and a new direction of the arts

When Cardinal Mazarin died in 1661 Louis XIV (1643–1715), then aged twenty-three, announced his intention to dispense with the services of a first minister and to take over personally the governing of France. He chose Jean-Baptiste Colbert as his assistant and advisor. These two events marked the beginning of a new and spectacular age in France. Under Colbert's able administration the monarchy became absolute and France became the most powerful nation in Europe. The age of the private patron and of the individual artist came to an end, for Colbert believed that all the arts should be concentrated on one purpose – the glorification of the king and France. To achieve this he systematically set out to control the arts in exactly the same way as he directed politics and economics, by means of a highly organised central administration.

Colbert began in 1661 by giving a completely new significance to the Academy of Painting and Sculpture. This had been established in 1648 on Italian lines and had helped to improve the status of the artist; Colbert turned it into a kind of state school responsible for the training of young artists who were taught according to rigidly laid down principles. The doctrine that was expounded in the lectures and discussions gave an official direction to art both in theory and in practice. This Academy system was soon extended to include architecture and other forms of art like music and drama, and a French Academy was opened in Rome to enable the best French students to study directly from antique art.

The foundation of the Gobelins factory, which was planned to provide furnishings of every description for the king, enabled Colbert to impose a similar discipline on the minor arts. Colbert's aim, however, was not limited merely to enriching the royal palaces, but was also to encourage these neglected industries and the Gobelins became a school of art for the training of young painters, sculptors, engravers, goldsmiths, silversmiths, cabinet makers, carpet weavers, tapestry embroiderers and dyers. Charles Le Brun, the king's first painter, was appointed director and so complete was his control that every design or project that was produced at the factory was either approved or designed by him. The result was an uniformity of style and a standard of technical skill of unparalleled excellence.

As the court was now the only important patron all the main commissions came through the official channels of the Academies and the Gobelins. This centralisation was so successful that the doctrines of Colbert and Le Brun became virtually dogma and no independent artist or style appeared, either in or outside Paris, till after Colbert's death in 1683.

Louis XIV and his palaces

Louis XIV believed himself to be the greatest monarch of the century and he chose as the symbol of his greatness Apollo the sun god; to celebrate this new cult a temple was needed. Colbert wished to make the Louvre the royal headquarters, and new designs were requested from French and

144
LOUIS XIV AS A CHILD
c. 1643
Jacques Sarrazin 1588–1660
bronze
Louvre, Paris

This portrait bust, which was probably made shortly after Louis became king in 1643 at the age of five, formerly decorated the apartment of the Queen Mother, Anne of Austria, in the Palais Royal. Sarrazin's work is parallel with that of Poussin and François Mansart; his interest in classicism is particularly apparent in the style he has adopted here, a Roman hero crowned with laurel leaves.

Italian architects to complete and modernise the old palace. Bernini, the most celebrated architect of the century, was invited to come to France but his plans were too grandiose for the practical Colbert and the only result of his visit was the marble bust he made of the king. Eventually in 1667 a team of Frenchmen, Le Vau, Le Brun and Claude Perrault, produced the design for the east front, which is notable for its great colonnade of free-standing paired columns. Though Baroque in some of its treatment, the Louvre façade is more strictly classical than any earlier French building; this particular combination of classical and Baroque elements became the style of Louis XIV.

Before the colonnade was even finished the king decided to move the court and government from Paris to Versailles. The same team that had worked for the financier Fouquet at Vaux-le-Vicomte transformed the small hunting lodge of Louis XIII into the most splendid palace in Europe, Le Vau as architect, Le Brun as designer and Le Nôtre as gardener. The palace was designed in several stages; after Le Vau's death Jules Hardouin Mansart, the great-nephew of François Mansart, added on the Galerie des Glaces and the huge north and south wings. Although these additions spoilt the scale of Le Vau's original design on the garden front, Mansart's special contribution was to give a vastness and visual splendour to the whole ensemble. He was the perfect official architect, not brilliant but quick and competent and possessing an ability to provide a suitable royal setting for the king.

The enormous park which took André Le Nôtre twenty-six years to create provided the perfect setting for the architecture. Its huge formal flower beds, its sheets of water and its parallel and radiating avenues between tall, trimmed hedges were formal in shape and geometric in pattern, and the same mixture of classical order and symmetry with Baroque scale and variation that characterised Mansart's architecture was extended to the gardens. Occasional pavilions that were used as pleasure retreats from the formality of court life and numerous fountains and ornamental sculpture formed an essential part of this layout.

The most important part of the palace was the interior which had to provide a fitting stage for the reception of foreign ambassadors and the innumerable grand ceremonies. Le Vau provided a magnificent suite of six rooms which, starting from the Salon de Vénus, led up to the focal point of the throne room in the Salle d'Apollon. The decoration of these rooms was Le Brun's greatest work. He himself made sketches for every part of the decoration and a vast team of artists and craftsmen helped to carry them out. Le Brun was not a particularly imaginative artist but he was a magnificent organiser and had an amazing ability to create and blend all the different arts into an harmonious ensemble of great richness and splendour. His designs for the walls and ceilings of the Salon de la Guerre and Galerie des Glaces, added on by Mansart, were richer, more complex and much more plastic than the earlier flat painted panelling; and his use of materials with the introduction of patterned velvets, mirrors and many-coloured marbles was much more varied.

In theory Le Brun and the Academicians preached a far stricter adherence to classicism than was actually achieved in practice. For the guidance of students strict rules were worked out down to the last detail and the ancients as well as Raphael and Poussin were upheld as masters. Although this classical style was in fact more suited to small paintings than large-scale decorations, the easel paintings, such as *Chancellor Séguier* by Le Brun and *Comte de Toulouse as Cupid Asleep* at Versailles by his chief but dull rival Pierre Mignard, were freer in composition and colouring than the

145

139

132

154

145

BUST OF LOUIS XIV

1665, marble
Gianlorenzo Bernini 1598–1680
life size
Versailles

This is probably the grandest piece of portraiture of the Baroque age; here Bernini brilliantly achieved his intention to convey grandeur, nobility, pride, heroism and majesty as well as the king's character. The impressive pose, the turn of the head and the sweeping drapery give an amazing liveliness to the marble.

146

PARADISE

1708, fresco
Antoine Coypel 1661–1708
ceiling of the chapel at Versailles

Coypel was one of the three important artists who, at the end of the century, helped to change the trend in French painting from the classical to the Baroque. This huge fresco which covers the ceiling of the royal chapel is painted in melodramatic trompe-l'oeil and is the most completely Baroque decoration in French art.

147

LOUIS XIV VISITING THE GOBELINS FACTORY

c.1667, tapestry
designed by Charles Le Brun 1619–90
193 × 270·5 in (489 × 685·7 cm)
Musée des Gobelins, Paris

This tapestry is one of a series of fourteen, all designed by Le Brun, known as *L'Histoire du Roi*, the most famous series manufactured at the Gobelins. The scene shows the king on a visit to the factory in 1667, inspecting the wide range of objets d'art, furniture, paintings, tapestries, carpets and silver objects made there.

official doctrines advocated and show that theory only went so far.

The main role of sculpture during this period was, as in painting, a decorative one. Fountains, figures and other ornamental sculpture were made in immense quantities in marble, bronze and lead to decorate the gardens and to a lesser extent the rooms at Versailles. The two most notable sculptors were François Girardon and Antoine Coysevox. Girardon was the more esteemed of the two as his sculptural groups of *Apollo tended by the Nymphs* and *The Rape of Persephone* in the gardens at **148** Versailles and his tomb of Richelieu in the church of the Sorbonne followed Poussin and the classical theories of the Academies more closely than the work of any other sculptor. Coysevox on the other hand showed a Baroque richness and freedom of invention in his decorations for the Galerie des Glaces and the Salon de la Guerre and a liveliness and nobility **132, 150** in his portrait busts that obviously derived from Bernini.

The enormous requirements for Versailles gave a new encouragement and importance to the industrial arts. Colbert's aim to make France independent of foreign craftsmen and foreign products was so successful through the foundation of the Gobelins that during the second half of the century France became the leading producer in Europe of tapestries and furniture. Great series of tapestries with subjects such as *L'Histoire* **147** *d'Alexandre*, *L'Histoire du Roi* and *Les Indes*, the majority of which celebrated Louis XIV's greatness, were designed by Le Brun, and are now lent out by the factory museum. The grandeur and quality he gave to the large figure compositions surrounded by rich borders make them closer to paintings than decorative wall hangings.

The greatest stimulus, however, was in furniture design. The former solid shapes were reduced in size and lightened by twisted, fretted forms. A new concern for comfort stimulated new shapes and even new types of furniture, such as the sofa and the chest-of-drawers, that were utilitarian in purpose. Their enrichment consisted not only of an abundance of animal forms, human figures and naturalistic foliage but also a wide use of different materials, of solid silver, copper, gilded woods and marquetry. André-Charles Boulle was the most brilliant furniture designer of the time; he developed to a high degree of perfection a type of furniture **141, 143** inlaid with copper and tortoiseshell. The granting of special monopolies also encouraged other arts outside Paris; rich silks and brocades were produced at Lyons, porcelain at Rouen and Moustiers, lace at Alençon, **142** and carpets at the Manufacture de la Savonnerie.

When Louis XIV came to the throne the royal collection of paintings started by Francis I was very small compared to the rich collections of some of his subjects. Colbert applied the same determined energy to amassing a collection of suitably regal proportions as he had done to providing a royal setting for the court. Famous collections were acquired, like those of the Cardinal Mazarin and of the banker Jabach, both rich **137, 138** in paintings of Titian, Raphael, Giorgione and Correggio that had been in **151** Charles I of England's collection. Works by the best contemporary artists were purchased; the most famous of these many acquisitions were thirteen paintings by Poussin which included *The Four Seasons* bought from the Duke of Richelieu. Visiting ambassadors and foreign princes, as was the custom, presented works of art as diplomatic gifts, and even the king's **164** own courtiers offered their respect in this way. By the end of Louis's reign the paintings in the royal collection, which had numbered only two hundred in the middle of the seventeenth century, had been increased to over two thousand; these later became the nucleus of the Musée du Louvre. The classical bias which dominated the art of this period is clearly

APOLLO AND THE NYMPHS
OF THETIS

1666, marble, life size
François Girardon 1628–1715
gardens of Versailles

This group, showing Apollo being tended
after his day's work of driving the sun
chariot across the sky, is the most famous
of many sculptures designed by Girardon
to decorate the Versailles gardens. Its
original setting, now replaced by picturesque rocks and ruins, was an enclosed
niche in a grotto of shells within which
the figures were arranged in a highly
classical manner.

149

LOUIS XIV

1701
Hyacinthe Rigaud 1659–1743
oil on canvas
110 × 74·75 in (279 × 189 cm)
Louvre, Paris

This state portrait of the ageing king with
its imposing stance and swirling draperies
epitomises Louis's sense of monarchy and
majesty and created a type of court
portrait popular throughout Europe during
the eighteenth century. Louis was so
delighted with the result that he abandoned
his original intention of presenting it to
Philip V of Spain and hung it instead in
his own throne room at Versailles.

apparent in the choice of paintings acquired; buyers showed a marked
preference for the Italian Renaissance and for the more classical of Italian
and French contemporary painters.

Changing attitudes

During the 1680s the tight control which had been exercised over the
arts was loosened and new and more varied tendencies began to appear. A
series of events contributed to this change of situation. Colbert's death in
1683 brought to an end Le Brun's complete dictatorship over the arts as
François Louvois, Colbert's successor, favoured another painter, Pierre
Mignard. Furthermore the authority of the Academies had been under-
mined by the violent quarrels of the 1670s which had split them into two.
The orthodox Academicians on one side supported the ancients and
Poussin while the more avant-garde members favoured the moderns and
Rubens.

The great quarrel in the Academy of Painting during the 1670s had been
over colour and form. This had arisen out of an increasing admiration by
certain artists for Venetian painting and led not only to a greater
importance being given to colour but also to the substitution of Rubens
as the greatest master in place of Raphael and Poussin. Rubens's great
series of decorations painted for the Luxembourg Palace, which had been
neglected by French artists for fifty years suddenly became the object of
highest esteem. This interest in Rubens and the northern artists generally
was reflected in the later purchases for the royal collection which began
to include such paintings as *The Kermesse* by Rubens and *Portrait of the
Artist as an Old Man* by Rembrandt. A wide range of non-classical

influences appeared in painting: Charles de la Fosse painted colourful religious scenes like *The Presentation of the Virgin*, now in the Musée des Augustins in Toulouse, in the manner of the Venetians, while Antoine Coypel dramatically opened up the vault of the Versailles Chapel to the skies in the Roman Baroque tradition of illusionistic painting. The rich colours and Baroque formulas of Rubens and Van Dyck inspired such portrait painters as Largillière in his *Charles Le Brun*, and Rigaud in his *Louis XIV*, both now in the Louvre. There were variations of style even within the works of individual artists. Both the painter Rigaud and the sculptor Coysevox show in their portraits that the more formal Baroque style was reserved for the state portraits of the king and his courtiers while a new naturalism, intimacy and sensitive characterization, at times reminiscent of Rembrandt, was given to the portraits of their friends and bourgeois patrons, as can be seen in Rigaud's *The Artist's Mother* and Coysevox's *Robert de Cotte*.

A different attitude at court helped this new Baroque movement to be accepted even in official art. The king had become religious and totally autocratic and the emotional qualities of the Baroque style were more suited to his new state of mind than the rational qualities of classicism.

This change in taste was also significant in sculpture. Girardon's popularity at the court began to wane and the more Baroque sculptures of Coysevox came into favour, such as his equestrian statues of Mercury and Fame made for the royal château of Marly (now in the Tuileries Gardens). Likewise Pierre Puget, the most Baroque of all French sculptors who had been ignored previously by Colbert, had two figure groups including the *Milo of Crotona* accepted for the gardens at Versailles.

In architecture the new pronounced tendency towards the Baroque was strongest in ecclesiastical art due to Louis XIV's changed attitude to religion, and the two most important public buildings of the last years of his reign were the chapels for the Invalides and Versailles built by J. H. Mansart, who remained official architect. Ambitious town planning schemes that were Baroque in scale and grandeur were created, such as Mansart's public squares for Paris, the Place Vendôme and the Place des Victoires, and the laying out of the Place de l'Etoile and Avenue des Champs-Elysées, designed by Le Nôtre as a magnificent vista approach to the Tuileries Palace. Towards the end of the century, however, commissions from the crown itself diminished due to the king's involvement in ruinous wars, and private patronage in Paris became more widespread. The court however remained the largest and most influential patron but it was the younger members of the royal family who created the initiative. Attempts made in the interior decoration of the smaller royal châteaux to break away from the ostentatious formality of Versailles led to a more frivolous fashion that was to be developed under Louis XV; the heavy grandeur of Le Brun's interiors was replaced by a new lightness and gaiety.

During the major part of the seventeenth century Rome was the un-rivalled centre of the artistic world and her art and artists were held in the highest esteem. The first indication of change was in 1667 when the three Frenchmen Le Vau, Le Brun and Claude Perrault had their design for the Louvre accepted where Bernini had failed. The creation of Versailles took this a stage further when the palace became a model of taste and fashion which was imitated throughout western Europe. During the very last years of Louis XIV's reign with the development of the new style in decoration France began to take the lead in artistic creation and the change of roles between Paris and Rome became complete.

Mary Whiteley

150
BUST OF COLBERT
c. 1685
Antoine Coysevox 1640–1720
marble, h. 31·5 in (80 cm)
Louvre, Paris

Jean-Baptiste Colbert, Marquis de Seignelay (1619–83), was known in his day as 'the man of marble'; he was however an indefatigable servant of Louis XIV and devoted his great ability and extra-ordinary energy towards the better management of the state. Coysevox gave a new freedom of movement and sensitive modelling to the French portrait bust and was undoubtedly inspired by Bernini's bust of the king at Versailles.

151
COUNT
BALTHAZAR CASTIGLIONE
c. 1513–16
Raphael 1483–1520
oil on canvas, detail
32·25 × 26·5 in (82 × 67 cm)
Louvre, Paris

Castiglione was one of the most accomplished and cultured men of his age. Raphael painted this sympathetic portrait of him when he was the duke of Urbino's envoy to the papal court. It is one of the most outstanding portraits of the Italian Renaissance and was first brought to France by Cardinal Mazarin, passing into the royal collection in 1661.

152
THE MARRIAGE OF HENRY IV TO MARIE DE' MEDICI

1622–25, Peter Paul Rubens 1577–1640, oil on canvas
155 × 116·25 in (394 × 295 cm), Louvre, Paris

Rubens was commissioned by Marie de' Medici to paint twenty-one large canvases depicting the main events in her life to decorate her new and favourite palace of the Luxembourg. This scene shows her marriage by proxy in Santa Maria del Fiore in Florence in 1600, a ceremony which Rubens himself had attended.

153
GALLERY OF THE HOTEL LAMBERT

c. 1650–60, Louis le Vau 1612–70 and Charles le Brun 1619–90, Paris

Galleries were popular features of mid-seventeenth-century Parisian houses and this one, built by Le Vau for a private patron, Jean Lambert, is the most magnificent room of the period to survive. Its decoration is dedicated to Hercules and consists of bronze and gold stucco reliefs alternating with landscape paintings on the walls and a vast ceiling decoration painted by Le Brun which is strikingly Baroque in its illusionism.

154 *right*
THE CHANCELLOR SEGUIER

1660, Charles le Brun 1619–90, oil on canvas
116 × 137·5 in (294 × 364 cm), Louvre, Paris

This life-size portrait of the artist's first protector, the powerful chancellor Séguier, shows the latter taking part in the state entrance of Louis XIV and his bride into Paris in 1660. The painting remained in the Séguier family until 1942. The carefully balanced grouping of the equerries strung out across the picture resembles an antique frieze, but the warm colouring and naturalistic treatment of the materials are far from classical.

155 *centre right*
THE PEASANTS AT SUPPER

1642, Louis le Nain c. 1593–1648,
oil on canvas
38 × 48 in (96·5 × 122 cm), Louvre, Paris

Louis le Nain was one of three painter brothers who came to Paris from Laon. He usually portrayed simple peasant scenes, a subject more common in Dutch seventeenth-century painting than in French. He neither caricatured nor idealised his humble sitters but treated them with complete detachment, giving even to the poorest a sense of gravity and dignity.

156 *bottom right*

ULYSSES AND THE SIRENS

after 1635, tapestry
designed by Simon Vouet 1590–1649
157·5 × 126 in (400 × 320 cm)
château de Cheverny, Loir-et-Cher

This tapestry, showing Ulysses successfully resisting the enticing songs of the sirens, is one of a series of eight which Vouet probably based on his own paintings of the history of Ulysses which decorated the gallery of a Paris house. The influences absorbed by the artist during his stay in Rome and Venice are reflected in the playful exuberance of the border amours and the light gay colouring.

157

FIRING SQUAD OF ARQUEBUSIERS

1633, engraving, Jacques Callot 1594–1635
Bibliothèque Nationale, Paris

One of eighteen prints from the series of the *Miseries and Misfortunes of War* made by Callot during the Siege of Nancy. He reports on the calamities of war without comment or moralisation but with acute observation and finesse; his method of isolating the main drama from the massed groups on either side heightens the poignancy of the scene.

158

MAISONS-LAFITTE

1642–46, François Mansart 1598–1666

The château of Maisons, seen here from the garden side, was built for a member of the new middle class, René de Longueil. It consists of a free-standing block with a prominent central frontispiece and is the finest and most complete example of Mansart's architecture on the interior as well as the exterior. The decoration composed of classical orders is complex yet severely restrained and kept within the main masses of the building.

160

MILO OF CROTONA

1671–83
Pierre Puget 1620–94
marble
h. 8 ft 10.5 in (270 cm)
Louvre, Paris

This large group which originally stood in a prominent position
in the gardens of Versailles, shows the famous Greek athlete
with his hand caught in a tree trunk, being torn to pieces by
a lion. The sharp twisting movement and the emotional strain
introduced by the sculptor come closer to the feeling of baroque
Roman sculpture than any other French art.

161 *opposite*

CHURCH OF THE INVALIDES

1680–91
Jules Hardouin Mansart 1646–1708
Paris

This magnificent church which dominates the skyline of Paris
was added by Mansart to the vast building built ten years earlier
by Liberal Bruant to house disabled soldiers. The plasticity
and dramatic grandeur of the architecture, the richness of the
decoration and the upward soaring movement produced by
the strong vertical emphasis on the façade and dome make
this the most Baroque building in France.

159

MERCURY

1701–2
Antoine Coysevox 1640–1720
marble
Tuileries Gardens, Paris

Mercury, the winged messenger of the
gods, is one of a pair of equestrian statues
that were originally designed for the
gardens of the château of Marly, one of the
royal pleasure retreats, and now flank the
entrance to the Tuileries Gardens. They
are good examples of the enormous
quantities of decorative sculpture that
were designed to form an integral part of
Le Nôtre's geometric garden designs.

162

THE ARCADIAN SHEPHERDS

c. 1655
Nicolas Poussin 1594–1665
oil on canvas
33·5 × 47·4 in (85 × 121 cm)
Louvre, Paris

This painting, one of Poussin's most classical, is treated with great simplicity and dignity. A group of shepherds and shepherdesses are shown reading a tomb inscription which reminds them of the transience of life. In an earlier version Poussin had portrayed them in a state of agitation, but here they contemplate death with philosophical detachment. The painting was purchased for the royal collection in 1683.

163

VAUX-LE-VICOMTE

1657–61
Louis le Vau 1612–70

This château, built for Nicolas Fouquet, is the most splendid in France. The large free-standing block is set off by the magnificent formal gardens designed by Le Nôtre stretching far into the distance while the interior is richly decorated with sculpture and painted panels by Le Brun. A few years later at Versailles Louis XIV not only took over the magnificent splendour of the style of Vaux-le-Vicomte but also the same team of artists.

164

SEAPORT AT SUNSET

1639
Claude Lorraine 1600–82
oil on canvas
40·5 × 53·5 in (103 × 136 cm)
Louvre, Paris

The scene is typical of Claude in that he portrays a dream rather than a real port. He uses the ships, buildings and people as a medium to show the poetic effects of golden light from the setting sun. This painting, together with its companion piece *The Village Dance*, was given as a present to the king by his landscape-gardener, André le Nôtre.

The last years of the reign of Louis XIV were a period of depression and anti-climax. France was poverty-stricken and demoralised by successive military defeats. The last great projects of the reign, the chapel at Versailles and the royal chapel at the Invalides, were finished in sumptuous Baroque style after the War of the Grand Alliance, although they had been begun before. The richness and decorative splendour of these buildings seems to have been designed to conceal the disastrous decline in the fortunes of the state. For the last time, the absolutist monarchy of Louis XIV impressed the nation with the glorious symbolism of church and state, heavenly and earthly power combined.

With the first reverses of the war the splendour of Versailles grew dim. The silver furniture was melted down and in the new decorations cheaper materials were substituted for bronze and expensive imported marble. For a short period gilding was banned and the Gobelins factory was closed down. The court itself and with it the splendid ceremony that had given the great palace its meaning began to evaporate. The younger members of Louis's family began to build new houses in Paris. Before they deserted the court entirely, they played a large part in the development of the new style, the Rococo, so-called from the meaning of the word 'rocaille', artificial rockwork and shellwork of the kind used in grottoes in the sixteenth century.

The king's retreat in the grounds of Versailles itself, the Grand Trianon, was devoted to pleasure, ease and domestic privacy. Here some of the first signs of a new, more delicate ornament came into being. This single-storey building with its very tall windows and mirrors was a model for the ease of the private houses of the next generation. Everything was designed for the pleasure of the occupants, not for the display of a court eager to impress foreign ambassadors. The influence of the young Duchess of Burgundy was more important than the moderation and economy of Mme de Maintenon. The old Menagerie at Versailles was redecorated for her amusement at the expense of the state. The king, as always, inspected the designs himself. One scheme submitted in 1698 was solemnly allegorical in the old court style and Louis inscribed on it: 'Youthfulness must be brought into the work that is to be done'. The spirit of youth showed itself more and more frequently in the last years of the reign. It was the king's own idea in 1700 to decorate the Salon de l'Oeil de Boeuf with what seems to be a gilded trellis in front of which children, modelled in low relief, run and dance and play musical instruments.

The artists responsible for the new decorations were designers in the studio of Jules Hardouin Mansart. The designer Bérain introduced arabesque C- and S-curves in walls and on ceilings that broke up the rigidity of the old geometrical décor. A revolution soon took place: fanciful decorations and arabesques were installed in royal and private houses alike. Gracefully curving ornament was intertwined with a profusion of delicate curving forms from nature, shells, foliage and flowers inhabited by all manner of diminutive monsters, monkeys, orientals, lovers, nymphs and satyrs. These motifs appeared in the painted and lacquered panels of walls and in the inlay of furniture. The greatest of the specialists in this style was Claude Audran I who employed the young Watteau in his studio.

An important stimulus to the new decoration came from the importation of large quantities of oriental lacquer and porcelain. Chinese gods appeared among the many exotic figures of ornament and even the popular 'singeries' (comic monkeys) in wall decorations were prompted by the Chinese taste. Chinese work was widely imitated and gave rise to the creation of porcelain all over Europe in the eighteenth century. The

The Last Years of the Monarchy

1700–1789

165
PORTRAIT OF
MADAME DE POMPADOUR
1756
Maurice Quentin de la Tour 1704–88
pastel
69 × 50 in (175 × 128 cm)
Louvre, Paris

This pastel portrait is one of La Tour's most brilliant highly finished pieces. The pastel technique allows a great lightness of colouring and was imitated widely by painters in oils. Mme de Pompadour is shown here as a patroness of learning and the arts. The Encyclopaedia of Diderot and d'Alembert is at hand, emphasizing her political alliance with the powerful, progressive intellectuals of the enlightenment, the 'philosophes'.

most beautiful Chinese porcelain was often mounted in French gilt-bronze mounts.

With the gradual return of the nobility to Paris and the demand for new houses by the rich middle class, new suburbs were opened up, notably the Faubourg St Honoré and the Faubourg St Germain. Here great princes rubbed shoulders with neighbours who were merchants, soldiers or perhaps wigmakers, like Peyrenc de Moras, who built the beautiful hôtel which is now the Musée Rodin. What is now the Place Vendôme was begun as the Place Louis XIV with an equestrian statue of the king in its centre. Financially the project was taken over by the city of Paris. Royal dignity demanded a unified palatial appearance, but bourgeois individualism insisted on the right of each proprietor to build his house behind the façade according to his own taste and requirements. The new power in the land, the financiers, lived in this urban, middle-class palace. They could afford to do what the court could not and used gilding quite freely in their new houses in spite of the royal prohibition.

167 One of the finest buildings of the period is the Hôtel Soubise, now part of the Archives Nationales. The wife of the Prince de Soubise had received numerous gifts from the king in secret. Thus enriched, they bought a very old house in 1704, the Hôtel de Guise, and had it transformed by Delamaire with a splendid courtyard, a new entrance and a magnificent façade in the style of Mansart. Delamaire intended to make a grand suite of rooms with their doors aligned 'en enfilade', so that there would be a long perspective view right through the house in the manner of Versailles. The courtyard displeased the princess and the construction of the rooms 'en enfilade' would have inconvenienced her son. He replaced Delamaire with Boffrand, who destroyed the great design by creating intimate oval rooms across Delamaire's perspective. Here one can see the triumph of the taste of the new generation. The exterior is public, **183** stately and Baroque; the interior, fantasy, private contentment and Rococo.

There were also changes in the taste for painting. The great decorators of the end of Louis XIV's reign, Charles de la Fosse and Antoine Coypel, had worked in a colourful, naturalistic style derived from Rubens and the great Venetians. There was no room for their large mythologies and allegories in the new intimate apartments. What was needed were small pictures for pleasure whose curves would fit in with the arabesques of the room decorations of the day. The style of Rubens and Veronese was reduced to a new, small scale by numerous French artists for little domestic scenes of amusement and sophisticated daily life. The models for this style were little pictures by the Flemish painter David Teniers or the seventeenth-century Dutch paintings of daily life and landscape. This taste was exploited by numerous French artists of the next generation, who combined the new curvilinear decoration with small naturalistic scenes. Their themes were no longer mythology and allegory or even the simple morality of the Dutch painters, but fashionable life, pastorals, children's amusements and scenes of love.

The regency of Philip, Duke of Orleans

The tendencies of the beginning of the century were given a new impetus when the regent abandoned Versailles for the Palais Royal in Paris. The nobility rapidly built up the new suburbs. With none of the pressures of court etiquette to restrain them, they emphasised domestic comfort in their new Paris villas. Both the nobility and the middle classes bought furniture and small ornaments in profusion, stimulating a great age in the decorative arts. Furnishings and paintings formed the framework of a

166
PORCELAIN
CELADON WARE CUP
(YUNG CHONG)
1723–35, gilt-bronze mount c. 1750
Musée Nissim de Camondo, Paris

The finest pieces of Chinese porcelain were often treated as ornaments. They were given exquisite gilt-bronze mounts, the most perfect examples of this especially French craft. The use of this cup is made impossible by the metal that surrounds the smooth porcelain; instead of a useful object it has become a precious ornament. When these mounts were made the taste for oriental objects had existed for about fifty years due to extensive trading contacts.

167
HOTEL SOUBISE
1704
René-Alexis Delamaire 1675–1745
Paris

This view shows the new entrance to the old Hôtel de Guise devised by Delamaire in 1704. The tall windows, the central pediment and the elegant Classicism of the façade reflect the architectural taste established by Jules Hardouin Mansart. The colonnaded courtyard, built in what was formerly a garden, was greatly admired for the new grandeur it gave to the old building. The courtyard of the old building can just be seen through an arched opening on the left of the façade.

168

CANDLESTICK

c. 1734–35
Claude Duvivier,
master 1720, after a design by Juste Aurèle
Meissonier 1693/5–1750
h. 15 in (38 cm)
Musée des Arts Décoratifs, Paris

This artist created the most irregular designs to be seen in Rococo art. His interior decorations carried asymmetry to new lengths, while his small gilt-bronze objects, like this one, reflect a desire for more and more naturalistic forms, even in everyday domestic things. This piece was probably made by the goldsmith Duvivier, like many of Meissonier's designs. Meissonier himself was at first a bronze-worker but later gradually became an architect of some importance.

luxurious life. The exteriors followed the style of the interiors. Columns and pediments were avoided and replaced by richly varied window shapes, decorative sculpture and the arabesques of ironwork balconies. They concealed lowpitched roofs in the fashionable Italian style behind balustrades. These pleasure houses, built for themselves, their lovers and mistresses, were lavishly decorated in the new style and with a new interest in comfort. The corridor replaced the enfilade, making more private apartments. Kitchens were brought closer to dining-rooms, so that food did not get cold on its way to the table. Chimneys were improved and attempts were made at sanitation.

In the midst of the ease of the nobility and the rich upper-middle class the French economy was in a most unhealthy state. The regent was persuaded by the Scottish adventurer, John Law, to issue paper money. All Paris gambled madly on stocks or at cards. Architects and art dealers grew rich very fast. The collecting of works of art increased and prices rose, especially for the popular Dutch and Flemish pictures. Architects built houses as speculations for immediate resale or for letting as apartments. Fortunes were made in a day and when the crash came in 1720 fortunes were lost overnight. For the rich this was an age of endless pleasure, of conversation, music, the theatre and hunting. Significantly the only grand monument of this period is not a private house but the vast stables built for the horses of Le Grand Condé at Chantilly, a Versailles for horses. In taste, there was no clear division between the classes. The great lawyers, that highly respectable class, the bankers, the tax-gatherers and the architects all profited from the new activity. Soon debt-ridden aristocrats–it was fashionable to be in debt–married the dowry-laden daughters of the middle class. They built, gambled, bought pictures and acquired new debts.

The regent initiated no public works. He formed a collection of the great classical masterpieces of Renaissance and seventeenth-century painting in the most famous gallery of the century. He owned some Dutch pictures, but none by Watteau. The only trace of his personal interest in the new taste is in the decorations of the Palais Royal executed in the most up-to-date manner. They were undertaken by Oppenord, who had just returned from Italy full of enthusiasm for the freedom of Italian design.

A most important group gathered round the rich Pierre Crozat, the tax farmer. His friends were connoisseurs, print dealers and art dealers. He had a magnificent collection of old master drawings and commanded the services of the elderly Charles de la Fosse. Thus he had his gallery decorated in a style that rivalled the great noble galleries of the seventeenth century. The greatest protégé of this circle was the young, moody and irresolute Watteau, who took over the decoration of Crozat's dining-room from De la Fosse. Watteau had struggled along in Paris, at first copying Dutch pictures for dealers, then working with Gillot, the painter of little pictures of stage scenes. Later he worked with the decorator Audran. Watteau's arabesques are delightful in their naturalism and fantasy. Undoubtedly one of the greatest artists of the century, his influence dominated Europe for fifty years or more.

Watteau's world appears to be all fantasy. Many of his characters and **172** his motifs–love, music and leisure–are taken from the ballet-operas or from the improvised, satirical commedia dell'arte. The Italian comedians who had introduced this kind of theatre to France were banned for their scandalous comments on the court. Watteau does not deal with morality. His realm is feeling and the most subtle nuances in the relationship of one

figure to another. There is an intense realism beneath the charming exterior. Watteau drew incessantly from nature and his figures are the result of his personal discoveries. Many sheets of drawings are covered with experiments, in which he seems to be searching for the precise gesture or the exact tilt of a head that would convey some subtlety of emotion. It is idle to look for the contemporary world in his paintings. He did not record the life but the ideals of his society. Contemporary life was recorded by other artists, by the genial Jean François de Troy and, later, by Carle van Loo. The taste for hunting shows in many of these pictures, as it does also in the game still lifes of Oudry and Desportes. Desportes even shows himself in his self-portrait, not hard at work at the **170** easel, but as a huntsman. When Watteau painted scenes of the hunt, he left out quarry, chase and hounds and painted the dalliance of people resting instead.

Watteau's middle-class patrons also welcomed to Paris two international personalities of the day, the Venetian painter Pellegrini and his sister-in-law, the pastellist, Rosalba Carriera. Pellegrini introduced a new freedom of handling and a brilliant luminosity of colour in his decoration of the ceiling of Law's bank, now destroyed. Rosalba painted many pastel portraits of fashionable Parisians and set a pattern for sweet, light coloured pastels that influenced the whole course of French work in this medium.

The beginning of Louis XV's reign

The end of the regency in 1723 had very little effect on the arts for a decade. The court returned to Versailles, but work there gained momentum slowly. Unlike his predecessor Louis preferred, all his life, to leave the details of public and artistic affairs to others. At the age of fifteen Louis married the Polish princess Maria Leczinska. Seven of their ten children, **169** all born within a short time, survived to maturity. After their birth in the 1730s the queen was retired in favour of a succession of mistresses.

In foreign policy Cardinal Fleury kept the peace and in the 1730s the Comte d'Orry kept a firm grasp on the purse. The only military disturbance was the War of the Polish Succession. The improvement in finances under Orry made royal patronage possible once more. The Chambre de la Reine at Versailles is a fine example of the mature Rococo style which had been developed in Paris in the regency period. The only great pictorial decoration of the period was the ceiling of the Salon d'Hercules **182** by François Lemoyne. When Lemoyne committed suicide in 1737 he left not only a fine piece of decoration but a group of highly talented pupils including Boucher and Natoire. These two painters soon demonstrated their talent in several decorative schemes and in their luminous and amorous mythologies. They provided the little paintings for the Chambre de la Reine and were among the group of artists who painted pictures for the Hôtel Soubise, the others being Trémolières and Van Loo. In 1732, the new Prince de Soubise married a beautiful young widow. The theme of love is carried through all the rooms of her apartment, the large Delamaire rooms and the smaller oval room built by Boffrand. The wooden carved panels in the large rooms are exquisite, but Boffrand's greatest achievement is the decoration of the Salon Ovale. Natoire's beautiful paintings of the story of Cupid and Psyche are surrounded by white and gilt stucco cupids, while all the details of mouldings are natural forms in elegant **18** profusion.

In all the arts the decorative curves, in use from the beginning of the century, became opulently three-dimensional in the 1730s, and increasingly naturalistic in their details and motifs. This can be seen in Cressent's **18** furniture. The extreme was reached in designs for interiors by Meissonier,

171
SYLVIA RUNNING FROM THE WOLF SHE HAS WOUNDED

1755, oil on canvas
François Boucher (1703–70)
48·5 × 52·5 in (123·5 × 134 cm)
Musée des Beaux Arts, Tours

Many of the tapestries designed by Boucher
were woven at Beauvais in a range of
brilliant but perishable colours. This
piece was woven at the Gobelins factory
in a range of more limited but better-
preserved colours. It is one of four scenes
based on Tasso's *Aminta*. The originals
were painted in 1755–6 for the Duc de
Penthièvre. The tapestries were commissioned by the Duke of Portland. Boucher
was director of the Gobelins factory from
1755 onwards and was responsible for
many designs for the decorative arts.

172
THE PILGRIMAGE ON CYTHERA

detail, 1717, oil on canvas
Jean-Antoine Watteau 1684–1721
51 × 59 in (129 × 149 cm)
Louvre, Paris

This was Watteau's diploma piece for
the Academy, where he was the first
artist to be received as a painter of 'Fêtes
Galantes'. The subject is taken from a
ballet-opera. Watteau painted several
earlier versions in which the setting is
obviously a stage; here the stage has given
way to a fantastic mountainous landscape,
and a chain of contented lovers winds
down to a boat surrounded by cupids.

which are filled with a swaying asymmetry. All his work is made up of spiral curves, transforming everything firm and solid into the forms of growing vegetation or of flames. The same tendency can be seen even in
168 his small objects, like gilt-bronze candlesticks.

Nature appears in a quite different guise in Chardin's paintings. His calm, lucidly organised still lifes are far from the spirited fantasy of the work of his contemporaries. Slow and patient, Chardin scrutinised appearances in the empirical spirit of the scientists of the eighteenth century. By the end of the 1730s he was painting scenes of life below stairs, quite different from the glossy scenes of fashionable life of Boucher and De Troy. He points no moral, although engravers of his work often added little verses to give his images a middle-class moral appeal. He simply shows servants patiently at work, perhaps peeling potatoes. Other pictures show the lady of the house taking tea or the children amusing themselves with tops or card castles. The domestic virtues of this middle-class painting were not unnoticed at court. The cult of moral sentiment
175 seems to have begun as early as 1740 when Louis XV bought *Le Bénédicité*.

Historical accident played its part in the development of the arts. At the outbreak of the War of the Austrian Succession, the king, unwilling to lead his armies, fell ill at Metz. He put the swash-buckling Maréchal de Saxe in charge in his place. He also turned unexpectedly pious, dismissed his mistress, and vowed to dedicate a church to St Geneviève if he recovered. The Maréchal's tomb is one of the most heroic in France. The building of
178 the church was to have started in 1755 by Soufflot. It is now the Panthéon. Both works are quite foreign to the languid and elegant Rococo, so dear to Louis' own court in mid-century.

Another, equally unforeseeable result was the creation of one of the greatest urban designs of the century, the Place Royal and the Place
184 Stanislas at Nancy, Lorraine. Stanislas, ex-king of Poland and established by Louis in Lorraine, on hearing of his son-in-law's famous illness determined to create a monument to him. The design was entrusted to Boffrand's pupil, Héré, who created a magnificent sequence of squares and palatial buildings which link the old and the new city. A great scheme had been undertaken earlier at Bordeaux by Jacques Gabriel and his son Ange-Jacques, but no later projects in the cities of France or in the metropolis equalled the grandeur of the Nancy design.

Mme de Pompadour and the later years of Louis XV's reign

165 The king's next mistress was the most famous, Mme de Pompadour. She took over the reins of power and has been much blamed for her interference in foreign affairs, the result of which was the loss of France's empire in Canada and India. In the arts, however, she was an energetic patroness. She encouraged artists of all kinds and took a great interest in porcelain and tapestry. Her chief artist was Boucher who was in full charge of the decorative arts for the royal houses. Her uncle Lenormant de Tournehem and then her brother the Marquis of Marigny were put in charge of artistic affairs. Lenormant raised the tariffs for history pictures and thus encouraged anew a more serious kind of painting.

Marigny was fitted for his position as no-one had been before him. He was sent to Italy in the company of Abbé Leblanc, a connoisseur and critic, Cochin, an engraver, and Soufflot, a young architect from Lyon. During his grand tour they gave him instruction and he rewarded them with friendship and patronage in Paris. His mentors were in the vanguard of the attack on Rococo which began in the late 1740s. Critics began to favour a return to natural simplicity and to the dignity of antique art. This view was in general a product of the Enlightenment, the search for

173
THE BATHERS *detail*
c. 1765–70, oil on canvas
Jean Honoré Fragonard 1732–1806
25 × 31 in (65 × 18 cm)
Louvre, Paris

Not only did Fragonard learn from Boucher the secrets of a warm, sensuous palette, he also exploited them with a new freedom of handling. This is a brilliant sketch in which form and space are subservient to the effects of colour and the rhythm of the brush. Fragonard was one of the greatest masters of the impromptu in eighteenth-century art. The picture may have belonged to Mme du Barry, who in 1773 rejected a series of Fragonard's pictures in favour of paintings by Vien.

174 *opposite*
ST DENIS PREACHING

1767, oil on canvas
Joseph-Marie Vien
264 × 144 in (671 × 366 cm)
left transept, church of St Roch, Paris

This picture was painted for the church of St Roch and exhibited at the Salon of 1767, where it was retouched by Vien before being installed in the church. Critical acclaim was divided between this classical masterpiece and its companion piece by Doyen *St Geneviève succouring the plague stricken*. Diderot admired the simplicity and grandeur of its figures. He compared Vien's style with that of Domenichino or Le Sueur. It belongs to the calmest aspect of Neo classicism and Diderot complained of Vien's lack of verve.

175

LE BENEDICITE

1740, oil on canvas
Jean-Baptiste Chardin 1699–1779
19 × 15 in (49 × 39 cm)
Louvre, Paris

Louis XV bought this painting in 1740
and later versions found their way to the
courts of Sweden and Russia. The Dutch
artist Jan Steen had painted the same
subject in the preceding century. Chardin
treats the child-like innocence of the
subject with calm sobriety. The sentiment
is that of the eighteenth century, but the
colouring and handling are personal to
the artist. Unlike Boucher, he was not
satisfied with simplification of colours
into smooth brilliant generalities; each
delicate touch here helps to reconstruct the
complexity of real light and colour.

laws founded on nature, which could be applied to all human activities.

Mme de Pompadour was associated politically with Voltaire and other
philosophers, but not with the new classical taste for which they prepared
the way. She favoured the artists who could provide the best entertainment, for her chief aim was to prevent the king from becoming bored.
Boucher grew ever more rhapsodic in his treatment of mythology and **185**
continued to pour out a succession of sensuous paintings, tapestries and
designs for porcelain groups. With this armoury at her disposal Mme de
Pompadour could hardly fail to triumph over the pious and perhaps rather
boring queen.

Although privately Marigny still preferred Rococo painters, in public
he sponsored the birth of Neoclassicism in France. While the Renaissance
had been based on Roman art the new antiquity was that of Greece. The
wonders of Pompeii and Herculanaeum were revealed and travellers
began to visit Athens in search of the source of antique art. The monuments
themselves are not enough to account for the movement; the causes lie
primarily in contemporary concern with natural simplicity, the ideal of
liberty of the ancient republics and a respect for ancient morality and law.

The rich amateur, the Comte de Caylus, published a great collection of
antiquities. He bullied the artists he patronised to work in an antique
style. The most compliant was Vien who painted versions of antique
pictures and Grecian girls sacrificing at altars, a theme which also appears
in Carle van Loo's paintings. At the Academy, Caylus delivered a dis-
course on the virtues of Homeric subject matter and although the academicians did not like this sort of interference, surprisingly many of them
began to paint subjects from ancient poetry and history. However they
often relied on the style, sentiment and pathos of the Rococo, not on the
heroic qualities that the critics envisaged. Even Fragonard, Boucher's
successor in the field of Rococo fantasies, painted in the mid-1760s a few
history pictures of this kind. His *Corrhesus and Callirhoe* of 1765 sent
Diderot into raptures. Two years later the sensation at the Salon was the
appearance of the two vast pictures for St Roch, Vien's *St. Denis* and **174**
Doyen's *St Geneviève*. Both paintings are on a new heroic scale.

The revolution in architecture began earlier and was less tentative.
A.-J. Gabriel's Place de la Concorde was planned in 1755. Much of the
originality of this finely conceived open square lies in the simplicity of the
colonnading of the buildings on its north side. Gabriel used the same new
simplicity in the Petit Trianon at Versailles, at the château of Compiègne
and in the lucid volumes of the Ecole Militaire in Paris.

A new rectilinearity and restraint in ornament can also be seen in
furniture of the 1760s, though the process of change of style was slower **186, 188**
in the decorative arts. The private house began to be a classical villa in
the 1770s and especially in the imaginative and expensive transposition of
classical forms in the works of Ledoux.

Even among painters of a pure Rococo style, like Fragonard, one can
trace a gradual movement towards simple, smooth modelling and a
purity of line. Fragonard began with a style very like Boucher's. In
Italy in the early 1760s he studied the great decorative painters, not the
classical masters, and painted some spontaneous and luminous landscapes
in company with the painter of ruins, Hubert Robert. In Paris Fragonard
created a series of masterpieces of pure brilliance of colour and vigorous,
virtuoso handling, products of a warm and sensuous humanity. Many of **173**
his subjects are frankly erotic, while others reflect the tradition of Watteau
in their treatment of scenes of open-air entertainment. Later, he painted a
number of pictures that do not fall into these Rococo categories. They

177 show scenes of country life or the delights of families of numerous children. Fragonard, like Greuze, was clearly affected by the wave of sentiment about natural man that stemmed from Rousseau's writings of the 1760s.

However important the influence of Rousseau may have been in French thought before and during the Revolution, Diderot's effect on the arts was more direct. He proclaimed a new category of painting, 'moral painting', which was characterised in the 1750s and 1760s by Greuze. This artist's earlier pictures have a delicate colouring reminiscent of Dutch painting. They were devoted to the virtues of family life and virtuous simplicity of the provincial middle classes. Diderot had formerly admired Chardin, but he now found Chardin's subjects too trivial and preferred the explicit morality of Greuze. Partly as a result of this critical hostility, Chardin gave

187 up his genre scenes and turned to still life again. He returned to favour with a series of piercingly honest pastel portraits in his last years which are as intimate and realist as those of any eighteenth-century portraitist and beside works like these it is Greuze's pictures of sentiment that look trivial to us today.

Louis XVI and the end of the monarchy

The intellectual activity of the preceding period culminated in the Revolution of 1789. Louis XVI was more irresolute and more cut off from the nation than his predecessor. The small-scale Petits Appartements

189 at Versailles are the main monument of his reign. The classical style in these delicate rooms is spindly and fragile in the so called Pompeian manner and the finish is incomparable. Its thin, straight lines finally replaced the curves of the Rococo. Classicism on a grand scale existed in the minds of Ledoux and other architects and in their drawings. They dreamed of great symmetrical cities, geometrical in their forms and devoted to an ideal of liberty, justice and equality for their inhabitants. The beginnings of such a scheme still exist at Chaux.

D'Angivilliers, the new Directeur des Bâtiments, was as tyrannical in the artistic sphere as other ministers were in the political. Classicism became the only acceptable official creed. All opposition was suppressed and rival Salons were banned. Even the nude was abolished and the sensuous exterminated. Everywhere history pictures and classical subjects abounded and nowhere more than in the work of the painter Vincent, David's true predecessor.

Before Greuze painted his well-known sentimental figures of Grecian dressed maidens, he had failed in a final attempt to gain recognition from the Academy as a history painter. He quarrelled with the Academy, with Diderot and all except his noble acquaintances and exhibited at his own

179 house. There in 1777 and 1778 he exhibited *The Father's Curse* and *The Son's Punishment*. These reproachful domestic tragedies are couched in a heroic style derived from Poussin and the antique. In these pictures the modern genre scene takes on a new glory. Greuze anticipated the vigorous morality and the classical language which was to be used by the great painter of the

180 Revolution. Jacques-Louis David in the famous *Oath of the Horatii* signed the death warrant of Rococo and perhaps also the monarchy. His morality, described through classical drama, was immediately understood as a call to patriotic combat against tyranny, in which the three brothers of the picture are a striking symbol of unity and equality. The call was answered within four years.

Anthony S. G. Green

176

BUST OF
JEAN-JACQUES ROUSSEAU
c. 1778, terra-cotta
Jean-Antoine Houdon 1741–1828
h. 25 in (65 cm)
Louvre, Paris

Houdon's portraits were famous for their life-like quality and for the delicacy of their surface treatment, which made marble appear as soft and resilient as flesh. Rousseau was one of the most important influences on French educational and political thinking, while his cultivation of idealistic sentiment was widely influential on the arts.

177

THE FAIR AT ST-CLOUD
c. 1775, oil on canvas
Jean Honoré Fragonard 1732–1806
85 × 131 in (216 × 335 cm)
Banque de France, Paris

Like his great English contemporary, Gainsborough, Fragonard emulated the luminous naturalism of the great Dutch landscapists. The fantastic forms of his golden trees and billowing clouds, together with this vast episodic composition of amusements marks this out as a fully Rococo picture. Like Gainsborough, too, Fragonard exploits a free and improvisatory technique. The picture was painted for the Duc de Penthièvre and installed in the Hôtel de Toulouse, the Banque de France since 1808.

178

THE PANTHEON

foundation stone laid 1764
Jacques-Germain Soufflot 1713–1780
Paris

Formerly dedicated to St Geneviève, the patroness of Paris, the church was commissioned by Louis XV, and is a great achievement of eighteenth-century science as well as of art. The Greek colonnading of the interior is combined with Gothic lightness of structure. Soufflot took infinite precautions in the selection of stone, in laying foundations and in the system of masonry. The giant pediment is held together by an elaborate system of iron ties.

179 *above*

THE SON'S PUNISHMENT

1778, oil on canvas, Jean Baptiste Greuze 1725–1805
51 × 65 in (130 × 163 cm), Louvre, Paris

Greuze is best known for his sentimental pictures of young girls, and the one-time popularity of these has obscured his real importance, as a painter of genre scenes. Greuze aspired to be a painter of histories; both this picture and its companion *The Father's Curse* are full of quotations from antique sculpture and from Nicolas Poussin. They are the artist's most formidable attempt to combine a heroic style with domestic tragedy. Greuze exhibited this picture in his own studio, since he had quarrelled with the Academy.

180

OATH OF THE HORATII

1784–85, oil on canvas, Jacques Louis David 1748–1825
129 × 167 in (333 × 425 cm), Louvre, Paris

This picture was inspired by a performance in Paris of Corneille's drama *Les Horaces*. David finished the picture in Rome amid the monuments of antiquity. He exhibited in Rome and then in Paris in 1785 where the painting created a furore, the content being recognised as patriotic and revolutionary. The style is completely free of Rococo tendencies, the space is measured, the light rational, the forms hard, sculptural and monumental. In spite of its revolutionary message the work was bought for Louis XVI and was exhibited again after the Revolution had begun in 1791.

181
COMMODE

c. 1740, Charles Cressent 1685–1782, Louvre, Paris

Furniture makers as well as painters employed the gracious Rococo curve. Cressent's work is among the finest in mid-eighteenth-century furniture; the naturalistic curving bronze-gilt mounts echo the three-dimensional curves of the finely inlaid cabinetwork. Even the theme of the swing is characteristically Rococo. French furniture reached its zenith in the eighteenth century in response to the new taste for domestic luxury. Cressent was famous in his day for the moving parts of his furniture, which often incorporated secret drawers.

182
APOTHEOSIS OF HERCULES *detail*

1733–1736, François Lemoyne 1688–1737, oil painting
55 × 60 ft (15.66 × 18.29 m), Salon d'Hercules, Versailles

This important painter created the last great pictorial decoration at Versailles in the years 1733–36. Continuing the tradition of De la Fosse, he formed his style on the example of the great Venetian and Flemish colourists. In this ceiling piece, the light and airy colouring derives more from the eighteenth-century Venetians, Pellegrini and Sebastiano Ricci. This is his largest work, containing a hundred and forty-two figures. In mid-century it was much admired by the Comte de Caylus as a masterpiece of decorative painting.

183 *opposite*
SALON DE LA PRINCESSE

1737–40, Germain Boffrand 1667–1754
Hôtel Soubise, (Archives Nationales), Paris

This is the richest and most colourful of all surviving Rococo French interiors. It was decorated for the bride of the Prince de Soubise, a young widow. The wood-carving was probably executed by Herpin who had been working at the hôtel for some years. The paintings by Charles Natoire (1700–77), showing the story of Cupid and Psyche were executed between 1737 and 1740. The walls appear to dissolve into light, because of the many windows and mirrors. The remaining solid parts of the structure are turned into a rich fantasy of organic life, which spreads over the walls, through the wavy cornice and into the ceiling, transforming the room into a garden bower.

184 *opposite*
WROUGHT IRON GRILLE

c. 1751, Jean Lamour 1698–1761, Place Stanislas, Nancy

The idea of open spaces joining the old and new towns was first thought of by Stanislas in 1745. Emmanuel Héré (1705–61) made the designs in 1751, and the Lorrainer, Lamour, designed fine ironwork balconies and executed the grilles for the corners of the main square. These linked the buildings; a triumph of eighteenth-century craftsmanship, they show a characteristic insistence on ornament even in a vast architectural scheme.

185 *below*
AURORA AND CEPHALUS

1763, François Boucher 1703–70, oil on canvas
55 × 43 in (140 × 110 cm), Louvre, Paris

A late masterpiece exemplifying the splendidly luminous quality of Boucher's art. The figures appear to float not so much in space as in radiant zones of colour. Boucher used colour rather than gesture or expression to convey the content of his mythological paintings, many of which, like this one, involved the deities of air or light.

LOUIS XV'S WRITING DESK
1760–69
François Oeben c. 1710–63, Jean-Henri Riesener 1734–1806
mahogany with various inlays and gilt-bronze mounts
59 × 72 in (126·2 × 172·7 cm), Versailles

This is one of the finest pieces of French furniture of the eighteenth century. It was begun by Oeben for Louis XV in 1760 in a style still noticeably fond of Rococo curves, especially in the design of the gilt-bronze ornaments. Unfinished at his death it was completed in 1769 by his pupil Riesener, who was to become one of the leading exponents of the later Neoclassical furniture style.

187

BASKET OF PLUMS

1758–9, oil on canvas, 14 × 17·5 in (36 × 45 cm)
Jean-Baptiste Simeon Chardin, 1699–1779
Musée des Beaux Arts, Rennes

The simple objects are shown in broken touches of clear colour against a golden brown ground. Chardin allowed for the full effect of multiple reflections and the glow of colour over softly lit surfaces. Contours disappear and volumes are constructed entirely in terms of colour. His achievement in still-lifes like this is as great as that of the Impressionists of the nineteenth century.

188

SEVRES VASE *1783, Louvre, Paris*

From the 1770s onwards furniture, porcelain and the decorative arts tended towards an elegant classical style, encouraged by many connoisseurs and by Mme du Barry. Many objects were made to look like those of antiquity found at Herculaneum. In stone, the materials used were often of the hardest and most richly coloured, and these were extensively imitated in marble. Porcelain was frequently fitted out with gilt-bronze mounts in the specifically French tradition, as in this piece. These were based on classical examples and show the decisive change from the free vegetable forms of the Rococo.

189

MARIE-ANTOINETTE'S BOUDOIR

c.1780, Richard Mique 1728–94
Versailles

The refinement of fine detailing is typical of the style of the late eighteenth-century Petits Appartements at Versailles. Louis XVI's Austrian queen Marie-Antoinette adopted Mique and the style he had created for the king's sisters. The antique motifs, slender and symmetrical, are contained within narrow rectangular borders. This style represents the nearest approach of the court to Neoclassicism and is carried through into the furniture designed by Reisener. The desk and writing table are inlaid with mother of pearl.

David's *Brutus* was painted in the year of the Revolution; its full title makes clearer the painting's relevance to the events of 1789. The citizens of what was to become a new republic identified themselves constantly with the earlier republicans of Rome and Sparta. For Roman liberty read French liberty. Brutus condemning his sons stood for the Frenchman devoted to the concept of liberty and to a nation whose demands were to supersede those of the individual. If 1789 did not see the establishment of liberty, it certainly saw the birth of nationalism.

Three years later France was at war. The Assembly's 'Declaration of the Rights of Man and of the Citizen' had been intended not for Frenchmen alone but for all men. The powers of the European Coalition were committed to defend themselves, by attack if necessary, against a nation and an ideology. In 1794 the tide of war turned in France's favour and by 1811 the Napoleonic empire covered the whole European mainland with the exception of the Balkans. Behaving surprisingly like a conquering prince for the liberator of Europe and leader of a nation of free men, Napoleon arranged for the transportation to Paris of works of art and objects of curiosity. By 1794 the Convention had already begun to requisition works of art from the Low Countries, and armistice agreements made in 1796–97 provided for the submission of works of art from Italy in lieu of war taxes. A commission of experts selected works from the galleries of Parma, Modena, Milan, Cremona, Bologna and Perugia. In 1798 works of art were requisitioned from the states of Rome and of Venice and in 1800 from Florence and Turin. The first consignment arrived in Paris by water in July 1798 and was carried in Roman-style triumph through the streets to form a circle of wagons around the statue of Liberty in the Champs de Mars. Several works of Greek and Roman art were preceded by a standard on which was written, with unfounded optimism: 'Yielded up by Greece, lost by Rome, their fate has changed twice and will not change again.' Free men, it was implied, were the proper guardians of great art.

Napoleon and the national museum

While this situation was made possible by military conquest, the concept of centralising collections and safeguarding works of art which justified it was a product of Enlightenment thinking. The idea of a great national public collection in the Louvre had been canvassed under the ancien régime as early as 1747. By 1789 various projects for the practical improvement of the Louvre and of its collections were already under way. But if the concept and the structure of the gallery were already prepared, it took the fervour of the revolutionaries to create from these beginnings the first national museum. 'It should foster the fine arts, offer diversion to amateurs and serve the tastes of artists; it should be open to everyone . . . the institution shall be national and there shall be no-one who has not the right to enjoy it.'

On 18th of November 1793 the Muséum Central des Arts, created by decree of the Convention, was opened in the Louvre. The latinised name testifies to its Neoclassical bias. The first works to join the former royal collection in the Louvre had been those seized from the nobility, including a large number of minor Dutch and Flemish works whose selection by the newly elected commissioners bore witness to the pervasiveness of a taste which had ruled during the ancien régime. But after 1798 works began to pour in from Italy. The connoisseurs and artists whose tastes were guided by antiquity admired Raphael above all, sharing the view held by Vasari and furthered by Winckelmann that with Raphael and the painters of the High Renaissance art had reached a plateau. They saw Raphael as the heir to antiquity, the law-giver of a new

The Founding of the National Museums
1789–1871

190

J. BRUTUS FIRST CONSUL
1789
Jacques Louis David 1748–1824
oil on canvas
127·5 × 166·5 in (325 × 423 cm)
Louvre, Paris

The full title of this painting is: *J. Brutus first consul, on his return home after condemning his two sons who had joined the Tarquins and conspired against Roman liberty: Lictors bring in their bodies for burial.* A 'historical' subject used to make a political gesture. The political and social upheavals of France were mirrored within the Academy where a conservative faction attempted to have David's name struck from the lists before the Salon. The *Brutus* was banned, but was admitted and protected by art students in the uniform of the newlyformed national guard. By the next Salon, two years later, the Academy had lost control. Huge crowds which included workers and peasants packed in to see the paintings of David and his followers. A major victory had been won in the democratisation of taste in high art.

classicism. 'To proceed by the ancients and Raphael is to be truly an artist,' David had written. The first paintings chosen for despatch to Paris by the commission of experts in Italy were thus principally of the sixteenth century. Among the works displayed in the Grande Galerie of the Louvre at Napoleon's marriage in 1810 to Marie-Louise of Hapsburg were Raphael's *Madonna della Sedia* from Florence, his *St Cecilia* from Bologna, and his *Coronation* and *Transfiguration* from Rome, Leonardo's *La Belle Ferronnière* and Correggio's *Leda and the Swan* from Potsdam. There were also several canvases by Rubens, briefly out of favour under the revolutionary governments but reinstated as Bonaparte's court assumed princely trappings. Elsewhere in the Louvre the collections of classical sculpture were displayed, with the *Apollo Belvedere* and the *Laocoön* as the star pieces. A Musée des Antiques, forerunner of the Greek and Roman antiquities department of the Louvre, was founded in 1800.

At this time of territorial expansion, some magnificent private collections were also assembled and in perhaps the most remarkable of these it was Raphael once again who figured. J. B. Wicar, whom David had taken to Rome as a pupil in 1784 and who had remained in Florence to make drawings of the works in the Palazzo Pitti, assembled three collections of Italian drawings between 1784 and his death in 1834. The first was stolen, the second was sold to an English dealer and the third, which contained some items recovered from the first, was left to his home town of Lille. From the many drawings by Raphael and Michelangelo in Wicar's collection, there are several in the Louvre quite apart from the thirty-eight works definitely attributable to Raphael among the thirteen hundred drawings bequeathed to Lille. Other collections were formed by members of Napoleon's armies in Spain and it was at this period that Maréchal Soult acquired the two Murillos, *Immaculate Virgin* and *Immaculate Conception*, which entered the Louvre in 1817 and 1852.

If this wholesale displacement of works of art seems immoral to modern eyes, it seemed less so to contemporaries. The officers in Spain were buying not looting; the states annexed by conquest were usually only too happy to be allowed to pay their levies in works of art rather than in cash; many of these works were cared for by the French authorities in the Louvre as they would never have been in their former settings. Of the ten days in the revolutionary week while the Louvre was open to the public, two were reserved for cleaning and restoration of the collection. Works which had been dimly lit and near invisible in Italian churches were viewed by thousands in the galleries of the Louvre. The intellectuals of Europe, to whom the French Revolution was not necessarily the disaster it seemed to their rulers, saw the Muséum Central as the fulfilment of a dream; a kind of European encyclopaedia of art, a place for study, for contemplation and for enlightenment. People travelled from abroad to visit the gallery and several editions of the catalogue were published in English. For a brief period it seemed that Paris would recreate one of the rôles of republican Rome by peopling Europe with loyal citizens of Paris.

Works of art were not in fact reserved for Paris alone. By a decree of 1800 fifteen departmental museums were created within the enlarged boundaries of France, and works by artists already adequately represented in the Louvre were chosen by lot and distributed among them. Nor was France alone intended to benefit. Napoleon may have declared: 'My policy is France before all', but it was under his régime that both the Brera Gallery in Milan and the Accademia in Venice were established. Exchanges were made with the former; Italian paintings came to Paris, while the Brera gained some major works of the northern schools less well

191

THE APOTHEOSIS OF HOMER

1827, oil, 152 × 203 in (386 × 261 cm)
Jean Auguste Dominique Ingres 1780–1867
Louvre, Paris

Originally commissioned by the Director General of Museums as a ceiling decoration for the Musée Charles X, the painting entered the Louvre from the Luxembourg in 1874 and was exhibited in the same Salon as Delacroix's *Death of Sardanapalus*. Ingres and Delacroix stood for rival approaches to painting during the middle of the nineteenth century. *The Apotheosis of Homer* is a testament to Neoclassical loyalties and a reminder of the tastes of the Consulate and Empire; compare the Greek temple in Ingres' painting with the façade of the Madeleine, then under construction.

192

LA MADELEINE

1808–45
built from designs of
Pierre Alexandre Vignon 1763–1828
Paris

Napoleon is said to have chosen the design of the Madeleine between two battles. More a temple of glory to the everlasting memory of the hero Bonaparte than a church for Christian worship, the building is a close, if heavy, version of the conventional Roman temple. Nothing could testify more accurately to the image of himself which Napoleon wished to project into the future through the arts he patronised.

193

L'OPERA, PARIS

1861–75
architect Charles Garnier 1825–98

An opulent monument for an opulent Paris. While Haussman restyled the centre of Paris for the wealthy bourgeoisie, Garnier designed this monument to their recreations. The Napoleon III style, so far as it was a style at all, evoked the Renaissance and the Baroque to create an impression of luxury and overt grandeur which accorded ill with what remained of classical balance and order.

represented in Italy. These exchanges were in line with the policy of comprehensive representation of all schools which was vigorously pursued by the first great director of the Louvre, Baron Vivant Denon. It was Denon who recognised that among the welter of paintings by Raphael, Correggio and Veronese the earlier Italian schools were sadly neglected. He decided to devote one room of the Louvre to 'painting since its renaissance in the thirteenth century'. Denon was the prototype for the ideal museum curator; a man with an extraordinary eye for quality and historical importance to which he was able to subordinate his own preferences. His taste among the earlier Italian and Flemish painters was encyclopaedic rather than enthusiastic, but his acquisitions were nevertheless brilliant. In 1814 an exhibition was held at the Louvre of 123 paintings, including Cimabue's *Madonna of the Angels*, collected by Denon in 1811 on **207** a mission to Italy to acquire works of the earlier schools.

If Denon was the first to give public expression to the reappraisal of the Italian primitives, the true revolutionaries in the matter of taste were, like the Chevalier Artaud de Montor, distinguished amateurs. De Montor published in 1808 his *Considerations sur l'état de la peinture en Italie dans les quatres siècles qui ont précédé celui de Raphael*. Significantly, he also published a translation of Dante, who had come to fill for the Romantics of the early nineteenth century the place held in the hearts of the Neoclassicists by Homer. Paillot de Montabert, another amateur, published in 1812 a work on the Gothic painters which marked in the history of European taste the turn of a tide which had been flowing since the time of Vasari: 'Around the sixteenth century, the art of painting, which achieved so much in terms of imitation and execution, in fact lost in dignity, in naivety and in beauty.' This was the first blow to Raphael's reputation for almost three centuries. If there were still by the end of the Napoleonic period archclassicists such as Quatremère de Quincy to uphold the principles of Winckelmann, they came to seem increasingly conservative figures.

The Romantic Museum

The Revolution had promoted republican ideals and encouraged identification with the classical world, but it had also promoted the ideal of individual freedom. In terms of the arts this involved freedom for the artist to express his personal dreams and aspirations. The new Romantics, reacting against the constraints of the classical style, were attracted by the spiritual honesty and directness of the Italian primitives. The confrontation in the Salon of 1827 between Ingres's *Apotheosis of Homer* and **191, 196** Delacroix' *Death of Sardanapalus* was symbolic of the clash between the public and private consequences of the Revolution. If Ingres's painting can be seen explicitly as the expression of a Greek classical ideal, and implicitly as a hail and farewell to the dead Napoleon and to the republican dream, Delacroix gave rein on a public scale to darker and more private fantasies.

Despite the acquisitions of Denon, the Louvre was bound by the scope of its major holdings to retain to a large extent its bias towards the classical periods. It was another institution that was to indulge and stimulate the tastes and curiosities of the Romantics and of the new generation of collectors. Soon after the Revolution a certain Alexandre Lenoir had been placed in charge of a depôt to which had come from all over France the sculptures and architectural fragments confiscated from the nobility or removed from the churches. Through Lenoir's efforts much was thus saved from vandalism. In 1792 the collection became, by decree of Convention, the Musée des Monuments Français. The museum with its garden was arranged with sculpture, stained glass and metalwork shown **194** in settings believed appropriate to their various periods. The Romantic and the historian were able to browse through Lenoir's museum or through his Jardin Elysée, and feel themselves in touch, through the objects displayed, with the period of their manufacture. As the great national collection in the Louvre satisfied republican ideals, so the Musée des Monuments Français catered for the private reveries of the independent intellect.

The enthusiasm of Lenoir's collecting drew protests from Quatremère de Quincy who held and published the unfashionable view that works of art should be left in their geographical and spiritual settings. Already under some restraint, Lenoir's museum was dissolved at the Restoration in 1815. The small number of works not returned to their original owners went to form the basis of the medieval and Renaissance sculpture collections in the Louvre. Some of the sepulchral monuments were transferred to the Père-Lachaise cemetery. The life of the Musée des Monuments was short but its influence was considerable. The study of the evolution of art owes much to Lenoir's romantic historicism.

Many tastes were formed or directed by the Musée des Monuments Français, among them that of Alexandre du Sommerard, Balzac's 'Prince du Bric-à-brac'. Several collections of medieval and early Renaissance art were formed in the second quarter of the nineteenth century, but none so extensive as his. In 1832 he acquired the former abbey of Cluny in Paris **212** and filled this appropriate building with furniture, faïence, armour and ivories. It was a romantic collection in the tradition of the Musée des Monuments, albeit Du Sommerard was more acquisitive than educated. The abbey had been accessible to amateurs, to artists and to the merely curious for several years when Du Sommerard died in 1842, and under considerable pressure from those who knew the collection the state bought the 1,434 items and the building that housed them for a total of 590,000 francs. In 1844 the Musée des Thermes et de l'Hôtel de Cluny opened to the public under the curatorship of Du Sommerard's son.

The Restoration

The Louvre paid heavily for Napoleon's hundred days. In 1815 the allies were in a harsher mood than they had been a year earlier when the commissioners had ordered only those works not on exhibition to be returned to their countries of origin. In November 1815 Lavalée, the Secretary General, listed as reclaimed from Paris a total of 5,233 works. A heartbroken Denon was able to keep for the Louvre a mere 100 canvases and 800 drawings, the former including 29 paintings of the period before 1500 abandoned as valueless by the Florentine commissioners, many of these collected by Denon on his expedition in 1811. Veronese's *Wedding at Cana* was considered too large to transport and the commissioners representing Venice accepted a painting by Le Brun in exchange. The provincial museums fared much better and this accounts in part for the extraordinary **211** wealth in French provincial collections of first-rate works by second-rank artists and second-rate works by first-rank artists. The masterpieces by major painters had been reserved for the Louvre and were thus for the most part returned.

The collections of the Republic were sadly depleted by the Restoration, but the concept of the museum was firmly implanted. In 1818 Louis XVIII established in the Luxembourg a museum of contemporary French art from which paintings were to be transferred to the Louvre after a respectable lapse of time. This had a considerable effect on the Louvre in the 1860s, when the masterpieces of the early nineteenth century, works **205** by David, Géricault, Delacroix and Ingres, became due for transfer. But this was a long-term benefit. Academic taste persisted under Louis XVIII. **200** Louis-Philippe, although he made acquisitions among the Spanish schools,

194
THE DYING SLAVE
c.1515
Michelangelo Buonarrotti 1475–1564
marble
Louvre, Paris

Among the works confiscated from the French nobility at the time of the Revolution, this priceless sculpture, with its companion *The Rebellious Slave*, (plate **125**) once adorned one of the several properties of the Richelieu family. They are among the masterpieces now in the Louvre which found a temporary home in the Elysian Fields of Lenoir's Musée des Monuments Français. Among others were the twelfth century column figures from Corbeil and the Diane d'Anet by Goujon (plate **130**).

195
BEDROOM OF
THE EMPRESS JOSEPHINE
AT MALMAISON
c.1810
Musée National de Malmaison

Bought by Josephine in 1799 during Bonaparte's Egyptian campaign, and transformed at the Emperor's command by Percier and Fontaine, Malmaison was for the ten years until the divorce both a temple of the arts and a political centre. In various hands after Josephine's death in 1814, the château was reclaimed by Napoleon III and refurbished as a memorial to the Consulate and the Empire by the Empress Eugenie. It was opened as a museum in 1906. The decoration of the bedroom illustrates superbly the luxurious and classical taste of the Empire. The bed, signed by Desmalter, is that in which Josephine died. The carpet is Beauvais.

196
THE DEATH OF SARDANAPALUS

Salon of 1827–28, oil on canvas
Eugène Delacroix 1798–1863
155·5 × 195 in (395 × 495 cm),
Louvre, Paris

If Neoclassicism was in part an expression of national ideals, the Romantic movement was international. This painting was dedicated to Goethe and its theme was taken from Byron. The subject – King of Nineveh, besieged, ordering the slaughter of his entire retinue – came ready to hand, but the claustrophobia and turbulence of the painting express an involvement which is highly personal. The *Sardanapalus* was bought by the Louvre in 1921 for 8,000,000 francs after being in the hands of various dealers and collectors during the nineteenth century.

197 *bottom*
LA GRANDE ODALISQUE

1814, oil on canvas
Jean Auguste Dominique Ingres 1780–1867
35·75 × 24·5 in (90·8 × 62·2 cm)
Louvre, Paris

Originally painted in Rome for Queen Caroline of Naples who never took delivery, the painting was exhibited in the Salon of 1819 where it was not greatly admired, and purchased by the Chamberlain to the King of Prussia. It changed hands several times until it was acquired by the baron Seillières in the 1860s. Ingres became the leader of the Neoclassicists, but he was also superbly equipped to satisfy the luxurious tastes of the wealthy Second Empire collectors. The *Grande Odalisque* was bought by the Louvre in 1899 for 60,000 francs.

198
LE DEJEUNER SUR L'HERBE

1863, oil on canvas
Edouard Manet 1832–83
84·25 × 106·5 in (214 × 270 cm)
Jeu de Paume, Paris

Exhibited in the Salon des Refusés in 1863, this painting caused a scandal due largely to the realistic treatment of the model as seen in a clear light and to her nudity in the company of clothed men. In fact Manet longed for nothing so much as the official recognition which was denied him so long. The composition is taken from an engraving after Raphael and the subject and treatment relate to Titian's fêtes champêtres. Manet's painting is an example of the revival of interest, during the later nineteenth century, in Italian painting of the sixteenth. The painting entered the national collection in 1906.

was chiefly interested in his Musée des Gloires de la France at Versailles.

If the Louvre made few major acquisitions under the restored monarchy, it was at least able to broaden its scope and to consolidate its status. The Egyptian campaigns of Napoleon had drawn attention to the art of the Middle East–an attention which bore strange fruit in the eccentric architectural schemes of Claude Nicolas Ledoux–and in 1826 the Department of Egyptian Antiquities was established in the Louvre. This was followed in 1842 by the arrival of the first Assyrian collections. In 1848 under the revolutionary régime the Louvre was reorganised and hung by schools, thus preparing the national collection for the major acquisitions of the Second Empire.

Private collections

Louis Napoleon Bonaparte was elected for the magic of his name by a vast majority of Frenchmen, who looked back with longing to the age of conquests and of greatness. In taste too they reverted. The world of antique Greece had been the ideal in 1800. The people of the Second Empire took to their hearts the softer arts of the Greek baroque: the *Winged Victory of Samothrace* and the *Venus de Milo*. In 1852 Napoleon III completed the project for the extension of the Louvre which his predecessor had begun. But the country had long since wakened from the great republican dream which had made the earlier Neoclassical style so fervid an expression of the ideals of its practitioners. The new Bonaparte, presiding over a period of economic growth, encouraged the accumulation of large private mercantile fortunes, and under his direction Baron Haussman restyled the centre of Paris, catering for the requirements of a wealthy bourgeoisie which had become the ruling class in matters of taste. The collectors of the first Napoleonic period had been adventurous amateurs, men of vision and ideas. The collectors of the Second Empire were financiers whose tastes ironically recalled those of the ancien régime. The school most widely represented in these collections was seventeenth-century Dutch, always a favourite with bankers. Baron James de Rothschild owned paintings by Hobbema, Ruysdael, Rembrandt, Hals, de Hooch and Van de Velde. The later Italian painters also returned to favour. At a time when one could still buy a Fra Angelico for the equivalent of five hundred pounds, a Hobbema or a Bronzino might cost ten times as much. Of contemporary painters, every rich collector would have his Meissonier and his Delaroche, possibly one of Ingres's more luxurious odalisques, rarely a Delacroix, never a Courbet. French painting of the eighteenth century underwent a dramatic return to favour. In 1820 a Watteau could be had for a few pounds. In 1860 it might have cost a few thousand pounds.

Watteau figured largely in one of the major collections of this period. The collection of Dr La Caze, assembled with the intention that it should pass to the Louvre, formed what the present director has described as 'the most important donation ever made to a European museum'. Apart from a large number of eighteenth-century French and seventeenth-century Dutch paintings, there were works by Ribera and Velasquez and by the later Italians, among them Tiepolo and Guardi. Shortly before this in 1861 the Louvre had benefited from the acquisition of a very different but equally important collection belonging to the Marquis of Campana, who had acquired a huge number of Italian works of art. Napoleon III, successfully cutting out the Russian authorities and the British Museum, bought the collection including 640 paintings of varying quality, for slightly over four million francs. Of these 169 found a permanent home in the Louvre, while the remainder were dispersed to the various provincial

199

THE CARD-PLAYERS *detail*

c. 1665, oil on canvas
Pieter de Hooch 1629–85
26·5 × 30·5 in (66·7 × 77·5 cm)
Louvre, Paris

Not all the works imported for the Louvre in its early days were seized or requisitioned. *The Card-players* was bought in 1801. Its acquisition bears witness to the survival, even into Napoleon's Consulate, of what was essentially an ancien régime taste–a taste, moreover, that was to be revived under the Second Empire, as the wealthy bankers and merchants aped the style of the nobility whose fall had permitted them to rise.

200

JUSQU'A LA MORT

1796
Francisco Goya y Lucientes, 1746–1828
71·5 × 49·25 in (181 × 125 cm)
Musée des Beaux Arts, Lille

Acquired in Spain in the mid 1830s, this was one of the few purchases made for the Louvre under Louis Philippe (1830–48) who, so far as he was interested in painting, admired the Spanish school. Unlike its companion, *The Young Women*, this picture, sometimes known as *The Old Women*, was not popular and the pair were sold in London in 1853. In 1874 they were bought by subscription for the museum at Lille, founded in 1795 under the Revolutionary régime.

201

**BONAPARTE CROSSING
THE BRIDGE AT ARCOLE** *detail*
1796, oil on canvas
Jean Antoine, Baron Gros 1771–1835
28·75 × 21·25 in (73 × 59 cm)
Louvre, Paris

An early portrait of Napoleon, and one
that was understandably popular with the
emperor. It was engraved at his request
and provided a prototype for a number of
later portraits. Gros propagandised
Napoleon not as he was but as he wished
to be seen and as the French people
wished to see him – as the archetypal
romantic hero. Not surprisingly Gros
received several commissions from the
emperor.

202 PORTRAIT OF EMILE ZOLA
1868, oil on canvas, 57 × 45 in (145 × 114 cm)
Edouard Manet 1832–83
Jeu de Paume, Paris

Exhibited in the Salon of 1868 where it
was badly received, the portrait was given
by Manet to Zola and bequeathed to the
Louvre by his widow. It was painted in
gratitude for Zola's spirited defence of
Manet's art. 'M. Manet's place is marked
out in the Louvre,' Zola had written,
'as is that of Courbet and of every artist
of a strong and unyielding temperament.'
Zola is shown in his study, with a print
by Utamaro on the wall. This was the
period of the spread of Japanese influence;
in 1871 the dealer Bing opened a shop in
Paris specialising in oriental goods.

museums. The main strength of the collection lay in Italian painting of
the fifteenth century, thus filling a gap in the national collections.

A new concept

The sums spent by La Caze and the amount paid for the Campana
collection bore witness to the fact that there was a good deal of money
available for art of proven value. But those with money to spend were
generally unwilling to invest in advanced contemporary art. The creative
French painters were the last to benefit. The Revolution had freed the
artist from the patron's dictation, but in so doing had broken the consensus
of taste between patron and artist which had guaranteed the satisfaction of
the one and the income of the other. David and Gros were propagandists
for the Revolution and for the Consulate, and as such had been sure of
success during the life of the régimes which they supported. In exhibiting
his *Rape of the Sabines* and charging for admission, David was able to quote
a classical precedent to which his potential audience would respond
sympathetically. The Romantics, in exploring more private visions,
could count on no such ready response in an audience which neither
shared those visions nor understood them. The concept of great painting
as the skilful interpretation, or perhaps modification, of a known style
gave way to a new concept in which individual sincerity of expression
was offered as the criterion. Art could no longer be seen as the extension
of a certain taste and a certain mode of decoration, or as the pleasant
accompaniment to a genteel way of life. The purchase of a romantic or
a realist painting was in part a gesture of commitment. The word 'patron'
was inappropriate for the new generation of collectors. The supporters of
Courbet or of Manet, men like Bruyas or Zola, were men of like ideas who
responded to the painters as intellectual equals. Courbet rather than
David should be seen as the originator of the modern one-man exhibition.
In responding to the rejection of his major works by the jury of the World
Fair in 1855 by setting up at his own expense his Pavillon du Réalisme he
was asserting the modern artist's right to be accepted on his own terms.

Courbet, having taken as his motto Proudhon's dictum that property is
theft, could hardly have objected when so few people appeared prepared
to acquire his works, but in fact the situation of the original artists became
desperate as the gap widened between their individual vision and the
demands of a bourgeois public with a conservative taste. Ingres and
Delacroix were major exhibitors at the World Fair, but the prizes went to
Gérôme, Cabanel, Meissonier and Bougereau. In the next few years
Manet and the young Impressionist painters suffered continual rejections
from the Salon. When in 1863 Napoleon III responded to complaints
about the harshness of the Salon jury by sanctioning the Salon des
Refusés, he succeeded unconsciously in bringing matters to a head. The
nature of the misunderstanding between the Impressionists and their
reluctant audience became increasingly well defined. On opposing sides
the advanced artists and the entrenched public closed their ranks. War was
declared and the concept of the avant garde was born. It was soon to
become a point of honour for the original artist to keep at least one step
ahead of his public. Taste in the eighteenth- or early-nineteenth-century
sense was on the way out. The task that had been begun during the
Revolution was a fair way to completion by 1871.

The nineteenth century saw the birth of two vitally important concepts:
the national museum and the one-man exhibition. The private ownership
of works of art will always be a privilege of the rich. What was achieved
between 1789 and 1871 was the liberalisation of the most important
aspect of art: the pleasure that it gives.   Charles Harrison

203 *below*

THE PAINTER'S STUDIO

*subtitled 'a real allegory summarizing a phase in my artistic life
that lasted seven years.' 1855
Gustave Courbet 1819–77
oil on canvas
Louvre, Paris*

This was painted at Ornans, rejected by the Salon of 1855 and shown in Courbet's Pavillon du Réalisme at the World Fair. It was bought by the Louvre in 1919 for 900,000 francs. The artist painted himself at the centre of his own world, surrounded by his canvases, his neighbours and his friends. Bruyas, his patron, Proudhon, his mentor and the source of much of Courbet's socialism, and Baudelaire, critic and poet are among those represented in this gathering. Courbet described them as 'the people that serve me, that support me in my ideas and participate in my actions'.

204 *left*, THE BELLELI FAMILY

*c. 1858–60, oil on canvas
Edgar Degas 1834–1917
78·75 × 98·5 in (200 × 250 cm)
Jeu de Paume, Paris*

An early work which nevertheless shows the extraordinary strength of Degas' drawing and composition, the result in part of his study of the Italian masters. The informality of this group is very far removed from the portraiture of the earlier nineteenth century and perhaps reflects a change in the status of the artist. What Degas sought was an art 'in which the truth about life is expressed without compromise'. The painting was bought for the Musée du Luxembourg in 1918 and transferred to the Louvre in 1929.

205 *top*

THE RAFT OF THE MEDUSA

*Théodore Géricault, oil on canvas
194·25 × 275·25 in (491 × 716 cm)
Louvre, Paris*

Both in his choice of subject – the terrible aftermath of a recent disaster at sea – and by his treatment of it, Géricault was exposing inhumanity and illustrating suffering. The theme was public but the emotion was highly personal. Paintings of this sort were unlikely to find 'patrons', but the *Raft of the Medusa* attracted great attention in the Salon of 1819 and was later exhibited in London. In 1824 it was bought from the estate of the artist by Charles X for the Luxembourg Palace, from whence it passed to the Louvre *c.* 1850.

206

VENUS DE MILO

c. 200 BC, marble, Louvre, Paris

The statue was discovered on the island of Milos in 1820 and transported to Paris by the French ambassador to the Ottoman court. A masterpiece of Hellenistic art, it was celebrated in a pamphlet of 1821 by the classicist Quatremère de Quincy who welcomed its arrival in France while criticizing the removal of Gothic works for Lenoir's romantic museum. The statue reached its peak of popularity during the mid-nineteenth century when it was moved to a prominent position in the Louvre.

207 *opposite*

MADONNA OF THE ANGELS

c. 1300, Cimabue, active 1240–1302, panel
167 × 108·5 in (424 × 267 cm)
Louvre, Paris

Formerly in the church of San Francesco at Pisa, the painting was acquired in 1811 for five francs by Vivant Denon from among the property of the suppressed religious houses of Tuscany. It entered the Louvre in 1813, was exhibited a year later and was left in the museum by the Florentine commission at the time of the Restoration as being a work of no value. It is now priceless. Those who are disposed to cavil at what might be seen as commandeering on the part of Denon and others can weigh rival claims to guardianship over works like this between the enlightened curators and conservers of the Louvre and the Italian authorities who failed to see its worth.

208

SACRA CONVERSAZIONE

c. 1500, oil on canvas
Vittore Carpaccio, active 1490–c. 1525
38·5 × 50 in (98 × 127 cm)
Musée des Beaux Arts, Caen

Bought by the Marquis of Campana in Rome in 1845 from the collection of Cardinal Fesch, the painting entered the Louvre in 1863 after Napoleon III had acquired the entire Campana collection. It was consigned to the Musée de Caen in 1876; one of the finest paintings from the Campana collection to have been allowed to leave the Louvre.

209 *left*

BATHSHEBA

1654, oil on canvas
Rembrandt van Rijn 1606–69
56 × 56 in (142 × 142 cm), Louvre, Paris

The private collectors of the Second Empire favoured the Dutch masters – to this day an expensive taste. In the second half of the nineteenth century collecting paintings became a highly expensive, if often profitable pastime. Louis la Caze, who bequeathed this painting to the Louvre in 1869, was one of the most discriminating collectors of his time. The Bathsheba had been in London in 1837 and was acquired by La Caze at the Perier sale in 1843.

FRIEZE OF ARCHERS OF THE GREAT KING

from the palace of Darius at Susa
fifth century BC, enamelled terra-cotta bricks
height of archers 4 ft 10 in (147 cm)
Louvre, Paris

Susa was excavated by the French from
1662 onwards. This frieze is from the
Achaemenid palace, built after the fall of
the Assyrians and inspired by their palaces.

211 *below*

THE RESURRECTION

c. 1460, panel
Andrea Mantegna c. 1451–1506
27 × 34.75 in (68.6 × 88.3 cm)
Musée des Beaux Arts, Tours

This is a predella panel of the altarpiece
by Mantegna in the church of San Zeno,
Verona. The entire altarpiece was
transported to Paris in 1799 and placed
on exhibition in the Louvre. The panel
of the *Resurrection*, and its companion
The Agony in the Garden were sent to
Tours a few years later and thus escaped
repatriation in 1815 when the altarpiece
itself, which had remained in the Louvre,
was returned to Italy.

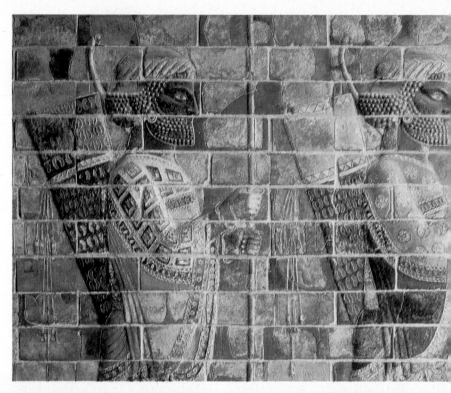

212 *below*

ALTAR FRONTAL

offered by the Emperor St Henri to the cathedral of Basle c. 1019
gold
Musée de Cluny, Paris

Alexandre du Sommerard is remembered as the creator of the collection now housed in the Musée de Cluny, but in fact many of the most splendid acquisitions were made by his son Edouard, including this masterpiece of early Romanesque metalwork and several magnificent tapestries. The extent to which Edouard upheld the spirit of his father's interests may be judged by the fact that the catalogue of 1883, two years before his curatorship ended, lists over ten thousand items.

213

THE BATTLE OF SAN ROMANO

c. 1451
Paolo Uccello 1396/7 – 1475
panel
71 × 125·5 in (180 × 316 cm)
Louvre, Paris

One of three panels rediscovered in 1784, long after they were presumed lost, in the furniture store of the Medici family. The others are now in the Uffizi and in the National Gallery, London. The Louvre panel was bought by the Marquis of Campana with misappropriated funds and entered the Louvre when his collection was acquired by Napoleon III. In 1862 the collection was divided between the Louvre and sixty-seven provincial museums, with the former skimming most of the cream.

Politically the period from 1871 to the present day coincides almost exactly with the lifespan so far of the Third, Fourth and Fifth French Republics. The Third Republic, proclaimed during the Franco-Prussian War of 1870, was made virtually a clause of settlement in the victorious Bismarck's peace treaty and was formally established in 1875. A hostile balance between France and Germany remained a constant feature of the European scene in the nervous years of tension and rearmament between 1871 and 1914, and the opposition of these two nations was a central axis in both of the great wars of the twentieth century. The cost of republican status and of wars has made its impact on the worlds of art and patronage. When national art collections depend directly upon the national economy of a republic under stress, instead of on the purse of a self-glorifying monarch and his nobility, a decline in available funds is predictable.

The unsettled mood of the intervals of peace was also reflected in art and period taste: in a taste for the exquisite decadence and stagey mysticism of Art Nouveau in the 1890s and in the several shades of theatrical hysteria of Dada, Surrealism and Art Déco in the 1920s. There was a spirit of dissatisfied restlessness, of social and political change, throughout the first quarter of the century. The dialogue between this spirit and modern art is clear enough: the infectious, nervous energy that Picasso brought with him to Paris from anarchist Barcelona is a powerful instance. Perhaps it is also expressed in the modern speculative instincts of artist and collector.

European culture is no longer a tightly-knit cell. The last hundred years have witnessed an interest in other artistic traditions, increasing almost in proportion with their distance in time and spirit from the European tradition. The long-term interaction with other cultures that started with the Parisian vogue for Oriental art of the 1860s and 70s has expressed itself not only through its influence on the arts, but also in the furnishing of collections and appropriate museums. Paris's ethnographical museum the Trocadéro (now the Musée de l'Homme) which in the days when Picasso went there to look at Negro sculpture had been a random disarray of exhibits, was completely reorganised in 1928 to take full advantage of its increased possessions and of refined scholarship in the field. France took a leading role in excavations and exploratory missions throughout the world and particularly in Asia and Africa, but two of the outstanding discoveries of this century occurred on or under French soil. The famous *Lespugue venus* discovered in 1922 and the painted caves of Lascaux are now recognised universally as among the most important examples of prehistoric sculpture and painting respectively. The historicist urge to collect and document, largely the prerogative of individual passions since the eighteenth century, has become a national concern, more specialised and far-reaching. It has also become an area of great international rivalry.

France in a scientific world

The international character of the twentieth century with its unprecedented ease of communication and travel and the fluid interchange of ideas and influences has had a profound effect on the pace and currency of art at all levels. On the whole this development has not been to the French advantage. The country has not been in a position to compete for the highest fruits of the commercial art market. For the same reasons French private collectors have not featured largely among the business magnates and, since more often than not some national museum may eventually inherit a magnate's collection, this constitutes another major disadvantage.

The other general characteristic of the last hundred years to have a very significant bearing on the period's art and patronage is the ever-

219

4, 6

14

The State and the Individual

1871 to the present day

214

THE SWING

1876

Pierre-Auguste Renoir 1841–1919

oil on canvas

36·5 × 28·5 in (92·7 × 72·5 cm)

Jeu de Paume, Paris

One of the sixty-seven Impressionist masterpieces by Monet, Renoir, Pissarro, Sisley, Manet, Degas, Cézanne and others bequeathed by the painter and collector Gustave Caillebotte to the Louvre in 1894. Even at this date – twenty years after the first Impressionist Exhibition – public and academic feeling against the Impressionists still ran high enough for nearly half of the bequest to be refused. Of the painters represented only the works of Degas were all accepted. *The Swing* is a major example of Renoir's developed Impressionism. The sentimental mood of urban relaxation, the diffused and broken light, the soft reflected colour and the facility of his improvised brushwork typify his painting of the 1870s.

accelerating pace of technological and scientific progress. The conditioning of the modern way of life by scientific advance is probably its major definitive force. The conditioning of art by these elements is many-sided. Particularly important here is the role–so vital to the worlds of art, art commerce and art scholarship–of the modern publishing machine working through books, magazines and reproductions. New materials and more sophisticated techniques have opened very different fields to artist, designer and architect. The struggle between mass production and good design has been a feature of the history of applied art for more than a hundred years and in the twentieth century at least there has been a spirited exchange between fine art and the modern mass media. More than all these things, the effect of science on art has been to inspire a 'brave new world' ideology, an ambition to construct a new art that could embody the spirit and appearance of the modern technological age. The Eiffel Tower, symbol of the late nineteenth century's vision of the **215** future, was painted like a sacred icon by Seurat and Delaunay and later **216** venerated in the writings of the Russian sculptor Gabo as the first work of Constructivism.

The sweeping changes in Europe's social and political structure between 1870 and 1920 had far reaching importance. Declining nobility, overrun or powerless monarchies, massive shifts of population to industrial urban communities, these were the universal results of successive political and industrial revolutions. Their consequence for the artist was enormous. The era of Impressionism was as significant for the changes it witnessed in the pattern of an artist's working and living conditions as it was for the artistic innovations. The nineteenth century as a whole had seen the abuse and decline of the old systems of artistic authority and patronage. Now in the 1870s, a new system emerged which has remained fundamentally unchanged to the present day.

The isolation of the artist

The French Academy which for more than two centuries maintained responsibility for artistic theory and ideology, art politics and patronage had ensured its own decay. Two of the primary sources of established patronage–the aristocracy and the church–had virtually disappeared. The establishment was replaced by the newly prosperous, newly influential middle classes as a real force in society and consequently as direct and indirect patrons of the arts. State patronage, which, although it had concentrated on 'museum art', had at its best reflected the cultured taste of the aristocracy and the exclusive standards of the Academy, now reflected the standards of the bourgeoisie.

The combination of these two factors–a highly conservative academic governmental establishment leading and being led by a self-confident social majority that was intellectually lazy and aesthetically numb–formed the unenviable stage on which the young nineteenth-century artist was obliged to interpret his part. Both the elements he faced were predisposed to mistrust serious innovation. The gulfs between artist and public and artist and academies that grew up in the late nineteenth century and became firmly established in the first half of the twentieth undoubtedly have their origins in this situation. It was a vicious circle. The young artist with progressive ideas, debarred by a tangle of conventions and prejudice from the normal channels of his profession, created new channels for himself and his colleagues as best he could, sometimes organising his own exhibitions. Artists were and still are each other's best audience as theorist, critic and sometimes patron. This inbreeding has served to deepen the gulfs between artists and the general public.

215
THE EIFFEL TOWER
1909–10
Robert Delaunay (1885–1941)
oil on canvas
Musée National d'Art Moderne, Paris

Dealers, critics and collectors

A distinct feature of the last hundred years is that, compared with almost any other period in the history of art, dramatically few works have been commissioned. Artists, in the pursuit of their own ideas, produce paintings and sculpture which may or may not be purchased. The destination of the work of art appears as an increasingly separate aspect, irrelevant to that work's creation. The modern equivalent to traditional patronage consists firstly in history-conscious acquisition of works by museums and secondly in prestige-conscious collecting by private individuals. The highly specialised development of museums is a relatively modern phenomenon, but art-for-art's-sake collecting is by no means new.

The real innovation, and what has made it practicable for the artist to pursue his independent course and still make a living out of it, has been the appearance and entrenchment of the dealer-system. The dealer's role as 'middle man' was made possible and necessary by the inadequacies of the academic channels of exhibition and purchase. What is more it had considerable advantages to offer the young artist: a retainer (admittedly of variable regularity in the early years) in return for pictures to be painted and the opportunity to develop his ideas through a series of pictures rather than having to concentrate on the production of a single spectacular 'grande machine', as it was called, to catch the eye of jury and client at the annual Salon. Many young artists regarded the dealers as a temporary expedient until official recognition.

In any event the dealers' success hastened the downfall of the academic monopoly. A key factor in this success was that hand-in-hand with the dealer's rapid rise to a position of strength ran the similar fortune of the independent art critic. Their functions were to an extent interdependent. In effect the dealer replaced the patron, since it was he who actually acquired works direct from the artist. The late nineteenth-century critic replaced the high priest of the academy as theorist. With the dispersal of buying power to a wider and less educated public, the critic's potential influence was enormous.

This radical change of artistic-social structure applies generally to the whole European scene. Its particular application to France derives from the total dominance of Paris as the centre of artistic development at least until 1914 and to a lesser degree until 1940. Just as the roots of modern art lie in Parisian painting of 1870–1914, so the new system of 'marketing' just described owes its development to the Paris of the 1870s and 1880s. But housing the nucleus of the artistic avant-garde also entailed being the centre of public hostility and militant conservatism. It is one of the sad ironies of modern art history that the country which produced modern art's greatest early achievements was perhaps the slowest to recognise and preserve them. Those treasures of late nineteenth-century art that are now in French public collections are there despite the opinion of the majority at the time. For example the Louvre's Museum of Impressionism in the Jeu de Paume, Paris, owes a colossal debt to the perception and subsequent bequests of a handful of private collectors for its present riches.

Four bequests deserve particular mention. The legacies of the painter Caillebotte (1894), the biographer Moreau-Nélaton (1906) and the collector Count Isaac de Camonde (1908) between them contributed 140 of the outstanding paintings in the collection. The more recent donations by the family of Dr Gachet, if smaller numerically, nevertheless account for nearly half of the Van Goghs and nearly a third of the Cézannes in the national museum. The fate of Caillebotte's legacy illustrates contemporary feeling. When the news broke that he had left his collection of sixty-seven

216

THE EIFFEL TOWER
1887–89
Gustave Eiffel 1832–1923
iron
Paris

At the time of its completion and for many years after the Eiffel Tower was acclaimed by artists and architects as a milestone. Eiffel, the engineer of bridges, stations and viaducts throughout Europe, made this his tour de force and it stood as a symbol of modern technology in France. The 1889 World Fair for which it was constructed was dominated by feelings of nationalism (the centenary of the French revolution) and modernism. During the exhibition, the Tower was ablaze with electric lights and at night a revolving tricolour searchlight at the top swept across Paris.

Impressionist paintings to the Louvre such uproar followed that only thirty-eight works were accepted.

The debt of the young artists to these collectors, in terms of moral as well as financial support, was probably as great as the French nation's debt is to them now. There were a number of such benefactors and their help and interest was shared among the Impressionist and Post-Impressionist generations to a remarkable degree. Cézanne's constant supporter Victor Chocquet is known to have helped Renoir and Monet as well. There were a very few heart-warming incidents like Chocquet's successful refusal to lend from his collection of period furniture to the Paris World Fair of 1889 unless at least one of Cézanne's canvases was hung in the exhibition of painting. Manet shared a successful exhibition with Rodin at a dealer's gallery in 1889 and a painting by Renoir, *Jeune filles au piano*, was purchased by the state from the 1892 Salon. The few signs of improvement were tempered by the reaction to Caillebotte's bequest in 1894. Impressionism was meeting growing acceptance but was still unthinkable as a 'museum art'.

Another irony of this situation is that the Impressionist painters were in no sense misfits or rebels. With the exception of Renoir, they were all of the middle classes and their professional aspirations lay within the accepted structure as they found it. Finding themselves ostracised, however, they were obliged to accept their rebel status. Holding their own exhibitions (there were eight of them between 1874 and 1886) seemed the only solution to the stalemate of Salon rejection. At the same time some of them continued to submit works to the Salon for official approval; Renoir sometimes went out of his way to meet it, as Manet had done before him. Others shared Pissarro's semi-political belief that it was a matter of principle *not* to exhibit at the Salon. The usefulness of group activity, apart from bolstering morale, lay primarily in establishing a public name (whether it was respected or not mattered less than its establishment). By the 1880s this function was accomplished and the group dissolved. Nevertheless the principle remained. Group exhibitions and manifestoes have become, and still are, a regular feature of twentieth-century French art.

Paul Durand-Ruel was the outstanding dealer in Impressionist paintings. He had entered the market dramatically by anticipating with immaculate timing the popularity of the Barbizon painters. He followed this with his purchase from the luckless Manet of twenty-two paintings in 1871 at very moderate prices, and then in 1876, with a daring foresight, invited the Impressionists to hold their second independent exhibition in his own galleries. When he could afford to, he applied the policy of sole rights to Monet, Pissarro and others by paying them a monthy advance. At times his existence was as precarious as theirs, but by a mixture of shrewd artistic judgment, genuine sympathy with their ideas and a masterly speculative instinct for the moment to hold back and the moment to push particular works, he emerged at the head of the market in the 1880s.

A consequence of his campaign and a cause of its success was the awakening of foreign interest. English and German attention exceeded the French and as far as the Americans were concerned it was the thin end of a very big wedge. By the 1890s Durand-Ruel's rivals included several American dealers based in Paris, agents for American museums as well as for private collectors. Claude Monet's sponsorship of a subscription to buy Manet's *Olympia* for the nation was inspired by rumours of an imminent American purchase. French national conscience was awakening, but too late in most cases.

217

LURISTAN BRIDLE PLAQUE
c. 1000 BC
Persian
bronze
5·5 × 6·75 in (14 × 17 cm)
Louvre, Paris

Compared with plate **221** this piece of east Persian applied art decoration fusing animal and human forms demonstrates the more whimsical invention that was an almost constant characteristic of Mesopotamian art. This is one of several Luristan pieces, formerly in the Frenchman Coiffard's collection, that were acquired by the Louvre in 1958.

218

SEATED STATUE OF GUDEA I, FROM TELLO

c. 2275–60 BC
Sumerian, diorite
h. 17 in (45 cm)
Louvre, Paris

One of the few perfectly preserved examples among the many surviving images of Gudea, 'divine bailiff' of Lagash. This statue ranks among the major art treasures of Sumer, the father of Mesopotamian cultures. The enigmatic intimacy of the half-smile is characteristic of many Sumerian sculptures.

219

RELIQUARY FROM GABEN

date not known
wood, cane, feathers and other materials
h. 22·75 in (58 cm)
Musée de l'Homme, Paris

One of the most remarkable manifestations of the modern European interest in less sophisticated cultures has been the high regard for primitive African art. At the start of the century this rapidly developed from the chance appearance of masks and other objects brought home as sailors' mementoes to more systematic collection. The influence of this art, uninhibited by European conventions of naturalism and orthodox media, acted as a vital catalyst for artists during the revolutions in painting and sculpture of the 1900's. This reliquary was presented to the Trocadero in 1897.

220
THE WINGED VICTORY
OF SAMOTHRACE
c. 200 BC
marble
h. 96·5 in (245 cm)
Louvre, Paris

The epitome of 'Greek baroque' the
Winged Victory appealed to the expansive
tastes of the Second Empire bourgeois
who liked his classicism theatrical and
appealing, if not actually erotic. In the
1870s the statue was removed to its
present commanding position at the head
of a flight of stairs.

221
ACHAEMENID HEAD
sixth century BC, possibly Persian
white marble
11 × 9·5 in (28 × 24 cm)
Louvre, Paris

An impressive example of late Mesopotamian art, this fragment of an over-
lifesize royal statue combines a refined
naturalism of features with a decorative
and hieratic formality. It was presented
by the Société des Amis du Louvre in 1966.

Public suspicion of contemporary art

The imbalance between the attitude 'give the public what it wants' and
a progressive sponsorship of new painting prevailed among critics as
among dealers. Outstanding nineteenth-century critics included major
creative writers: Baudelaire, Mallarmé, Stendhal, Zola. Isolated examples **202**
of this sort of criticism have also occurred in the twentieth century. But
the more specialised world of modern art has tended to produce the
professional theorist-critic. Such men set out to inform the public.
Paradoxically, as their work has become more technical, analysing style
and method more than content, it has in consequence become less
accessible to a wide public. The critics' cult of obscurity for obscurity's
sake often exists only in the public mind. Nevertheless it has contributed
to the inbred appearance of the modern artist's world.

The foundation and survival of several semi-private, semi-memorial
museums of the work of individual artists from this era onwards also
reflects a division between artist and society. Their existence, it is true, is
very much a matter of chance. The most important to survive are the
Musée Gustave Moreau, the Musée Bourdelle and the Musée Rodin, all
in Paris, the Musée Toulouse-Lautrec at Albi and the more recent Musée
Léger at Biot. All of these are founded upon the artist's own work in his **250**
studio at, or before, his death. In Rodin's case the museum included his
collection of work by other artists; in Lautrec's case it has been significantly
expanded by subsequent donations. The evolution of the Moreau museum
was the most extraordinary. In his will he asked that his collection of his
own work should remain intact as long as possible and he seems to have
spent most of his later life preparing his house as a museum.

National museums

The Louvre maintained its position as the major national art collection,
but its constitution made no provision for the work of living artists. When
such work was bequeathed or, rarely, purchased, it was housed in the
inadequate annexes of the Palais du Luxembourg or the Musée des Arts
Décoratifs, a situation not rectified until 1939. The expansion of the
Louvre's historical collections between 1871 and the present day has
been, by comparison, consistent and impressive. The palace's exhibition
space has been considerably extended and modified to meet the growth of
established departments and the demand for new departments. For
example the Department of Oriental Antiquities, founded in 1881, was
fed by French excavations throughout Asia with a steady stream of major **217, 221**
examples of ancient art. The Mesopotamian civilizations were particularly
well represented. The most important examples now in the Louvre
include several carved images of the Sumerian king Gudea, the famous **218**
Victory Stele of Naram-Sin, three colossal winged-bull guardian figures
from the palace of Khorsabad and numerous examples on stone tablets
and baked clay cylinders of cuneiform writing.

The disadvantage suffered by the Louvre in being a national property
under the republics rather than the prestige-possession of a wealthy
monarch was that it was now just another state responsibility, and
indeed one of minor economic importance. The saving advantage lay in
the interest inspired by this new 'national-ownership' and, once more, the
generosity of interested supporters. The only Breughel in the Louvre was
donated in 1892 and the early achievements of the Société des Amis du
Louvre, founded in 1897, included acquisition of the superb *Avignon* **96**
Pietà in 1904 and of Ingres's *Le Bain Turc* in 1911. Poussin's *Inspiration
of the Poet* was bought in the same year out of a legacy of money. Other
private donations included Louis Le Nain's *La Charrette* in 1879. Without

such help, the Louvre on its relatively small budget could never have survived the fierce art-market competition among the major world museums before the First World War, even though this market was centred on Paris. Purchasing was concentrated on filling gaps in the magnificent historical collections amassed by successive monarchs and on bringing the French painting collections up to date. Particular effort was devoted to early Renaissance and primitive European art. The major purchases included Geertgen's *Raising of Lazarus*, Roger van der Weyden's *Braque Triptych* (1913), Dürer's 1493 *Self-Portrait* (1922) and works by Botticelli (1882), Pisanello (1893), le Maître de Moulins (1904) and Cranach (1910). The sudden European vogue for El Greco around 1900 was reflected in the Louvre's purchase of their first three works by him in 1893, 1903 and 1908.

Partisanship is a hallmark of any nation's art collecting. Its application to France both in public and private activity is particularly potent. The state purchase of Whistler's *The Artist's Mother*, engineered by Mallarmé in 1891, is only conceivable in terms of this painter's strong Parisian associations. This apart, the Louvre's purchase of works painted since about 1830 was almost exclusively French. Rousseau's *Avenue of Chestnuts* in 1912, Courbet's *The Artist's Studio* in 1919, Delacroix's *Death of Sardanapalus* in 1921 and Daumier's *The Washerwoman* in 1927 are among the most important purchases of their respective dates. Donations included two outstanding collections of mid-century landscape painting: Thomy-Thiery's magnificent collection of 121 paintings bequeathed in 1902 and the department store magnate Chaufard's 140 paintings (including Millet's *Angelus*) in 1910.

This pattern of generosity has prevailed, the most recent example being the bequest by the Mexican Carlos de Beistegui of his distinguished collection ranging from Rubens and Van Dyck to David and Goya. Goya's *Portrait of the Countess del Carpio* is now the Louvre's principal masterpiece by that artist. De Beistegui had formed his collection with the intention of donating it to the Louvre and he sometimes consulted the museum authorities about their special needs before purchasing works. The appearance of foreigners among the significant benefactors reflects both the Louvre's reputation as a museum and the infectiousness of the Frenchman's own feeling that France is where art belongs. Their gifts have not been limited to French art and some have simply left money for the purchase of pictures.

The fluctuations of fortune and taste which determine a work of art's eventual destination and its value can never entirely disappear; such is the unpredictable nature of collecting and, perhaps, of art. In 1941 the Louvre acquired its only Velasquez, an otherwise unexceptional portrait. What is remarkable is that it was acquired in an exchange with the Prado museum for a major Murillo altarpiece, *The Immaculate Conception*, bought by the Louvre at great expense in 1860, but no longer in fashion.

The exclusive quality of the French art world is heightened by the fact that, more often than not, for 'France' we may read 'Paris'. The designation of the modern French school as 'Ecole de Paris' is very relevant and its significance is not confined to the post-war era. The self-centred attitude of the Parisian academic establishment in the nineteenth century, virtually ignoring the provinces, contributed to its own weakening and downfall. This was to a degree put right by the broader organisation of the Musées Nationaux and similar reorganisation in art education, both of these being aspects of a more democratic political structure. The Conseil des Musées Nationaux is a body responsible for the budget and policy of all state art

222 SELF-PORTRAIT

1493, vellum mounted on canvas
Albrecht Dürer 1471–1528
22·25 × 17·75 in (56·5 × 44·5 cm)
Louvre, Paris

During the first quarter of this century a great deal of museum purchasing was concentrated on the early Italian and North European Renaissance masters. This betrothal portrait, painted by Dürer when he was twenty-two, before his art had been transformed by Italian influence, was one of the Louvre's major purchases in this field. Previously in a private Parisian collection it was purchased from a sequestrator in 1922 for 300,000 francs.

223 ARRANGEMENT IN GREY AND BLACK NO. I THE ARTIST'S MOTHER

c. 1870, oil on canvas
James Abbott McNeill Whistler 1834–1903
57 × 64·5 in (145 × 164 cm), Louvre, Paris

First exhibited at the Royal Academy in London, 1872, and then at the Salon in Paris, 1883, this outstanding example of Whistler's mature art was purchased by the French state in 1891 after energetic canvassing by leading French artists and sympathisers, Mallarmé at their head. The nature of Whistler's paintings–refined arrangements of muted tonal colour which he titled 'harmony', 'symphony', 'caprice', etc.–were far more sympathetic to Parisian late-nineteenth-century ideas than to the art of London, his reluctantly adopted home.

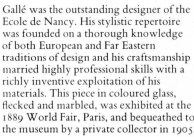

224

ORPHEUS AND EURYDICE
1888–89
Emile Gallé 1846–1904 and
Victor Prouvé 1858–1943
vase in coloured glass
h. 10·25 in (26 cm)
Musée des Arts Décoratifs, Paris

Gallé was the outstanding designer of the
Ecole de Nancy. His stylistic repertoire
was founded on a thorough knowledge
of both European and Far Eastern
traditions of design and his craftsmanship
married highly professional skills with a
richly inventive exploitation of his
materials. This piece in coloured glass,
flecked and marbled, was exhibited at the
1889 World Fair, Paris, and bequeathed to
the museum by a private collector in 1905.

225

THE 'NYMPHEAS' CYCLE *detail*
1920–26
Claude Monet 1840–1926
oil on canvas mounted on a curve
length approx. 14 ft (4·20 m)
The Orangerie, Tuileries Gardens, Paris

After discussions with the critic Roger-
Marx and with his friend Clemenceau
around 1917, Monet offered to present a
group of paintings to the state to
commemorate the Armistice. In 1920 he
decided that it would be a series of twelve
watergarden canvases, each nearly
fourteen feet long, to be housed in the
gardens of the Musée Rodin; their present
location in the Orangerie of the Louvre
was decided upon in 1931. Monet worked
on the paintings under extreme difficulties
and had to abandon them in September
1922, almost blind from double cataracts.
After an operation in 1923 which restored
sight to one eye, he continued work. The
Nymphéas cycle—an extraordinary
combination of Impressionist illusionism
and expressive mural decoration—was
dedicated in 1927.

226

OLYMPIA

1863, oil on canvas
Edouard Manet 1832–83
51 × 74·75 in (129 × 189 cm)
Jeu de Paume, Paris

Manet considered this his masterpiece
and in terms both of the extreme public
hostility it aroused at the Salon of 1865
and of its revolutionary implications of
tonal values, composition and technique,
it is historically his most important work.
Still in his studio at his death, in 1889 under
the threat of imminent foreign purchase,
Monet mounted a private subscription to
purchase the work for the state. In 1890 it
entered the Luxembourg Palace. It was
transferred to the Louvre in 1907.

227 *below right*

THREE BATHERS

c. 1879–82, oil on canvas
Paul Cézanne 1839–1906
19·5 × 19·5 in (49·5 × 49·5 cm)
Musée de la Ville de Paris (Petit Palais)

Purchased by Matisse from Cézanne's
dealer Vollard in 1899 at a time of great
personal hardship, this canvas symbolises
the transition from the last great era of
nineteenth-century French art to the first
uninhibited statements of modern painting.
Matisse said on presenting it to the Paris
Museum in 1936: 'I have owned this canvas
for thirty-seven years . . . it has sustained
me spiritually in the critical moments of
my career as an artist; I have drawn from
it my faith and my perseverance.'

228 *right*

THE SCHUFFENECKER FAMILY

1889, oil on canvas
Paul Gauguin 1848–1903
28·75 × 36·25 in (73 × 92 cm)
Jeu de Paume, Paris

Emil Schuffenecker was one of the minor
artists who became Gauguin's disciples
and were influenced by the simplified
'Synthetist' painting technique that
Gauguin evolved in 1888–89. This portrait
was painted during a visit to Schuffenecker's
Paris apartment that followed Gauguin's
tragic stay with Van Gogh in Arles. It
passed from Schuffenecker to the Japanese
collector Prince Matsukata. In 1952 it
entered the Louvre as part of the
Franco-Japanese peace treaty.

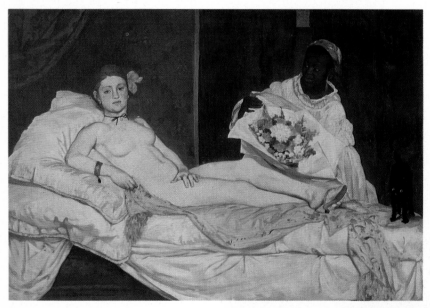

229 *right*

PORTRAIT OF DR GACHET

1890, oil on canvas
Vincent Van Gogh 1853–90
26·75 × 22·5 in (68 × 57 cm)
Jeu de Paume, Paris

Of the fifteen Van Goghs in the Jeu de
Paume, eight were at one time in
Dr Gachet's collection and seven of these
were presented to the museum by Gachet's
family in the 1950s. Gachet (1828–1909),
amateur painter and etcher under the
pseudonym Van Ryssel, collector and
friend of many artists, is himself
represented in the Jeu de Paume with
five canvases. He looked after Van Gogh
during the painter's last months in Auvers
in 1890, and taught him etching. This
image, which for Van Gogh contained
'something of the heart-broken expression
of our times', is an outstanding example
of his melancholic, proto-Expressionist
late works.

230 *centre*

THE CIRCUS

1891, oil on canvas
Georges Seurat (1859–91)
73 × 59·4 in (185 × 150 cm)
Jeu de Paume, Paris

231 *left*

DECORATIVE FIGURE ON AN ORNAMENTAL BACKGROUND

1927, oil on canvas
Henri Matisse 1869–1954
51·5 × 38·5 in (97 × 129·5 cm)
Musée National d'Art Moderne, Paris

Purchased in 1938 when Matisse was nearly seventy, this was only the second of his paintings to be bought by the state. Despite extensive purchasing after 1945, this remains the outstanding example of Matisse's art in the museum. A masterpiece of his mature art, it marries a respect for the monumental tradition of figure painting with his instinct for luxuriant decoration and with all of the modern painter's technical freedom and discipline.

centre

The Circus was the last of the seven major canvases from Seurat's tragically curtailed working life and is the only one still in France. Its presence in the Louvre is due to the bequest of an American collector, John Quinn, in 1925. It was earlier in the possession of Seurat's friend and disciple Paul Signac. Based on studies made at the Cirque Fernando, Paris, the painting demonstrates Seurat's ambition to reconcile the popular urban life of his day with the formal and theoretical disciplines of high art.

232

THE VIRGIN AND CHILD
WITH ANGELS,
ST ANTHONY OF PADUA AND
ST JOHN THE EVANGELIST

1437–44, oil on wood
Sassetta (Stefano di Giovanni) c. 1392–1450
centre panel 81 × 46·75 in (205 × 119 cm)
side panels 76·5 × 23·25 in (194 × 59 cm)
Louvre, Paris

These are the three main panels from the
reverse side of Sassetta's masterpiece,
a large polyptych painted for the church
of San Francesco, Borgo San Sepolcro.
In a French collection since at least 1900,
they were acquired by the Louvre in 1956.
In 1965 a predella panel from the same
altarpiece was presented to the Louvre
by the Société des Amis du Louvre and
there are some other small panels in the
Musée Condé at Chantilly.

233

HELLENISTIC WINE VESSEL

before AD 79
silver
Louvre, Paris

One of over a hundred pieces of fine
silverware presented to the Louvre in
1895 by the Baron Edmond de Rothschild.
The collection is known as the 'Boscoreale
Treasure' after the town near Pompeii
destroyed by Vesuvius in AD 79. They
were discovered there concealed in a
cistern on the site of a house. The treasure
includes outstanding examples, in almost
perfect condition, of the Hellenistic taste
for precious objets d'art.

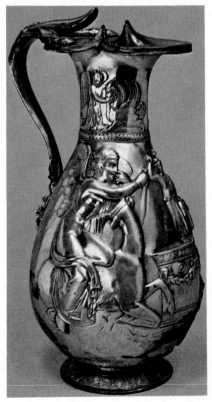

museums. It was founded in 1895 and since then the provincial museums have benefited from the national system of distribution. Pride in local achievement is often reflected in collections; there are Courbets and Bazilles at Montpellier, Lautrecs at Albi, Picassos at Cannes, and a Musée de l'Ecole de Nancy at Nancy.

Actual commissions of important artists in the late nineteenth century were few and relatively insignificant. There were portraits of course; it was largely in this way that Renoir achieved his breakthrough to official recognition, and very occasionally the Impressionists were commissioned to undertake specific decorative schemes for private houses. This latter field became particularly rewarding for the Nabis in the 1890s: the early art of Bonnard, Vuillard and their associates lent itself especially well to this function. The exceptions to the rule include Puvis de Chavannes whose murals in the Panthéon, Paris (1874–1898), the Hôtel de Ville, Paris (1889–93), and elsewhere inspired the modern revival of this genre. But for the most part commissions only offered outlets that lay outside the artist's normal channels of activity: poster design, book illustration, theatre design. The revived interest among painters in graphic media derived in part from economic necessity. But in the case of artists like

235 Toulouse-Lautrec, Jules Chéret and Bonnard the graphic media benefited enormously. They were employed by sheet music publishers, book and magazine publishers and cabaret owners and among them they stretched their media to a new directness of public communication. This phase in the history of graphic art inaugurated the most important modern version of the artist's role as propagandist.

Sculpture and architecture

Rodin was the major sculptor of the period; after an initial phase of fierce opposition to him, he received a string of public and private commissions. Many of these were to end in dispute with the patron. Two of his outstanding commissioned works, *The Burghers of Calais* (begun

240 1884) and the *Monument to Balzac* (1884–98) were refused on completion because of their unorthodoxy. Both are now erected in public sites, *The Burghers* in Calais as intended and the *Balzac* overlooking a Paris boulevard. His *Gate of Hell*, a doorway commissioned for the Musée des Arts Décoratifs, Paris, was still unfinished at his death. Rodin's contemporaries and immediate successors were overshadowed by his success and achievement. Maillol's best-known commissions were the *Monument to Blanqui* (1905–6) for Blanqui's birthplace Puget-Théniers near Grenoble, and the rather conservative *Monument to Cézanne* in the Tuileries Gardens. Bourdelle executed several public monuments and contributed murals and relief decoration to Perret's Théâtre des Champs Elysées, Paris. This last was almost a collective enterprise, the brainchild of the theatre's president, Gabriel Thomas. Other collaborators included Maurice Denis and Vuillard. Portrait sculpture has remained a fairly constant field of patronage. Rodin was prolifically successful in the genre and Despiau made his living from it in the 1920s. The modern phenomenon of the painter-sculptor like Degas and Matisse has encouraged the transformation of the art of sculpture from an essentially public medium to a more subjective activity increasingly comparable to modern painting, the public commission being the exception more than the rule.

In the exotic world of Art Nouveau there was a novelty-conscious demand for the work of furniture designers and interior decorators. One of the main centres of French Art Nouveau was not Paris but Nancy, a fast developing provincial city in the 1880s, whose mood of vital growth provided stimulus and patronage for an extraordinary outburst of

234
JANE AVRIL
AT THE JARDIN DE PARIS
poster, 1893, lithograph
Henri de Toulouse-Lautrec (1864–1901)
51 × 37·5 in (129 × 95 cm)

All of Lautrec's art was concerned with the world of Parisian entertainment. In the 1890s when the commercial use of colour lithography was greatly expanding, Lautrec's inventive talent as a graphic artist was called on for illustrations, posters, menus, invitation cards and sheet music covers. Jane Avril, Loie Fuller, Yvette Guilbert, La Goulue, Marcelle Lender and Sarah Bernhardt were among the cabaret, theatre and music hall artists for whom he designed posters. They combine his incisive ability to achieve a likeness with his imaginative impulse to improvise in two-dimensional design.

inventive applied art activity. The star was Emile Gallé, a native of
224 Nancy. His brilliantly inventive work in glass–coloured, moulded or
incised–and his intricate inlaid furniture typify the best of French Art
236 Nouveau. This era is fully represented in the Musée de l'Ecole de Nancy at
Nancy and the Musées des Arts Décoratifs in Paris. The critical influence
of this bizarre phase on early twentieth-century art owes little to its
patronage. This sort of patronage of the arts was a short-termed and
relatively non-committal investment.

The same may be said even of architecture, the one medium which,
before and later, did offer the traditional artist-patron basis of working.
Such opportunities as did occur for the employment of new architectural
materials, methods and ideas were in impermanent structures. We owe
the existence of an outstanding landmark of nineteenth-century structural
216 engineering, the Eiffel Tower, to its survival from an international exhibition in Paris in 1889. Contamin's revolutionary Halle des Machines for the
same exhibition, a huge iron structure standing on giant casters and
'tethered' to the ground by light external walls, did not survive. Hector
Guimard's original entrances for the new Paris Métro system, built
between 1899 and 1904, are gradually disappearing. So are the great
Parisian department stores of the period whose façades and interiors of
exposed ironwork contributed to the modern architectural aesthetic of
functionalism, the marriage of structure to decoration. The archetypes
are gone. Eiffel's Bon Marché has been replaced and Jourdain's Samari-
taine modernised. It was an age of experiment and discovery in building
methods: reinforced concrete as we know it was perfected in France in
the 1890s but not significantly utilised there until late into the twentieth
century. Nevertheless France remained at the forefront of concrete architecture's development: Anatole de Baudot's church of St Jean de Montmartre, Paris, 1894–9, was the first important public building in concrete.

The twentieth century

The years 1900–1914 saw the heroic pioneer development of twentieth-
century painting and sculpture with the richest activity concentrated on
Paris. These were the great years of Bohemian Paris, the cosmopolitan
artist's colony. In terms of patronage it was perhaps the most disastrous
231 period from the French viewpoint. Matisse and Picasso and their respective followers were sustained by a small circle of dealers and collectors.
227 The outstanding dealers were the Frenchman Vollard and the German
Kahnweiler. The outstanding collectors were American (Gertrude Stein
and her relatives prominent among them) and Russian (notably Morosov
and Shchoukin).

There were no French collectors of this standing. When the French
state started to purchase the work of this historic era in the 1920s, the
cream was gone. Such purchasing as did take place then was concentrated
upon the more conservative fringes of the early movements. The only
important early Matisse to be bought (*Le Luxe*) was acquired in 1945 and
the sole Picasso actually purchased by the Musées Nationaux (a gouache/
collage of 1914) was acquired in 1950. The outstanding state commission
225 between the wars was for the *Nymphéas* cycle of murals in the Orangerie
of the Louvre from the aged Impressionist Monet.

Paris was to remain a key international centre of artistic activity
between the wars. Matisse and Picasso still worked there; it was
Mondrian's home from 1917 to 1938 and Kandinsky's from 1933 to 1944.
The Surrealist movement was founded there in 1924, the Abstraction-
Création group formed there in 1931. Public and private attitudes
towards the avant-garde were little changed. The Surrealists' best patrons

235

ILLUSTRATION TO
VERLAINE'S 'PARALLELEMENT'
1900, lithograph
Pierre Bonnard 1867–1947
page 11·75 × 9·5 in (30 × 24 cm)
Bibliothèque Nationale, Paris

The Paris dealer and publisher Vollard
employed Bonnard as an illustrator on
several occasions. Bonnard made a hundred
and nine lithographs for *Parallèlement*,
informal in their disposition on the page
and exquisitely sensitive in touch, revealing
his extraordinary ability to give precise
expression to the literature and at the
same time to complement the formal
character and lay-out of the type.

236

DINING ROOM
1903–06, cedar wood and other materials
Eugène Vallin 1856–1922 and others
Musée de l'Ecole de Nancy, Nancy

Vallin was a prominent member of the
group of designers known as l'Ecole de
Nancy, which was at the height of its
activity from 1895 to 1905, working at
all levels of applied art from architectural

237

THE STUDIO OF BRANCUSI
(*bequeathed 1957*)
Constantin Brancusi (1876–1957)
Musée National d'Art Moderne, Paris

Brancusi was one of the most original and influential sculptors of this century. Apart from visits to India and to his native Rumania in connection with commissions there, he spent his whole working life from the age of twenty-eight in Paris. His studio became a place of pilgrimage for younger artists. Shortly before his death he bequeathed its entire contents to the French state. This most valuable addition to the national collection of modern art illustrates the full range of Brancusi's new consciousness of form and of his sympathetic sensitivity to his media's properties, from coarse-grained wood to highly polished metals and stones.

façades and interiors to minute objets d'art. The organic vitality that pervades all the details of this interior is typical of continental Art Nouveau. Typical also is the co-operative nature of the project: the glass was contributed by Davin, the wood-carving and ceiling painting by Prouvé. The room was commissioned in 1903 by Charles Masson, transferred to his Paris apartment in 1917 and presented in 1938 to the town of Nancy.

and critics lay mainly among the painters and poets of the movement itself.

A common feature of most artists' ideologies in the restless period between the wars was a genuine socio-political idealism. Surrealist manifestoes and Mondrian's personal programme both originate from desires, very different but equally intense, to serve and improve society through art. The same inspiration lies behind much of the work of Léger and Le Corbusier and—in a less obvious way—of Matisse and Brancusi. If anything the gulf between artist and society widened. The aggressively exhibitionist façade of Surrealism was not tailor-made for public acceptance and the purist art of Mondrian was probably too deeply rooted within the complexity of modern art history to find much social contact. In fact his existence in Paris has been likened to that of a benevolent hermit and his work was seldom exhibited.

The applied arts and architecture

It was the theatre that provided the richest meeting point of artist and public and more particularly the aura of Diaghilev's Ballets Russes. Diaghilev's activities included publishing and mounting exhibitions. He had brought his first company to the Paris stage in 1908 and his spectacular productions, ballet and opera, continued through the 1920s and 30s, bringing together some of the period's outstanding writers, composers, musicians, choreographers, singers and dancers as well as painters. The artists he employed include Braque, Picasso, Matisse, Derain, Gris, Rouault and the Russians Larionov, Goncharova, Gabo and Pevsner. As far as the artists were concerned he first of all offered them experience in a field where it was possible to experiment completely free of fine art inhibitions. Secondly, his own dynamic empiricism acted as a catalyst on all those around him.

The field of illustration offered a similar opportunity and challenge to Bonnard, Chagall, Rouault, Picasso and others. Vollard was probably the **235** most enterprising Parisian publisher to employ artists. A lot of painters worked in fields even further from painting: tapestry, textile design, exhibition decoration, etc. The atmosphere of the 'twenties, optimistically reckless and frivolously fashion-conscious, again prompted an irresponsible attitude towards patronage of the arts.

Only in the patronage of architecture did the traditional situation of the patron commissioning the artist to fulfil a specific, long-term function prevail to any considerable degree. Architecturally Paris is one of the most impressive historical cities in Europe. Its rather conservative taste in buildings is conditioned by a history-consciousness. In this light it is hardly surprising, for example, that the successive revolutionary ideas on city planning of Le Corbusier of 1921, 1925 and 1937, all conceived with Paris in mind, should not find realisation there. Auguste Perret's early buildings, on the other hand, married a progressive attitude towards materials with a traditional sense of style and organisation successfully enough to be acceptable. The crowning recognition in the public field came with his appointment as chief architect for the post-Second World War reconstruction of Le Havre's residential areas which was started in 1947. Le Corbusier's important pre-war works in France were a succession of highly original private houses, each of them a landmark of twentieth- **241** century architecture; the Cité de Refuge (a hostel for the Salvation Army) in Paris 1929–33; and a residential block for Swiss students at Paris University in 1930–32. His basic credo of 'suitability to purpose' which underlies every aspect of his work and theory made Le Corbusier the perfect modern public architect. In this role his only important state commission in France was the Unité d'Habitation in Marseilles, 1947–52.

A complete social unit, this was the first practical demonstration of his ideas about large-scale planning. Outside Europe – in India, South America and elsewhere – he had the opportunity to develop these concepts to the full.

237 The sculptor Brancusi's most important commissions also came from abroad: from India and his native Rumania. An inhabitant of Paris since 1904, he acquired French nationality a few weeks before his death so that he could bequeath his studio and its entire contents to the French state. It is now reconstructed in the Musée d'Art Moderne and is probably the most important single acquisition by that museum in its history.

The Musée National d'Art Moderne

It is true to say that only the devastation of the Second World War created the opportunities for Perret at Le Havre and Le Corbusier at Marseilles. Conversely it is a positive rethinking by the French art establishment since the war that has brought about the changed attitude towards contemporary painting and sculpture. A clear expression of this change is the foundation and history of the Musée National d'Art Moderne, Paris. The museum's constitution was laid down in 1939, but the outbreak of war interrupted its development and the 'reopening' in 1947 marks the real beginning of the museum's history. Until 1939 most 'modern art', including the donated collections of Impressionist paintings, was housed in the Orangerie of the Palais du Luxembourg and a small annexe to it. In 1939 all foreign works were put in the Jeu de Paume and the Impressionist paintings went to the Louvre. In 1946 the Jeu de Paume became the museum of Impressionism, a category that stretches to include some of the Impressionists' predecessors like Boudin and Manet as well as the heroic Post-Impressionist generation of Cézanne, Seurat, Gauguin and Van Gogh. At the same time all more recent art was moved to the Musée d'Art Moderne.

The national collection of 'more recent art' at the time scarcely matched the ambition of the whole project. The respectability of the collection at its opening was made possible by a spate of donations including seven 242 Matisses and ten Picassos (the latter all given by the artist). Since 1947 effort has been concentrated on establishing an historical twentieth-century collection with the emphasis quite openly on the Ecole de Paris.

The postwar situation

Under the administration of André Malraux, Minister of State for 232, 238 Cultural Affairs, private support of the national collections has been 239, 246 sustained. State commissions like Chagall's ceiling for the Opéra, Paris, and a series of enterprising and ambitious exhibitions mounted in various Parisian museums also reflect his energy. It is difficult to measure the achievement of his aspirations as expressed in *Le Musée Imaginaire*. The old situation of art under the supervision of a government department is not attempted. The policy is one of sponsorship rather than control. The 'Biennale de Paris', founded in 1959, is an example of a more liberal outlook. Held in the Musée d'Art Moderne, this international exhibition open to artists under thirty-five years old has gone some way towards offsetting Paris's postwar decline as a centre of artistic importance. As a centre of art dealing, Paris's decline in favour of London and New York has been dramatic.

Outside the realm of state sponsorship, the most important patronage since 1945 has fallen into three categories dependent on the wealth and open-mindedness of commercial houses, the church and international 248 organisations. Representative examples of each are the extravagant Maeght Foundation; the chapels of Le Corbusier at Ronchamp, Matisse at Vence, Léger at Audincourt and the UNESCO building in Paris. The

238
PORTRAIT OF TITUS,
THE ARTIST'S SON
c. 1659
Rembrandt van Rijn 1606–69
28·5 × 22 in (72 × 56 cm)
Louvre, Paris

This is the most important recent addition to the Louvre's outstanding Rembrandt collection. Originally in France in the eighteenth century until it was bought by Catherine II of Russia in 1780, the portrait returned to a French collection in 1935, and was donated to the Louvre in 1948. It is one of eight known portraits by Rembrandt of his son, born in 1641. The gentle mood of this sensitive study stems from the facial expression and is maintained in the generous but controlled handling of the pigment. Since 1956 the painting has been on loan to the Rijksmuseum, Amsterdam, in exchange for a still life by the fifteenth-century French Master of the Aix Annunciation.

Maeght family business is a prominent art dealing and publishing house in Paris. The foundation was conceived primarily as a memorial to a deceased member of the family. The setting, the architecture and the scale of commissions within the project exude an atmosphere of self-conscious luxury and magnificence strongly reminiscent of papal, royal or titled patronage of past epochs.

There is a large element of this spectacular outward show about some of the bigger church commissions as well. Church patronage of modern architecture in France has a commendably progressive history. De Baudot's first concrete church of 1894–9 was followed in 1922 by Perret's Notre Dame, le Raincy, Paris. Le Corbusier's Notre Dame du Haut at Ronchamp, 1955, is a more than worthy successor to these in terms of its historical importance, but a dramatic contrast to them in terms of its departure from their strict code of architectural morality. Le Corbusier used the occasion, obviously with his patrons' approval, for an extreme gesture of individuality that was to originate a new direction in his own work and to wield considerable influence on other architects. The offer or approval of such freedom by the church as patron may be a calculated risk, but if the artist employed is a Le Corbusier or a Matisse the calculation is pretty sound and the potential yield in prestige enormous. The church is in a stronger position than a civic body to allow an artist to create an environment of essentially aesthetic impact more than of decorous utility.

The UNESCO building was in conception both a functional project as the Parisian home of the UNESCO secretariat and a showpiece. Its international origins and its multinational realisation are features of the contemporary art world. The positive intention here was to be widely representative and world-embracing. The Y-shaped building (1953–8) is the work of three architects, the Italian Nervi, the American Breuer and the Frenchman Zehrfuss. A committee of artistic advisers drawn from five nations commissioned its decoration in the form of works by Afro, Appel, Arp, Bazaine, Brassai, Calder, Matta, Mirò, Moore, Noguchi, Picasso and Tamayo. Predictably there is some lack of homogeneity, but the building is big enough and strong enough in its own character to absorb and contrast the pockets of individuality. In effect this building has provided Paris with its outstanding postwar monument and a very rich annexe to its museum of modern art. In its nature the whole project is a supreme example of the self-conscious grand gesture towards the arts by modern establishments in the rôle of patron.

If its attitude sometimes seems more patronising than patronage, the modern establishment is no better or worse in this respect than its predecessors. The motives underlying all these commissions are basically no different from the pride and prestige of possession that fostered much traditional patronage. The outstanding difference is that the church, for example, must accept the art-for-art's-sake pedigree of contemporary painting and sculpture if it is to be a realistic patron of the art of its time. As a result there is a much stronger influence than before of that additional prestige acquired by an élite minority among public bodies that champions a misunderstood avant-garde. In the modern context this almost moral righteousness has sometimes clouded the judgment of suitability to function. The artist, for the most part, cannot fail to benefit from an opportunity of scale and media not otherwise available. Occasionally, as at Ronchamp and Vence, the occasion and the achievement have been married with a harmony that is to the benefit of all concerned and wholly comparable to the greatest monuments of earlier French art.

Nicholas Wadley

239
ST SIMEON THE STYLITE
sixth century
silver, partly gilded
11·75 × 10·25 in (30 × 26 cm)
Louvre, Paris

The Greek inscription on this early Christian plaque from Syria is to God and St Simeon; it is probably part of a reliquary. The lack of refined classical craftsmanship is compensated by its fresh charm and vitality. The plaque was donated by the Société des Amis du Louvre in 1952. It represents St Simeon besieged by temptation.

240

BALZAC

1897
Auguste Rodin 1840–1917
stucco
h. 113·75 in (289 cm)
Musée Rodin, Paris

Rodin's final version of this posthumous Balzac monument
was rejected by the literary society which had commissioned
it. In 1898 the public exhibition of this definitive plaster at the
Société Nationale des Beaux Arts created a scandal. Rodin's
determination to build something monumental out of Balzac's
grotesque physique rather than make a banal idealisation, was
misunderstood and found unacceptable. Its expressiveness,
originality and colossal strength distinguish it as one of the
most remarkable nineteenth-century portraits. A bronze
version stands on the Boulevard Raspail in Paris.

THE VILLA SAVOYE, ('LES HEURES CLAIRES')

1928–30
Le Corbusier (Charles Edouard Jeanneret)
1887–1965
Poissy-sur-Seine

Commissioned by the Savoye family in 1928, this villa was to be an expression of the revolutionary blueprint for modern architecture that Le Corbusier evolved in the 1920s. It is also a building of great classical beauty, in which modern functionalism is married to modern aesthetics. The simple regularity of the exterior – a white cube cut across by ribbon windows and standing off the ground on legs – contrasts with the free asymmetry of the interior spaces, where a dominant diagonal ramp breaks the cool rectangularity. There is a free play between exterior and interior space below and above. Use of the flat roof for terrace garden, solarium and sometimes swimming pool rapidly became standard practice.

L'ATELIER DE LA MODISTE

1926
Pablo Picasso born 1881
oil on canvas
67·75 × 100·75 in (172 × 255 cm)
Musée National d'Art Moderne, Paris

This was one of the ten Picasso's donated by the artist to the Musée d'Art Moderne immediately prior to its post-war opening in 1947. Before this generous gesture, the state owned only two Picassos, both private donations. This large canvas represents a lesser-known aspect of his work of the 1920s, largely formal in its preoccupations and restrained in colour.

243, 244 UNESCO SECRETARIAT BUILDING
1955–56, Pier Luigi Nervi born 1891
Marcel Breuer and Bernard Zehrfuss, Place de Fontenoy, Paris

A major example of modern 'institutionalised' patronage:
many individual artists and designers working under the
multi-tiered umbrella of committees and consultants. Considering
this and UNESCO's ambition to cross-section modern art and
design in the process, the result retains a remarkably distinctive
character. The building complex is dominated by the Y-shaped
secretariat, standing some 19 feet off the ground on seventy-two
columns. The structure throughout is in concrete and demonstrates
Nervi's reputation as the greatest living exponent of the medium.
In the grounds are three sculptures, the marble reclining figure
by Moore (**243**), a bronze relief by Arp and an iron mobile by
Calder, a Bazaine mosaic, Noguchi's Japanese garden, and two
ceramic walls by Jean Miró which stand in a T-shape *right*.
The longer *Wall of the Sun* measures about 50 feet. Between
them they are built of five hundred and eighty-five ceramic
tiles, made for Miró by José Llorens-Artigas. As in much of
Miró's mature art, the intrinsic qualities of the medium,
irregularities of surface, colour, and luminosity, were allowed
to determine much of the work's character. In 1958 the walls
were awarded the Guggenheim International Art Award.
Picasso's untitled mural (**244** *below*) on an end wall of the
conference hall foyer is his only important public commission
in France and the only major work by him in a public French
collection. It was painted in 1957–58 on forty wooden panels
and measures approximately 30 × 35 ft (9·14 × 10·66 m). From
some viewpoints in the foyer the irregular shape appears as
a true rectangle. Stylistically it is austere and simple, but
nevertheless full of the expressionist improvisation that
distinguishes all his post-Cubist art. The content of the image,
dominated by the black-shadowed skeletal Icarus is also definitive
of his lifelong concern with life and death. There are also murals
in this hall by Tamayo and by Afro, Appel, Brassai and Matta
on the seventh floor.

245 *right* WALL OF THE MOON

246

CEILING DECORATION

1962–66, Marc Chagall born 1887
The Opéra, Paris

The ceiling was commissioned by André
Malraux in 1962. The choice of Chagall
to decorate Garnier's exuberant mid-
nineteenth-century Opéra was probably
the most controversial post-war event in
the official Paris art world. After fierce
press campaigns, questions in the assembly
and a written justification to De Gaulle,
Malraux conceded that the decoration
should be executed on a 'false' vault over
the existing surface. The painting is
characterised by the naïve poetry and
fantasy of Chagall's imagery so much
admired by the Surrealists in the 1920s.

247

THE CHAPEL OF THE ROSARY

1948–51
Henri Matisse 1869–1954, Vence

Matisse lived at Vence from 1943 to
1949. His design for the chapel has the
austere purity and simple genius of a
great artist's maturity. The black and
white linear mural of glazed tiles is
enriched and articulated by light shining
through the colour areas of the windows
and playing across its surface. One priest,
Père Cousturier, was largely responsible
for commissioning Matisse at Vence and of
Le Corbusier at Ronchamp. In the Second
World War he did much to safeguard the
interests of French artists during the
German occupation.

248

THE MAEGHT FOUNDATION

St Paul de Vence

The Maeght Foundation, inaugurated
in 1964, is a kind of cultural settlement,
endowed by the Paris art dealers
Marguerite and Aimé Maeght. The only
major new art centre built in France
since the war, its intended function is to
provide a stimulating retreat for invited
artists, poets, musicians, etc., and a
spectacular summer season of avant-garde
culture (concerts, ballet, exhibitions) open
to the public. The principle architect was
José Luis Sert, formerly a pupil of
Le Corbusier whose influence is apparent.
The building complex includes the chapel
of St Bernard (erected in memory of

Bernard Maeght), a gallery, libraries, a small cinema, a theatre and extensive living accommodation. The gallery is an exhibition space rather than a museum, but permanent exhibits in the Foundation include the Giacommettis in the Grand Cour, a wall by Tal Coat and a 'garden labyrinth' designed by Miró.

NOTRE DAME DU HAUT

1955, Ronchamp
Le Corbusier (Charles Edouard Jeanneret)
1887–1965

Designed ten years before his death, this chef-d'oeuvre marked a change of direction in Le Corbusier's architecture, away from the disciplined beauty of his mature functionalism towards a more personal extravagance of style. As in all his work, the eccentric individuality of smaller units contributes to the homogeneous totality. The interior is lit by scattered rectangles of stained glass, the apertures cut through the monumental concrete walls like the graphic punctuations of a modern musical score.

THE LEGER MUSEUM

Fernand Léger (1881–1955), Biot

After Picasso, Léger was probably the leading figure in French figurative painting since the First World War. Following his pioneer involvement with the Cubist movement he worked for the application of the cubist's formal freedom to a monumentalisation of mankind, a modern equivalent of nineteenth-century French Realism. In his occasional use of popular images he is hailed by some as a father of 'pop art'. His public commissions included work in the theatre, in cinema and his stained glass windows at Audincourt. This museum at Biot contains some 400 canvases as well as drawings and ceramics.

Museums
and Monuments

An index of museums, châteaux, churches and palaces listing some of the major treasures they house and arranged in geographical areas to correspond with the maps at the beginning and end of the book.

Illustrations on this page:
top
a Temple of Love, Versailles; F. Miqué
b Cour du cheval blanc; Fontainebleau
c Tapestry chair; L. Delanois and F. Boucher; Louvre
middle
b Diana bathing, *detail*; 1742; F. Boucher; Louvre
e La Grande Galerie du Louvre, *detail*; *c* 1801; H. Robert; Louvre
f Visigothic crown from Guarrazar; Musée de Cluny, Paris
bottom
g Reliquary of Ste Epine; Rheims cathedral
h Le Moulin de la Galette, *detail*; 1876; P. A. Renoir; Louvre
i Arc de Triomphe, Paris

Flanders Artois Picardy Ardennes

ABBEVILLE
1 **Château de la Bagatelle** Built 1645 for Abraham van Robais. Decorations in style of Huet and Boucher; Louis XV and Louis XVI furniture.
2 **St Vulfran** Rebuilding commenced 1488 in advanced Flamboyant Gothic style, but not completed. 2 towers surmounting fine façade with 3 portals.
3 **Musée Bouchier de Perthes** Prehistoric exhibits; paintings and decorative arts.

AMIENS
4 **Cathedral** Begun 1220; the architect Robert de Luzarches took Rheims as his model. Nave of 7 bays; crossing; choir with 4 bays and apse; transepts with aisles; 7 chapels round choir. Nave and transepts completed by 1236. Robert succeeded by Thomas de Cormont who completed triforium upwards; purest work of classic Gothic style.
5 **Musée de Picardie** Paintings: primitives from N France; French 18th C, Fragonard *Les Lavandières;* El Greco *Portrait of a Man.*

ARRAS
6 **Palais St Vaast** Treasure of Beaurains; 14th C funerary mask. Paintings: Dutch and Flemish 12th C to 18th C; French 17th C and 18th C.

BOULOGNE
7 **Bibliothèque Municipale** Illuminated MSS Gospels of St Bertin from St Omer.
8 **Musée Municipal** Greek vases; ethnographical collection; paintings.

LE CATEAU
9 **Musée Henri Matisse** Works of Matisse, donated by the artist.

COUCY LE CHATEAU
10 **Château de Coucy** Ruins of medieval castle; 13th C walls.

DOUAI
11 **Musée Municipal** Paintings: important Flemish works.

LILLE
12 **Musée des Beaux Arts** Major collection of paintings: Flemish; Dutch; Spanish, Goya *Las Viejas;* Italian; French; German. Drawings mostly Italian, collection of Michelangelo.

SAINT-OMER
13 **Musée des Beaux Arts** Paintings, particularly Flemish; ceramics; library of MSS and incunabula.

SAINT QUENTIN
14 **Musée Lécuyer** Paintings, particularly works by Quentin de la Tour.

VALENCIENNES
15 **Musée des Beaux Arts** Paintings: Flemish and French, works by Watteau, Harpignies, Carpeaux.

Normandy

ALENCON
16 **Notre Dame** Built in Flamboyant style, started 14th C, completed 1444. Flamboyant porch by Jean Lemoine (1409–1506); stained glass windows (1530).
17 **Musée de la Maison d'Ozé** Drawings and sketches, French 17th and 19th C; objects from Cambodia.
18 **Musée de la Peinture** Paintings; Alençon lace.

LES ANDELYS
19 **Château Gaillard** Built by Richard I of England, 1196. Dismantled by Henry IV. Mainly ruins though keep in good condition.

BALLEROY
20 **Château de Balleroy** Built 1626–36 by F Mansart for Jean de Choisy. Fine interior decorated with paintings by Lemoine.

BAYEUX
21 **Notre Dame Cathedral** Mainly 12th C, surviving parts of Romanesque building consecrated 1077 include nave arcades; large crypt; parts of crossing and w tower. Remainder in Norman French Gothic; 22 chapels; much Rayonnant tracery.
22 **Musée de la Reine Mathilde** Bayeux tapestry.

BERNAY
23 **Musée Municipal** Flemish and Spanish paintings; Rouen ware, including enamelled tiles.

BRECY
24 **Château de Brécy** Mid 17th C, built by F Mansart for Jacques le Bas. Classical main doorway.

CAEN
25 **La Trinité, Church of the Abbaye aux Dames** Founded by Matilda in 1062, Romanesque. Nave 11th C with 13th C Gothic vault; choir with early quadripartite vaulting (1100–10). Extensively restored in 19th C.
26 **St Etienne, Church of the Abbaye aux Hommes** Founded by William the Conqueror, dedicated 1077. Romanesque with Gothic and later additions; towers Romanesque bases with 13th C spires; notable apse; 12th C nave; 13th C (earliest Norman Gothic) choir.
27 **St Pierre** Principal parish church. Tower and spire 1308; Flamboyant porch; early Renaissance apse by Hector Sohier 1518–45; extensively damaged 1944.
28 **Musée des Beaux Arts** Important painting collection: Van der Weyden *Virgin and Child;* works by Perugino, Veronese, Tintoretto, Carpaccio, Rubens, Poussin, Tiepolo, Boucher; collection of engravings, Dürer, Rembrandt, Callot; ceramics.

CARROUGES
29 **Château de Carrouges** Medieval, Renaissance and 17th C building. Fine entrance gate; 16th C pavilion; wrought iron. Salon des Portraits and other rooms decorated in 16th, 17th and 18th C.

CLERES
30 **Château** Medieval fortress in ruins; 15th C château with 16th C dormer windows; 16th C manor house.

COUTANCES
31 **Cathedral of Notre Dame** Built 1254–74. Fine design of two w towers, spires and octagonal lantern tower over crossing.

DIEPPE
32 **Musée du Vieux Château** Paintings including Boudin, Pissaro, Sisley, Courbet, Sickert; collection of ivories.

EVREUX
33 **Cathedral of Notre Dame** Destroyed c.1200 and rebuilt, finished late 15th C. N side restored 1511–31; damaged during 2nd World War. Flamboyant work including important screens in side chapel; 14th C stalls; important rose window (1511–31).
34 **Musée Municipal** Prehistoric; Gallo-Roman objects; medieval enamels and objets d'art.

FALAISE
35 **Château de Falaise** Castle where William the Conqueror was born. Late 11th C square keep with Romanesque windows; Tour de Talbot (130 ft high) 15th C.

FONTAINE-HENRY
36 **Château** Built on the remains of an old fortress (13th C cellars) in 15th and 16th C. Gothic pavilion with Italianate ornament and large roof; Renaissance well; Francis I staircase.

LE HAVRE
37 **Musée des Beaux Arts** Modern paintings; 295 works by Boudin.

HONFLEUR
38 **Musée des Beaux Arts** 19th C paintings.

JUMIEGES
39 **Abbey Church of Notre Dame** Important ruins of abbey built 1040–67, consists of large roofless nave and parts of transept and choir. 2 Romanesque octagonal towers on square bases and decorated with blind arcading flank w porch and are the oldest in France.
40 **St Pierre** Leading off ruined abbey is a small church, also in ruins. Part of nave Carolingian, includes a triforium gallery with twin arches separated by a column (c.940).

LOUVIERS
41 **Notre Dame** Originally built 13th C, celebrated for its façade and 15th C porch, magnificent example of exuberant Flamboyant style.
42 **Musée Municipal** Furniture; faience.

MESNIERES-EN-BRAY
43 **Château des Mesnières** Renaissance, built 1540–46. Main building has end pavilions and round towers with pepperpot roofs. 18th C staircase; Renaissance chapel; stained glass.

LE PIN AU HARAS
44 **Haras-du-Pin** Stud farm. Buildings designed by J Hardouin Mansart, construction begun in 1714.

ROUEN
45 **Cathedral of Notre Dame** All periods of medieval architecture represented. Romanesque building destroyed 1200; rebuilding started 1201 under Jean d'Andelay; basic work finished 1260. N and s fronts of transept important examples of Rayonnant style, as is lady chapel (1320–20). Flamboyant style blind tracery and gables on w front.
46 **Palais de Justice** Built under Louis XII by Roland le Roux in late Gothic style. Central part of edifice has richly ornamented façade.
47 **Church of St Maclou** Rich example of florid Gothic style, begun 1437 by Pierre Robin. Elaborate w portal with pentagonal porch; spire above crossing completed 1868; reliefs on wooden doors attr. to Jean Goujon; fine Last Judgment bas-relief on tympanum. Gothic staircase 1518–20 leading to organ loft; stained glass 15th C to 16th C.
48 **Musée des Beaux Arts et de la Céramique** Paintings: works by Fragonard, Monet, Perugino, Marten de Vos, Veronese, Velasquez, Gerard David *Virgin and Saints.* Ceramics: Rouen faience from 1550–1800.
49 **Musée Départemental des Antiquités de la Seine-Maritime** Roman and Merovingian exhibits; Grecian vases; Etruscan ceramics.

SAINT GERMAIN DE LIVET
50 **Château** 15th C and 16th C walls have chessboard pattern, white stone alternating with green and red enamelled tiles.

VARENGEVILLE
51 **Manoir d'Ango** Fortified manor built first half of 16th C. Four sided with central courtyard; s wing contains Italian style loggia.

Ile De France

ANET
52 **Château d'Anet** Renaissance building commenced 1548 by Philibert de l'Orme for Henry II. Decorations by Jean Goujon, Germain Pilon, Jean Cousin. Extensively damaged during the Revolution. Chapel with circular nave.

ASNIERES
53 **Abbaye de Royaumont** Cistercian abbey founded by Louis IX in 1228; greater part demolished after Revolution. Remains include cloister, Gothic refectory, kitchens.

BEAUVAIS
54 **Cathedral de St Pierre** Gothic, begun 1227 with apsidal chapels; main structure of choir 1247–72. Intended to be tallest cathedral but two falls of vaulting stopped work. Reconstructed, finished 1500. Flamboyant chapel by Martin Chambiges 1501–48; Renaissance sculptured wooden doors (1535).

CHAALIS
55 **Musée Jacquemart-André** In 18th C abbey of Chaâlis designed by Aubert. Paintings; tapestries.

CHAMPS SUR MARNE
56 **Château** Early 18th C building and garden; architect J-B Bullet. Furniture; paintings; decorations by Oudry, Huet, Desportes.

CHANTILLY
57 **Musée Condé** In Petit Château built c.1560 by Jean Bullant; 18th C furniture; porcelain; paintings and drawings: many by Jean and François Clouet, Poussin. Library: illuminated MSS Très Riches Heures du Duc de Berry.

CHARTRES
58 **Cathedral of Notre Dame** Uniquely important Gothic building, notable for sculpture (nearly 2,200 figures) and stained glass. Main rebuilding after a fire, 1194–1260. First building to make full constructional use of flying buttresses, increasing size of clerestory windows. 2 strongly marked transepts, each terminated by 2 towers;

E towers never completed; W front 3 portals and much sculpture; S porch (1224–50) dedicated to New Testament; N porch c. 1230 dedicated to Old Testament and coming of the Messiah. Magnificent rose window in transept; Statue of St Peter middle doorway of N transept.

59 **Musée Municipal** Medieval sculpture; paintings; tapestries.

CHATEAUDUN
60 **Château de Châteaudun** Impressively situated above Loire valley. 12th to 16th C, recently restored. 12th C round keep. Sainte Chapelle contains 15 15th C statues.

COMPIEGNE
61 **Château** Built on site of royal hunting lodge; reconstruction ordered by Louis XV in 1738; work undertaken by Jacques Gabriel but not completed until 1785. Marie Antoinette's games room and 1st and 2nd Empire apartments furnished with original fittings and furniture.

62 **Musée National du Palais de Compiègne** 18th C royal and imperial palace with period interiors and furniture, and works of art.

63 **Musée Vivenel** Prehistoric and Egyptian exhibits; Lucien Bonaparte collection of Greek vases.

COURANCES
64 **Château de Courances** Built in 1550, reconstructed in the 17th C by Claude Gallari. Subsequently abandoned and restored at end of 19th C. Park designed by Le Nôtre.

DAMPIERRE
65 **Château de Dampierre** Built 16th C, reconstructed 1675–83 by J H Mansart. Much 17th C decoration; Salle des Fêtes with murals by Ingres. Park designed by Le Nôtre.

DREUX
66 **Musée Municipal d'Art et d'Histoire** Romanesque capitals from church of St Etienne; modern paintings.

ERMENONVILLE
67 **Château** Built 1763 onwards for Marquis de Girardin. Park: tomb of J-J Rousseau, attr. to Hubert Robert.

ETAMPES
68 **Notre Dame du Fort** 12th C, once fortified. Fine Romanesque tower; sculpture on S portal comparable with Royal Portal, Chartres.

FLEURY EN BIERE
69 **Château** Started by Cosmo Clausse at end of 16th C; large courtyard closed by brick wall.

FONTAINEBLEAU
70 **Palace** Dates mainly from reign of Francis I and Henry IV; interior decorated in style of Guilio Romano; apartments of Marie Antoinette decorated by Blondel; Galerie de Henri II by Primaticcio; Galerie de François Ier by Rosso.

GUERMANTES
71 **Château de Guermantes** Early 17th C, reconstructed late 17th C. 2 Louis XIII rooms with original woodwork and ceilings; wing added late 17th C; gallery Belle Intuile by Robert de Cotte c. 1709. Park laid out by Le Nôtre.

JOSSIGNY
72 **Château de Jossigny** Built in 1743 in classical style of Louis XV for Claude-François le Conte. Rococo façade on garden side; pagoda-like roof profiles; contemporary furniture and fittings.

JOUARRE
73 **Abbey of Notre Dame** Crypt of abbey one of the oldest religious monuments in France. Contains various sarcophagi including tomb of Theodochilde, 1st Abbess; Merovingian marble columns.

LAON
74 **Cathedral of Notre Dame** Important early Gothic building which had considerable influence. Begun c. 1160, work progressed on choir, transept, nave, W front and central tower (completed 1205). Good illustration of full development of church type with galleries above aisles. Capitals of the arcades have foliated ornament. Beautiful W front (c. 1200) divided into 3 parts by buttresses to take internal thrusts.

75 **Musée Municipal** Prehistory; paintings by the brothers Le Nain.

MAINCY
76 **Château de Vaux-le-Vicomte** Important

building, designed by Le Vau for Nicolas Fouquet. Constructed 1656–61. Large rectangle with corner pavilions with circular domed pavilion in centre of façade. Decorations by Le Brun. Contemporary tapestries, carpets and furniture. Garden designed by Le Nôtre, restored in 1875.

MAISONS-LAFFITTE
77 **Château** Built 1643–51 by François Mansart. Mansart's chef-d'oeuvre. Outstanding example of French classical building. Contemporary decorations, paintings and sculpture.

NOYON
78 **Cathedral of Notre Dame** Influential Early Gothic building. Begun c. 1150 on site of earlier building. Choir completed by 1185, transepts built c. 1170; W end not finished until 13th C. Built with alternate round and compound piers to carry sexpartite vault which collapsed 1293; replaced by a quadripartite one. Vaulting of crossing replaced 1460–62.

PIERREFONDS
79 **Pierrefonds Castle** Reconstruction by Viollet-le-Duc in 1857 of a late 14th C fortress. Originally built by Charles of Orleans from 1390 onwards, dismantled by Richelieu. An irregular pentagon with crenellated walls and tall round towers.

RAMBOUILLET
80 **Château** Residence of the President. Original building 14th C, single tower remaining; restored and enlarged at various periods. Panelling, tapestries, furniture.

ROSNY
81 **Château de Rosny** Built early 17th C in Louis XIII style by Maximilian de Béthune, Duke of Sully. 17th and 18th C tapestries; woodwork; contemporary furniture.

RUEIL-MALMAISON
82 **Palais National de Malmaison** Bonaparte's favourite residence 1800 to 1805. Josephine died here in 1814. Art and history of the Napoleonic times. Original furnishings.

SAINT-DENIS
83 **Basilica of St Denis** Burial place of the French monarchs. Ends of the church, façade and apse 1132–44, important examples of early Gothic. Remainder rebuilt 1231–81. Royal tombs: tomb of Louis XII, Anne of Brittany by Jean Juste (1516–32); tomb of Henri II and Catherine de Medici designed by Primaticcio 1560–73.

SAINT GERMAIN EN LAYE
84 **Musée des Antiquités Nationales** In château built to designs of Pierre Chambiges for Francis I in 1539 on site of medieval castle; keep and chapel being retained. Chapel built c. 1230 by Pierre de Montreuil, architect of Sainte Chapelle in Paris. Later work in château carried out by Philibert de l'Orme, Guillaume Marchant, Le Vau, J Hardouin Mansart. Main French prehistoric museum; history of art in pre-Christian era.

SCEAUX
85 **Château and Park** Château designed by Perrault for Colbert; destroyed in 1798. Buildings remaining include Pavilion de l'Aurore with cupola by Le Brun; Little château and Orangery built in 1684 by J H Mansart. Present château built by the Duke of Trévise in the 19th C, contains Musée de l'Ile-de-France: political and artistic history of region.

SENLIS
86 **Château Royal** Dating from 4th, 11th and 16th C. Romanesque and Gothic buildings; bedroom and study of Louis IX

87 **Cathedral of Notre Dame** Built 1155–84. Spire on S tower of façade mid 13th C; central door in W façade c. 1185 has statues, a Tree of Jesse and outstanding Coronation of the Virgin on the tympanum. Transepts rebuilt 1530–56 in Flamboyant style by Pierre Chambiges. Upper part of nave rebuilt early 16th C in Flamboyant style; 16th C glass in clerestory windows.

SEVRES
88 **Musée de Céramique de Sèvres** History of ceramics. More than 30,000 pieces including 6 rare 16th C Florence porcelains.

SOISSONS
89 **Cathedral of St Gervais et St Protais** S transept (1175) early Gothic consisting of arcade, gallery, triforium and clerestory. Remainder High Gothic; choir completed 1212 nave 1230. Badly damaged in first world war and substantially restored.

VERSAILLES
90 **The Palace** Museum of 'all the glories of France'. Louis XIII established hunting lodge here in 1634, subsequently developed into château; renovated and embellished for Louis XIV by Le Vau and Le Nôtre (park) in 1661; further developed into a new palace; work was completed by François d'Orbay after Le Vau's death in 1670; remodelled by J. H. Mansart, 1676 onwards; subsequent Louis XVI additions by Gabriel. After execution of Louis XVI, contents were dispersed. Museum created by Louis Philippe. Important collection of paintings covering 16th to 20th C decorative paintings; sculpture; furniture; tapestries; objets d'art. Especially noteworthy rooms: Galerie des Glaces; royal apartments; chapel (begun 1699 by Mansart, completed 1710 by Robert de Cotte). The Petit Trianon and the Grand Trianon: royal residences with 17th C and 18th C woodwork.

VILLECONIN
91 **Château de Villeconin** Fortifications and keep built late 14th C by Jean de Montagu. Dwelling remodelled in time of Henry IV. Fine ceilings.

VILLERS-COTTERETS
92 **Château de Villers-Cotterets** Built for Francis I by Jean and Guillaume le Breton c. 1520; improved by Henry II. Plain façade in Renaissance style; outstanding main staircase under coffered ceiling with sculpture of fine workmanship.

VINCENNES
93 **Château and Musée Historique** Medieval fortress, keep begun 14th C, extended 1560–1614. Royal residence until removal of court to Versailles. Museum: history of the château.

Paris
94 **Arc de Triomphe** Commissioned 1806, built from designs of Chalgrin, finished 1836. Decorated with relief of *The Marseillaise* by François Rude.

95 **Hôtel des Invalides** Oldest institution of its kind, founded by Louis XIV, designed by Libéral Bruant, begun 1671, destined for 5000 old and wounded soldiers. Façade in 3 storeys, upper part of central pavilion holds equestrian figure of Louis XIV and bronze statues of Justice and Prudence by Cousteau.

96 **Dôme des Invalides** Designed by J H Mansart in 1675, finished 1735. Square pile surmounted by drum, on which rests dome, divided into 12 sections adorned with gilded trophies. Main façade consists of Doric columns with Corinthian above. Interior: in form of Greek cross; crypt containing tomb of Napoleon in centre; paintings by Coypel above high altar.

97 **Hôtel de Sully** Built 1624 by Jean Androuet du Cerceau, bought 1634 by Sully, minister of Henry IV.

98 **Luxembourg Palace** Commissioned by Marie de Medici; built by Salomon de Brosse 1615. Resembles Pitti Palace, Florence. Main façade often restored, though still reveals original design. Garden façade remodelled 1836–44 by A de Gisors.

99 **The Madeleine** Begun 1806 in style of Roman temple by Napoleon I; architect P Vignon; finished 1842 by Huvé. Relief in tympanum of façade, by Lemaire, represents Last Judgment.

100 **Notre-Dame** Early Gothic, 1163 onwards. Wide central nave with double aisles; chevet with double aisles and exterior chapels. W front and towers c. 1200–1250; W front, 'the grandest composition in France'. Rose window (1220–25), largest of its day and a remarkable structural achievement; S transept a fine example of mature Rayonnant. Between 1220 and 1330 chapels built on N and S sides and around choir.

101 **Church of the Sorbonne** Built 1635–59; begun by Cardinal Richelieu. Fine and conspicuous dome. Interior: R transept contains tomb of Richelieu by Girardon. Spandrels of dome painted by Philippe de Champaigne.

102 **The Sainte-Chapelle** Gem of Gothic architecture, old palace chapel, built 1245–8 by Pierre de Montreuil for reception of sacred relics brought back from crusades. Restored after 1837 by Viollet-le-Duc. Interior: 2 chapels, upper and lower. Upper chapel noted for superb stained glass, subjects chiefly biblical.

103 **St Etienne du Mont** Built 1517–1618; Renaissance façade (1618), choir mainly Gothic. Very fine interior consisting of nave and aisles of almost equal height. Slender round pillars united by gallery bear vaulting; choir enclosed by magnificent jubet (1600–5); interesting stained glass in upper windows (1568).

104 **St Germain des Prés** Founded 543 by Childebert. Interior: nave 11th c; choir, consecrated 1163, afterwards altered; much restored in 19th c; S transept contains tomb of Olivier and Louis de Castellan (d. 1644, 1669) with medallions by Girardon.

105 **St Roch** Fine Baroque church, built 1653–1740 from designs by Lemercier. Façade later, by Robert de Cotte. Interior: paintings by Doyen, Vien, Chassériau; Baptism of Christ in marble by J B Lemoyne.

106 **St Sulpice** Begun 1646 from designs by Gamard, continued 1655 by Le Vau and others. Completed except façade 1733. Façade by Servandoni, consists of a Doric and Ionic colonnade, one above the other. Interior: nave and 2 aisles with spherical vaulting. Contains many 19th c frescos, including a series by Delacroix in R aisle.

107 **Val de Grâce** Particularly fine dome, begun by F Mansart in 1645 on the model of St Peter's, Rome. Continued by Lemercier and others, completed 1665. Interior: dome decorated with fresco by P Mignard (1660) containing 200 figures; also much sculpture.

108 **Bibliothèque Nationale** Cabinet des Médailles et des Antiques: collection of medals, cameos and objets d'art. Cabinet des Manuscrits: vast collection of medieval illuminated MSS. Cabinet des Estampes: prints and drawings from all periods; many foreign works.

109 **Ecole des Beaux Arts**
1. Musée des Monuments Français, where smaller monuments, or parts thereof, are preserved and displayed.
2. Ecole des Beaux Arts. Replaces former museum. Prize-winning paintings.

110 **Les Gobelins** Museum: history of Gobelin tapestry works.

111 **Grand and Petit Palais** Built for Exhibition of 1900. Grand Palais: Palais de la Découverte – science museum and planetarium. Petit Palais: Musée des Beaux Arts de la Ville de Paris.

112 **Louvre** Originally built as fortress for Francis I by Pierre Lescot in 16th c. Work continued in 17th c by Lemercier, and for Louis XIV by Baroque architect, Le Vau, and Perrault. 19th c N wing by Percier and Fontaine, completed by Napoleon III.
Museum departments:
1. Greek and Roman antiquities: Venus de Milo; fragment of Parthenon frieze.
2. Egyptian antiquities: the Mastaba; stele of the Serpent King; stele of Princess Nefertabiet; statue, Crouching scribe; bas-relief of Seti I.
3. Oriental antiquities: the Vulture Stele; stele of Naram Sin; statues of Gudea; code of Hammurabi; frieze of archers; sarcophagus of Eshmunazar.
4. Sculpture: Middle Ages, Renaissance and 17th c: statues of Charles V and Jeanne de Bourbon 14th c; tomb of Philippe Pot, 15th c; tomb of Louis Poncher and wife; Michelangelo Diana, Two Slaves; Cellini, Nymph of Fontainebleau; Coysevox, Marie Adelaide de Savoie; Houdon, Diana.
5. Objets d'Art: statue, Virgin of Jeanne d'Evreux; Palissy tapestries; Louis XIV–XVI period rooms.

6. Paintings: all schools incl. prints and drawings: Mantegna, *Madonna della Vittoria*; Leonardo, *Mona Lisa*; Poussin, *Inspiration of the poet*; Holbein, *Anne of Cleves*; David, *Oath of the Horatii*; Titian, *Jupiter and Antiope*; Dürer, *Self-Portrait*; El Greco, *Crucifixion*; Veronese, *Suzanne au Bain*.

113 **Musée des Arts Décoratifs** Decorative arts of all periods; tapestries, ornaments, jewellery, sculpture, etc. Noted for furniture, foreign and French.

114 **Musée Bourdelle** Sculpture, paintings, drawings by Antoine Bourdelle, in the house where he lived.

115 **Musée Carnavalet** History of Paris.

116 **Musée Cernuschi** Important works from the great epochs of China and Japan.

117 **Musée de Cluny** House of the abbots of Cluny, 1485–1500. Museum devoted to medieval art: tapestries – *La Dame à la Licorne*; metalwork: gold altarpiece from Basle; pieces from the Guarrazar Treasure.

118 **Musée Cognac-Jay** Collection of 18th c art treasures.

119 **Musée Eugène Delacroix** Artist's studio, where he died.

120 **Musée Guimet** Major French museum for Far Eastern art. Collections of sculpture; painting; ceramics; from India; Indochina; Central Asia; Tibet; China and Japan.

121 **Musée de l'Histoire de France** (Palais Soubise, also houses National Archives).

122 **Musée Jacquemart-André** Collection of French and Italian works of art, middle ages to 18th c; painting; tapestry; furniture; bronzes etc.

123 **Musée du Jeu de Paume** Museum of Impressionist paintings: Manet, *Déjeuner sur l'herbe*, *Olympia*; Monet, *La Gare de St-Lazare*; Renoir, *Le Moulin de la Galette*.

124 **Musée Nissim de Camondo** 18th c period house. Furniture; 18th c objets d'art; Aubusson tapestries.

125 **Musée Rodin** (Hôtel Biron) Sculptures by Rodin: The Gate of Hell; The Burghers of Calais; The Kiss.

126 **Palais d'Art Moderne** comprises 3 museums:
1. Musée National d'Art Moderne – Braque *Ace of Clubs* (1911).
2. Musée des Beaux Arts de la Ville de Paris.
3. Musée du Costume de la Ville de Paris.

127 **Palais de Chaillot** comprises 4 museums:
1. Musée de la Marine.
2. Musée de l'Homme: ethnographical collections.
3. Musée des Monuments Français: sculpture, frescos.
4. Musée des Arts et Traditions Populaires.

Champagne Lorraine Alsace

CHALONS SUR MARNE

128 **Cathedral of St Etienne** Romanesque towers; choir renovated in late 13th c; ambulatory and chapels above choir renovated c. 1300.

129 **Musée Municipal** Indian objects; archaeology; Romanesque capitals; paintings.

COLMAR

130 **Musée Unterlinden** Mathis Grünewald *Isenheim Altar*, finished c. 1515; Alsatian primitives.

COMMERCY

131 **Musée de l'Hôtel de Ville** Oriental porcelain and ivories.

EPERNAY

132 **Bibliothèque de la Ville** Illuminated MSS Gospel Book of St Ebbo.

EPINAL

133 **Musée Départmental des Vosges** Paintings: Rembrant *Portrait of a Woman*; Georges de la Tour *Woman visiting a Prisoner*; Flemish and French 17th c paintings; 18th c French drawings.

FLEVILLE

134 **Château de Fléville** 12th c keep; façade of centre building in French Renaissance style (16th c).

HAROUE

135 **Château de Craon** Built by Boffrand 1720–31 in classical style. Wrought iron gates by Jean Lamour; statues in parks by Guibal; tapestries from cartoons by Le Brun.

LUNEVILLE

136 **Musée Municipal and Musée Delorme** In Neoclassical 18th c château, designed by Boffrand (1703–6) for Duke Leopold of Lorraine. Paintings; sculpture, ceramics.

LUXEUIL LES BAINS

137 **Musée Archéologique des Thermes** Gallo-Roman exhibits.

NANCY

138 **Musée des Beaux Arts** Paintings: French school and old masters, Perugino, Tintoretto, Rubens, Ribera.

139 **Musée Historique Lorraine** In 16th c palace of the dukes of Lorraine. Exhibits relating to the history of Lorraine; prehistory; tapestries; French paintings.

RHEIMS

140 **Cathedral (Notre Dame)** Gothic, begun 1241 from designs of Jean d'Orbais; continued by Jean le Loup, Gaucher de Reims, Bernard de Soissons, and Robert de Coucy. W front begun 1241; W towers completed 1430; severely damaged in first world war. Interior: W end 13th c statues; 13th c rose window, pillar capitals carved in foliage (outstanding vintage scene). Treasury: 12th c chalice; reliquaries; goldsmiths' work.

141 **Musée des Beaux Arts** Tapestries; 15th–16th c painted cloths; paintings, outstanding works by Corot, Cranach the Elder, Cranach the Younger, Holbein, Amberger.

142 **Musée Historique et Lapidaire** Prehistory; medieval and Renaissance sculpture.

RONCHAMP

143 **Notre Dame du Haut** Chapel designed by Le Corbusier, built 1950–54.

SARREBOURG

144 **Musée Régional** Gallo-Roman and Merovingian exhibits.

SAVERNE

145 **Château de Saverne** Large 18th c classical building built for Cardinal Louis de Rohan. Architect Nicolas de Salins de Montfort. Very impressive N façade.

STRASBOURG

146 **Cathedral of Notre Dame** Romanesque cathedral destroyed by fire 1176; apse and crypt still survive. Reconstruction begun 13th c; W portals completed by 1291; N-W tower in 1365; spire started 1399 by Urich d'Ensingen. Cathedral much damaged during Revolution. Outstanding W façade designed by Meister Erwin of Steinbach; W portal and rose window. Interior: stone pulpit by Jean Hammerer 1496; S transept, angel pillar 1230–50; astronomical clock, original 1352–54, redesigned 1574 by Conrad Dasypodius and constructed by Isaac Harbrecht.

147 **Musée du Château des Rohan** In the Château des Rohan built by Massol in 1728–41. **Musée des Beaux Arts**; paintings of all schools, important works by Thomas de Keyser, Corot, D Teniers the Younger, Hans Memling, El Greco, Conrad Witz and 6 cartoons from studio of Leonardo da Vinci. **Musée des Art Décoratifs**; clocks; Strasbourg and Niderviller porcelain. **Musée Archéologique**: prehistory; Gallo-Roman objects.

148 **Musée de l'Oeuvre Notre Dame** Important collection relating to Strasbourg in middle ages and Renaissance, located in houses dating from 1347, 1578–85 and 17th c. Romanesque rooms: *Wissembourg Head of Christ, c.* 1070, oldest stained glass with figure. Gothic rooms; 15th c rooms; Renaissance rooms.

TROYES

149 **Cathedral (St Pierre)** Gothic. Started 1208; consecrated 1429. Flamboyant W front by Martin Chambiges; stained glass of various periods, including rose window by Jehan Soudain 1546. Treasury: reliquaries etc.

150 **St Urbain** Small church founded 1262 by Pope Urban IV, left unfinished till 19th c. Considered a gem of pure Gothic architecture,

in style of Sainte–Chapelle, Paris. Portals of main entrance and transept have porches erected *c.* 1300. Windows with 13th and 14th C stained glass, notable for beauty of tracery.

151 **Bibliothèque Municipale** Illuminated MSS, Bible of St Bernard.

152 **Musée des Beaux Arts** Archaeology; paintings; Limoges enamels.

Brittany
CARNAC
153 **Musée Préhistorique** Prehistoric collection.

COMBOURG
154 **Château de Combourg** Medieval fortress, 11th to 15th C. Square with round crenellated and machicolated towers at each corner; 11th C tower.

FOUGERES
155 **Château** Built 13th C to 15th C. Crenellated and machicolated curtain walls; 11 towers: Tour Mélusine, Tour Gobelin.

156 **St Sulpice** Flamboyant Gothic. Begun 1410, completed 18th C (choir); 17th C slate spire; granite retables in aisles.

HAUTE-GOULAINE
157 **Château de Haute-Goulaine** Late 15th C elegant Flamboyant Gothic façade and towers; early 17th C wings.

JOSSELIN
158 **Château de Josselin** Medieval fortress was dismantled in 1629, only 16th C dwelling house being allowed to remain. Fine Flamboyant Gothic façade with much sculpture. Elsewhere, fortifications that still remain are severe (3 round towers and linking curtain).

NANTES
159 **Cathedral** Begun 1434 by Duke John V from plans of Mathelin Rodier, completed 19th C. Renaissance tomb of Francis II and Margaret de Foix (erected 1503–7); tomb of Général de Lamoricière (1865) by Dubois.

160 **Château de Nantes** Built by Francis II, Duke of Brittany, in 1466, continued by his son. Fortress-like exterior. Interior: palace with transitional Gothic-Renaissance façades; 15th C well; tower of the golden crown: loggias in the Italian style.

161 **Musée des Beaux Arts** Paintings of all schools, works by Murillo, Guardi, Perugino, Cosimo Tura, De la Tour, Ingres, Greuze, Dufy, Van Dongen, Rouault.

RENNES
162 **Musée des Beaux Arts** Paintings of all schools: Veronese, *Perseus and Andromeda;* Jordaens, *Christ on the Cross;* Georges de la Tour, *Nativity.*

VANNES
163 **Musée de Peinture et de Sculpture** Paintings, including Delacroix *Calvary.*

Loire Valley
AMBOISE
164 **Château of Amboise** Castle existed on site since 496; royal residence 1434 to 1560. Chapelle St Hubert, fine example of Flamboyant Gothic (*c.* 1490). Lintel: Vision of St Hubert and Legends of St Christopher and St Anthony. Logis du Roi, begun 1491, with state rooms.

165 **Château du Clos-Lucé** 15th C; given by Charles VIII to Leonardo da Vinci who died there in 1519. 16th C frescos; exhibits relating to Leonardo.

ANGERS
166 **Château** Rebuilt by Louis IX, 1228–38. 17 towers and linking curtain wall; 15th C chapel. Collection of tapestries, 14th to 16th C: *Apocalypse Tapestries* woven by Nicolas Bataille (1375–80) from cartoons by Henniquin of Bruges.

167 **Musée Archéologique Saint-Jean** Medieval objets d'art; glass; Anjou calicoes.

168 **Musée des Beaux Arts** Most of the works of the sculptor David d'Angers. Paintings: Italian primitives; Dutch and Flemish 17th C; Watteau, Fragonard.

169 **Musée Turpin de Crissé** Egyptian antiquities; Greek and Roman vases; Japanese prints; European drawings: 17th, 18th and 19th C.

AZAY-LE-RIDEAU
170 **Château** Built 1518–27; retains heavy machicolated cornice of medieval type. Contemporary furnishings.

BLOIS
171 **Château de Blois** Fine examples of architecture from 12th C to 17th C. Seat of French kings in 16th C. Galerie Charles-d'Orléans 1445. Salle des Etats 13th C; Francis I wing 1515–24; Gaston d'Orléans wing built by F Mansart 1635–38. In château, **Musée Lapidaire;** Renaissance and later sculpture and painting.

172 **Musée des Beaux Arts** Paintings: Italian primitives; Corneille de Lyon *Portrait of Madeleine of France;* Antoine Caron *The Torture of Thomas More.*

BOURGES
173 **Cathedral of St Etienne** High Gothic, commenced *c.* 1190 by Archbishop Henri de Sully. Very large crypt (end of 12th C) vaulted in masterly style; magnificent stained glass 1215–25 and 15th and 16th C.

174 **Hôtel Cujas** Early Renaissance building *c.* 1515; architect Guillaume Pellevoysin.

175 **Hôtel Jacques Coeur** 1440–50 Built for the treasurer of Charles VII. Leading example of civil architecture of the period; built partly as residence, partly as trading establishment. Romanesque and Gothic sculpture.

176 **Hôtel Lallement** Early Renaissance (1487–1518) built as a residence for Jean Lallement. Furniture, tapestries, objets d'art.

177 **Musée de Berry** Important archaeological collection; paintings.

BRISSAC
178 **Château de Brissac** Medieval in origin but rebuilt 1610–20 by Charles de Cosse-Brissac. Contemporary furniture and tapestries.

CELLETTES
179 **Château de Beauregard** Built 16th C to 17th C. Gallery with 363 historical portraits; Delft tiling; 16th C woodwork.

CHAMBORD
180 **Château de Chambord** Started for Francis I in 1519. Central keep; corner towers and lantern over a great double spiral staircase; much Italianate decoration; 14 grand staircases and 440 living rooms.

CHAMPIGNY
181 **The Sainte Chapelle** Built as part of a château 1508–43 in Renaissance style. Château was destroyed on the orders of Richelieu. Stained glass by Robert Pinaigrier 1560–97.

CHAUMONT SUR LOIRE
182 **Château de Chaumont-sur-Loire** Medieval in appearance, altered by Charles of Amboise 1465–1510. Renaissance windows, carvings and other details.

CHENONCEAUX
183 **Château de Chenonceaux** 'Queen of the Loire Valley', built 1513–21 by Thomas Bohier incorporating medieval keep. Bridge over Cher designed by Philibert de l'Orme. Two storeyed gallery added by Catherine de Medici. 16th C tapestries, paintings; furniture.

CHEVERNY
184 **Château de Cheverny** 17th C Neoclassical style, completed 1634. Contemporary furniture and decoration; tapestries from cartoons by Simon Vouet.

CHINON
185 **Château de Chinon** Composed of 3 medieval fortresses, Château de Coudray (towers); Château du Milieu; Fort St Georges (built by Henry II of England, dismantled).

CUNAULT
186 **Church of Notre Dame** 12th C: frescos, capitals.

ECUEILLE
187 **Château du Plessis-Bourré** Built by Jean Bourré between 1468 and 1473, not substantially changed. Guard room with painted ceiling; contemporary furniture and ornaments.

EVRON
188 **Abbey Church** 12th to 14th C, 13th C reliquary.

LA FERTE SAINT AUBIN
189 **Château** Built in Louis XIII style at end of 16th C and in 17th C.

FONTEVRAULT L'ABBAYE
190 **Abbey** Fine Romanesque building, consecrated 1119. Contains tombs of Plantagenets, including Henry II and Richard I. Other monastic buildings include Romanesque kitchen; unique in France in its construction with 5 fireplaces, 20 chimneys; 16th C chapter house.

FOUGERES SUR BIEVRE
191 **Château** Begun 1470, built in old style. Windows in Renaissance style and other improvements added 16th C.

GERMIGNY DES PRES
192 **Church** Built in the time of Charlemagne, only one of this period left in France, much restored, famed for its contemporary apse mosaic *Ark of the Covenant.*

GIEN
193 **Musée de la Chasse à Tir et de la Fauconnerie** In château, mostly dating from end of 15th C; Gothic doorways. Paintings by François Desportes.

LE GRAND PRESSIGNY
194 **Musée de Préhistoire** Prehistoric exhibits.

LANGEAIS
195 **Château de Langeais** Important fortified country mansion, built mid-15th C for Jean Bourré. Contemporary furniture and fittings. Consists of 2 wings at right angles, dominated by 3 round towers with conical roofs.

LASSAY SUR CROISNE
196 **Château de Moulin** Built between 1441 and 1500 by Philippe du Moulin. Façades, red brick and white stone.

LAVAL
197 **Musée du Vieux Château** In the château of Laval, medieval, altered 16th C. Prehistory.

LOCHES
198 **Château de Loches** Medieval fortress and royal prison. Massive late 11th C keep with semi-circular buttresses; 15th C round tower; royal residence 14th and 15th C. Agnes Sorel tower: tomb of Agnes Sorel.

199 **Church of St Ours** Romanesque, unique roof consisting of series of hollow spires composed of narrowing courses of stone, the work of Thomas Pactius 1168. 11th C fresco in crypt.

LE LUDE
200 **Château du Lude** Reconstruction begun by Jehan de Daillon in 1457. Rectangular with large round towers at corners; Gothic N façade; Renaissance S frontage; remainder in style of Henry IV.

LE MANS
201 **Cathedral of St Julien** Romanesque nave 11th C and 12th C; choir completed 1254; transepts and towers early 15th C. 12th C S porch flanked by statues. 12th C glass in W window; rose window 1430 in N transept; Gothic choir: double ambulatory of unequal height. Windows 13th and 14th C. Baptistery: Renaissance tombs Charles d'Anjou by Francesco Laurana (1473); Guillaume du Bellay.

202 **Musée des Beaux Arts** Paintings; goldsmiths' work; Plantagenet enamel (12th C).

MARCILLY SUR MAULNE
203 **Château** Built end of 16th C. Good example of transition to Classical style with central pavilion and pavilions at ends of wings.

MAZE
204 **Château de Montgeoffroy** Built 1775 by Barré for Marshal de Contades. Furniture by the *ébonistes* Garnier and Blanchard.

MENARS
205 **Château de Menars** Simple 17th C building completed in 18th C by Gabriel for Madame de Pompadour and by Soufflot for her brother the Marquis de Marigny. Temple of Love by Soufflot in grounds.

MONTREUIL-BELLAY
206 **Montreuil Castle** Founded 11th C, added to and altered in 13th, 14th and 15th C. 13th-15th C gatehouse. Little Castle with kitchen 15th C, copied from Fontevrault abbey; New Castle (15th C). Church of Notre Dame.

MONTSOREAU
207 **Castle** Built by Jean de Chambes in 1440, transition between Gothic and Renaissance. Main block flanked by pavilions; decorated sentry walk; ornamental sculpture.

ORLEANS

208 Cathedral of Ste Croix Begun 1601 by Henry IV after destruction of previous cathedral. Completed 1829 in Gothic style. Choir: early 18th c woodwork.

209 Musée des Beaux Arts Paintings, especially French school; 5,000 drawings; 35,000 engravings. Sculpture: Pilon, Carpeaux, Rodin.

LE PLESSIS-MACE

210 Château Founded in 11th c; renovated 15th c by Louis de Beaumont in Renaissance style. Stair tower; wooden balconies in courtyard; Flamboyant Gothic chapel.

PONCE SUR LE LOIRE

211 Château Renaissance building altered 18th c. Remarkable Renaissance staircase under coffered vaulting of white stone with very fine sculpture, more than 130 motifs.

RICHELIEU

212 Château de Richelieu Built by Lemercier for Richelieu in 1631 in Louis XIII style; much of it demolished after Revolution; remaining portions include monumental entrance; orangery; cellar; one of the domestic buildings.

RIGNY-USSE

213 Château d'Ussé Medieval fortress with Renaissance additions. Severely military exterior constructed 15th c, wing added in 17th c; 17th c staircase. Renaissance Chapel in park. Aubusson tapestries and other decoration of the period.

SAINT BENOIT SUR LOIRE

214 Monastery of St Benoit Important monastic school; 11th c Romanesque. Famous capitals of the Tower Porch of the basilica.

SAINT GEORGES SUR ERVE

215 Château de Foullertorte Built 1570 in granite. Severe façade, showing transitional features from Renaissance to Classical.

SAINT GEORGES SUR LOIRE

216 Château de Serrant Large castle built from 15th c to 18th c. Chapel built to designs of J H Mansart. Library; staircase; furniture; paintings etc.

SAUMUR

217 Church of Notre Dame de Nantilly Romanesque. Flamboyant s aisle. 13th c wooden statue of Notre Dame de Nantilly; tapestries 15th c to 17th c.

218 Musée des Arts Décoratifs In 15th c château. French ceramics 16th c to 18th c; Limoges enamels.

SELLES SUR CHER

219 Château Selles-sur-Cher Renaissance building, constructed for Philippe de Béthune. Consists of 2 tall pavilions joined by arcaded gallery. Coffered ceilings; gilded chimney-pieces; 16th and 17th c furniture.

SULLY SUR LOIRE

220 Château de Sully Medieval, mainly built before 1360. Rectangular building with round corner towers; living quarters built early 17th c; unique timber framing of 1363.

TOUR EN SOLOGNE

221 Château de Villesavin Built 1537 by Jean le Breton, overseer of Chambord. Evolutionary building as all elements of defence were dropped.

TOURS

222 Cathedral (St Gatien) First cathedral destroyed by fire in 1168, rebuilding started 1170: choir, apse, and E chapels completed c.1260, most of rest by 1266. W front completed 1500; upper part of towers in 1507. In spite of differing styles, appearance presents unified whole, and provides opportunity to study evolution of Gothic style. Good Renaissance work, organ gallery, cloister galleries (1450); fine stained glass 13th to 15th c.

223 Musée des Beaux Arts Paintings, including Mantegna: *Christ in the Garden of Olives;* Boucher; sculpture.

VALENCAY

224 Château de Valençay Built c.1540 by Philibert de l'Orme for Jacques d'Estampes on site of 12th c fortress; W wing added 17th c. Building acquired by Talleyrand in 1803. Early examples of classical style; furniture; objets d'art.

VENDOME

225 Abbey (La Trinité) Architecture representative of entire Gothic period; Romanesque belfry c.1150; 15th c choir stalls; 13th c polychrome statues; stained glass, including 12th c Virgin and Infant.

226 Château Stronghold of Counts of Vendôme, built 11th c, altered 14th c and 17th c. 16th c dungeons.

VILLANDRY

227 Château de Villandry Medieval fortress converted by Jean le Breton, in 1532. Renaissance gardens, reconstructed 19th c.

Burgundy
Franche-Comté

ALISE SAINTE REINE

228 Musée Alésia Gallo-Roman objects.

229 Musée Municipal Gallo-Roman objects.

ANCY-LE-FRANC

230 Château of Ancy-le-Franc Built 1546 to plans of Serlio, earliest classical Renaissance building in France. Decoration and paintings by Primaticcio and his pupils; tapestries.

AUTUN

231 Cathedral Built on the relics of St Lazare 1121–46. Famous Romanesque portal *Last Judgment* by Gislebertus; Gothic nave. Sacristy: museum of Romanesque sculpture from church.

232 Musée Lapidaire Saint Nicholas Important Roman remains.

233 Musée Rolin Burgundian Romanesque sculpture The Nativity attr. to Master of Moulins (1480).

AUXERRE

234 Cathedral of St Etienne Gothic built 1215, sculptured medallion on N Portal, Adam and Eve. Gallery of 18 Romanesque arches; stained glass in chancel.

235 Abbey of St Germain Part Romanesque, part Gothic. Famous for 9th c series of frescos of the Life of St Stephen in crypt.

BEAUNE

236 Collegiate church of Notre Dame Burgundian Romanesque, commenced 1120. 14th c Gothic porch. 5 tapestries (1474–1500) Life of the Virgin.

237 Musée des Beaux Arts Paintings, furniture, objets d'art, Gallo-Roman items.

238 Musée de l'Hôtel-Dieu Built between 1443 and 1451 by Nicolas Rolin as a hospital, for which purpose it is still used. Flemish inspired courtyard. Polptych *The Last Judgment* by Roger van der Weyden; tapestries.

239 Hospice de la Charité Wrought iron latticework; furniture; tapestries; objets d'art.

BERZE LA VILLE

240 Priory of Berzé Important Romanesque frescos in chapel, oriental themes.

BESANCON

241 Musée des Beaux Arts Drawings (over 3,800), 110 by Fragonard; paintings; prehistoric and Gallo-Roman collections.

242 Gallo-Roman remains Porte Noire and triumphal arch.

BOURG EN BRESSE

243 Brou Church Late Gothic (1513–23) with some Renaissance features; built to design of van Boghem by order of Margaret of Austria. Interior: conservative plan; star vaults; rood screen with three centred arches; elaborately carved choir stalls, misericords and canopies, The Correction; Altar of the Seven joys of Mary; tomb of Margaret of Austria; stained glass locally made. Church also contains **Musée de l'Ain** Paintings, various schools; Breughel *Stork Hunting;* Dürer *Adoration of the Magi.* Furniture of 16th and 18th c.

BUSSY LE GRAND

244 Château de Bussy-Rabutin Medieval with many 17th c additions; façade 1649; gardens laid out by Le Nôtre.

CHATEAUNEUF

245 Chateauneuf Castle Commenced 12th c with 13th c and 15th c additions; Gothic façades on inner courtyard.

CHATILLON SUR SEINE

246 Musée Archéologique The Treasure of Vix, 6th c B.C.

CLUNY

247 Abbey Church of St Hugh Abbey founded 9th c, prototype of Cluniac architecture. Twin towers over narthex; cluster of 4 spires at crossing; fine capitals representing the seasons. Largely destroyed in 19th c.

CORMATIN

248 Château de Cormatin Late Renaissance. 17th c furnished apartments; ceilings.

DIJON

249 Bibliothèque Municipale Illuminated MSS Bible of St Stephen Harding.

250 Musée Archéologique Gallo-Roman, medieval and Renaissance exhibits.

251 Musée des Beaux Arts Situated in palace of the Dukes of Burgundy (14th–18th c). Works of Chartreuse de Champmol including tombs, Philip the Bold by Claus Sluter and Claus de Werve; altar wings by Melchior Broederlam (1399); Flemish and German primitives; paintings of all schools; Medieval and Renaissance objets d'art.

252 Musée de Hospices Civils Medieval sculpture.

253 Musée Magnin Paintings: works by Poussin, Fragonard, David, Géricault.

254 Musée Rude Mouldings of principal works of sculptor Rude.

FAREINS

255 Château de Fléchères Built by Jean Sève 1606–10 to designs of Androuet du Cerceau. Good example of Henry IV style. Chimney-pieces and ceilings decorated with arabesques.

FONTENAY

256 Abbey Cistercian monastery founded by Bernard of Clairvaux 1118. Church and cloisters: commenced 1130, consecrated 1147. Unadorned, proportions laid down for the Order have been carefully followed.

GRAY

257 Musée Paintings, works by Prud'hon; 17th c Flemish.

LANGRES

258 Cathedral of St Mammès Built 12th c Transitional style. Classic façade with towers rebuilt 18th c. Imposing interior: monolithic columns of choir with fine capitals surmounted by Romanesque triforium with coupled columns. Chapelle des Reliques: paintings attr. to Rubens and Correggio. Alabaster figure of Virgin in Lady Chapel, Notre Dame de la Blanche (14th c). Renaissance font (1549) in N aisle.

MACON

259 Musée des Beaux Arts Paintings: Titian *The Doge Monigatti,* canvases by Van Goyen, Coypel, Greuze, Courbet.

MARTAILLY LES BRANCION

260 Château de Brancion 10th c keep. Remodelled in 14th c by duke Philippe le Hardi.

MONTCLEY

261 Château de Montcley Built 1778 by Bertrand. Main façade arc shaped; main portico with 4 giant Ionic columns surmounted by a pediment. Much original furniture remains.

NEVERS

262 Musée Frédéric Blandin Ceramics: Limoges enamels.

ORNANS

263 Musée Courbet Paintings by Gustave Courbet.

PARAY LE MONIAL

264 Basilica of the Sacré-Coeur Built 1109 by Cluniac monks, similar to Cluny in plan. 11th c s tower; 12th c N tower; façade and nave typical of Burgundian style.

SALINS LES BAINS

265 Hospital Apothecary's laboratory. Moustiers faience; 17th c woodwork.

SENS

266 Cathedral of St Etienne First large French cathedral; begun c.1140; extensively altered and restored. Flamboyant transepts by Martin Chambiges 1490–1500; central portal: statue of St Stephen, end of 12th c. Interior: glass 12th c to 17th c. Very rich treasury; tapestries and 15th c altar hangings; 10th c Byzantine casket; chasuble of St Thomas à Becket; ivories.

267 Musée Lapidaire Gallo-Roman mosaics.

TANLAY
268 **Château de Tanlay** Built *c.*1550, after Ancy-le-Franc, first building to be constructed in pure French Renaissance style. Built on site of a medieval fortress by François de Coligny d'Anderlot; additions by Le Muet 1643–48. Furniture; frescoes, allegory of political and religious problems of 16th c. Neoclassical pavilion.

TONNERRE
269 **Hospital** Founded at end of 13th c by Marguerite of Bourgogne. Main ward 100 metres long with oak vaulting.

TOURNUS
270 **St Philibert** Built 1009–19, huge building of Burgundian-Romanesque type; once used as fortress. Interior: nave with large round pillars and transverse vaulting; in s aisle, 15th c tomb and Byzantine statue of Virgin in wood.

VEZELAY
271 **Abbey** Built 11th and 12th c while abbey was under Cluny. Nave has round arches throughout; across nave are heavy transverse arches supporting a groined vault; narthex has much remarkable sculpture, Christ of the Pentecost on central portal; choir rebuilt late 12th c in new Gothic style with some transitional features.

Poitou Saintonge
CHARROUX
272 **Abbey** Much of the abbey demolished 19th c. Octagonal Romanesque lantern tower. Museum in chapter house: late 13th c statues.

DAMPIERRE SUR BOUTONNE
273 **Château** Built end of 16th c. Wings now demolished. Courtyard façade with double-storeyed gallery, the upper with coffered roof.

DISSAY
274 **Château de Dissay** Built 15th c, enlarged 18th c, extensively restored 19th c. 15th c oratory with 16th c frescos and stained glass.

NIORT
275 **Musée des Beaux Arts** Tapestries; paintings.
276 **Musée du Donjon** (in the keep, 12th to 14th c). Ethnography.

OIRON
277 **Château d'Oiron** Begun by Arthur Gouffier in 1518, continued by his son, Marquis of Carabas. Part Gothic, part Renaissance. Rich ceilings and chimneypieces; frescos of 16th and 17th c.

POITIERS
278 **Cathedral of St Pierre** Begun 1162 by Henry II. Some parts Romanesque but Angevin style predominates. Façade 14th c, partly restored 19th c; unfinished towers; 13th c Porte St Michel. Superb stained glass of 12th to 13th c, Crucifixion in central window of apse.
279 **Baptistère Saint-Jean** 4th c; oldest Christian building in France; contains Merovingian sarcophagi and Romanesque frescos.
280 **Notre Dame de la Grande** Romanesque-Byzantine style, rebuilt 11th c; remodelled 15th and 16th c. Superb w façade with 3 tiers of arcades, in lowest of which is a round arched portal. Upper tiers contain statues of saints and apostles; pediment shows Christ blessing; turrets and spire have conical fish scale roofs. Interior: nave with barrel vaulting; remains of 12th c fresco on vaulting of choir.
281 **Musée des Beaux Arts** 1st c statue of Minerva; paintings; Romanesque capitals from old churches in Poitou.
282 **Hypogée des Dunes** Early Christian archaeology.

LA ROCHEFOUCAULD
283 **Château de la Rochefoucauld** 11th c keep. Substantial alterations in Renaissance style; wings 1528 to 1538; Renaissance courtyard with 3 tiers of galleries; spiral staircase.

LA ROCHELLE
284 **Musée des Beaux Arts and Musée Archéologique** Paintings; prehistory.

SAINTE PORCHAIRE
285 **Château de la Roche Courbon** Medieval fortress with 17th and 18th c alterations. Staircases and gallery; furniture.

SAINT SAVIN SUR GARTEMPE
286 **St Savin** 11th to 12th c church of the abbey, noted for its Romanesque paintings (*c.*1100), the finest examples in France. Vault of nave decorated with scenes from Genesis and Exodus; crypt shows the martyrdom of St Savin and St Cyprien.

SAINTES
287 **Musée Archéologique** Gallo-Roman exhibits; ceramics.
288 **Musée des Beaux Arts** Paintings including Breughel *Autumn.*

VERTEUIL
289 **Château de Verteuil** Triangular fortress, in possession of the de la Rochefoucauld family for 900 years. Much of present building 16th c; 11th c Romanesque chapel.

Auvergne Limousin Perigord
AIGUEPERSE
290 **Château de la Roche** Feudal castle, 11th c. Arms, tapestries, stained glass of 15th and 16th c.

AZAY LE FERRON
291 **Residence and Museum** 15th c tower. Main building 16th, 17th and 18th c. Furniture including Empire bedroom and Restoration rooms.

BEYNAC
292 **Château de Beynac** 13th c castle dominating Dordogne valley. Interior being restored; Gothic frescos in oratory.

BORT LES ORGUES
293 **Château du Val** 15th c feudal castle.

CAHORS
294 **Cathedral of St Etienne** Built on site of 6th c church by Bishop Geraud de Cardaillac at end of 11th c. Choir mainly rebuilt 1285–93; chapels added 14th to 15th c; 12th c portal; 14th c w façade; 14th c paintings in choir and 1st cupola. Flamboyant cloister 16th c.
295 **Pont Valentré** Medieval bridge begun 1308. Gothic arches, 3 machicolated towers and crenellated parapets. Well restored 19th c.

CASTELNAU
296 **Château** 11th c keep; large castle triangular in plan, set in double wall with 3 round towers. Damaged by fire in 1851, restored 1896–1932.

CHATEAUROUX
297 **Musée Archéologique** Celtic and Gallo-Roman exhibits.

CLERMONT-FERRAND
298 **Cathedral of Notre Dame** Gothic. Begun 1248 by Jean Deschamps. 14th c side-portals with unfinished towers; façade with 2 towers completed by Viollet-le-Duc in 19th c.
299 **Notre Dame du Port** Founded in 6th c, rebuilt 12th c. Shows earliest type of Auvergne-Romanesque style. Nave borne by engaged columns with sculptured capitals; stained glass from Sèvres in choir; crypt contains 'black' image of Virgin.
300 **Musée des Beaux Arts** Prehistoric and Romano-Gallic exhibits; faience; Limoges enamels; paintings; sculpture.

CORDES-ORCIVAL
301 **Château de Cordès** Manor of 13th–15th c, restored 17th c; park laid out by Le Nôtre.

COURPIERE
302 **Château de la Barge** 13th c with major 16th c alterations. Chapel with Renaissance glass.

COUSSAC-BONNEVAL
303 **Château de Bonneval** Built 1350. Chimneypieces, contemporary furniture, tapestries.

CULAN
304 **Château de Culan** Part of 15th c fortress above Arnon valley. 3 towers on valley side of château act as buttresses; inner courtyard with square towers.

EFFIAT
305 **Château d'Effiat** Built 1627 by Marshal d'Effiat. Neoclassical gateway: façade with giant Doric pilasters. Chimneypieces, painted ceilings and furniture.

LES EGRETEAUX
306 **Château d'Usson** Built between 1536 and 1545 at Echebrune and moved to present site at end of 19th c. Good example of domestic Renaissance architecture.

LES EYZIES
307 **Musée National de Préhistoire** Housed in château des Eyzies. Important collection of prehistory.

GUERET
308 **Musée Municipal** Limoges enamels; shrine of St Stephen 13th c. 17th and 18th c Aubusson tapestries.

HAUTEFORT
309 **Château de Hautefort** Considered by some to be the most beautiful château in Périgord. Built on remains of medieval castle by Nicolas Rambourg in 17th c. Centre building supported by 2 large square pavilions from which wings project and are terminated by round, domed towers.

LANQUAIS
310 **Château de Lanquais** Rebuilt mid-15th c by Isabeau of Limeuil. Part standard 15th c with tower, bare walls and gateway, part Renaissance with Italianate decoration. Chimneypieces; contemporary furniture and fittings.

LAPALISSE
311 **Château de Lapalisse** Medieval castle transformed into Renaissance building late 15th c. 15th c Gothic chapel with tomb effigies. Tapestries, paintings.

LIGNIERES
312 **Château de Lignières** Started 1645 on site of medieval fortress. Designed by Le Vau; surrounding moats by Larivière.

LIMOGES
313 **Musée National Adrien Dubouché** Ceramic museum: collection of 10,000 pieces.
314 **Musée Municipal de l'Eveché** Egyptology; Limoges enamels.

MEILLANT
315 **Château de Meillant** Frankish fortress, restored 1127 and again early 16th c by Jacondo. Good example of transition from Gothic to Renaissance. Lion tower with rich external decoration; well; chapel; stained glass; 15th c retable.

MONPAZIER
316 **Château de Biron** Castle comprising medieval, Renaissance and 17th c buildings. Village was within fortifications. Place Centrale and houses 13th c; chapel and parish church 15th c.

MOULINS
317 **Cathedral** Flamboyant Gothic. Stained glass windows; in sacristy tryptych by Master of Moulins *The Holy Virgin.*
318 **Musée Départemental et Municipal** Tapestries; ceramics; Gallo-Roman bronzes; terracotta figurines.

PERIGUEUX
319 **Cathedral of St Front** Originally Augustine abbey-church founded 6th c; became cathedral 1669. Possibly 11th c; fine tower; 12th–14th c cloisters. Rebuilt Abadie 1858.
320 **St Etienne** Dates from 11th and 12th c; resembles St Front; almost destroyed by Huguenots 1577. Contains huge carved oak reredos (17th c) representing Assumption.
321 **Musée du Périgord** Important prehistoric exhibits.

RAULHAC
322 **Château de Messilhac** Medieval with much Renaissance addition, particularly at entrance, and 2 square towers.

RAVEL
323 **Château de Ravel** Medieval with Renaissance, 17th c and 18th c additions. Gothic frescos; 17th and 18th c furniture.

ROCHECHOUART
324 **Château de Rochechouart** 15th c; 13th c towers. Centre court has gallery resting on torso pillars. 16th c frescos.

SAINT-JEAN-LES-PINASSE
325 **Château de Montal** Outstanding Renaissance building, started 1523 by Jeanne de Balsac for her son, Robert de Montal. Only 2 of 4 sides completed; dismantled 1879; restored 1908. Exterior, fortress-like. Interior richly sculptured.

SAINTE-MONDANE
326 **Château de Fénelon** Medieval fortress

with outer defences. 15th c dwelling with 16th c wings.

SAINT NECTAIRE

327 **Church** 11th to 12th c in typical Auvergne-Romanesque style. Contains 13th c reliquary of St Baudime; 12th c statue of the Virgin.

SOUVIGNY

328 **Musée Lapidaire** In Cluniac church of St Pierre 1100, rebuilt 1440. Tombs of Louis II of Bourbon (d. 1410) and Charles I (d. 1456).

TOURNEMIRE

329 **Château d'Anjony** 15th c fortress, with single square keep and round corner towers. Chapel and hall with 15th c frescos; 18th c rooms with contemporary furniture.

VILLARS

330 **Château de Puyguilhem** Early Renaissance building built 16th c by de la Marthonie. Hairpin shaped, with fat round tower; 18th c wing; rich decoration and sculpture.

VILLEGONGIS

331 **Château de Villegongis** Built c. 1530 on foundations of medieval castle, architect Pierre Nepveu. Much of decoration inspired by Chambord; very well designed roofs and chimneys; typical Renaissance staircases.

Lyonnais Savoie Dauphine

AIX LES BAINS

332 **Musée du Docteur Faure** Modern paintings and sculpture; many works by Rodin.

AMBIERLE

333 **Musée d'Art Sacré** (In 15th c church). Stained glass; choir stalls; retable by Master of Ambierle.

CHAMBERY

334 **Castle of the Dukes of Savoy** Founded 1232; rebuilt in 15th c; restored in 19th c. 14th c Tour des Archives; 13th c keep.

335 **Musée d'Histoire et d'Archéologie** Archaeology and prehistory.

GAP

336 **Musée des Hautes-Alpes** Principal exhibit: Jean Rochier, Mausoleum of Duke Lesdiguières.

GRENOBLE

337 **Musée Fantin-Latour** Works of Fantin-Latour.

338 **Musée de Peinture et Sculpture** Richest modern collection after Musée d'Art Moderne, Paris. Masterpieces of Italian school: Tintoretto *Holy Family*; 18th c; Canaletto *View of Venice*; modern French: Bonnard *White Interior*, Matisse *Pink Nude*, Picasso *Woman Reading*.

GRIGNAN

339 **Château de Grignan** Predominantly Renaissance (façade); Medieval foundations; Gothic courtyard; Louis XVI wing.

LYONS

340 **Musée des Beaux Arts (Palais des Arts)** Outstanding general collection. Paintings: Tintoretto *Danae*; Cranach *Portrait of a Woman*; El Greco *Christ Stripped by the Soldiers*; Gauguin *Nave Nave Mahana*, and many other important works of every period. Sculpture: *Attic Kore* of 6th c; Rodin *Walking Man*, etc.

341 **Musée Lyonnais des Arts Décoratifs** Furniture; applied arts.

342 **Musée Guimet** Egyptology; arts of the Far East.

343 **Musée Historique des Tissus** Remarkable collection of materials; Coptic; Byzantine, Sassanid, etc.

MONTBRISON

344 **Musée Municipal d'Allard** Small Greek and Roman gold exhibits.

VALENCE

345 **Musée** Paintings; 96 red chalk drawings by Hubert Robert.

VIENNE

346 **Church of St Maurice** All periods represented, central portal of w front good example of late Gothic. Mausoleum of Cardinal de Montmorin (1713); modern font.

347 **Temple of Augustus and Livia** Built c.A.D.41, resembles Maison Carrée, Nimes, but less well preserved.

348 **Musée d'Art Chrétien** Merovingian, Carolingian, Romanesque and Gothic sculpture; primitive Christian inscriptions.

349 **Musée Lapidaire Romain** In 6th c church of St Pierre. Gallo-Roman exhibits.

Guyenne Gascony

AGEN

350 **Musée Municipal** Greek statue, Venus of the Mas; Celtic treasures; paintings, 5 by Goya.

ALBI

351 **Cathedral of Ste Cecile** Fortress church in pink brick 1282–1512. Large vaulted hall with apse; series of 29 chapels. Very important rood screen with Flamboyant statuary; 16th c choir stalls.

352 **Musée Toulouse Lautrec** Extensive collection of works by Toulouse Lautrec; works by contemporary painters.

BAGNERES DE LUCHON

353 **Musée du Pays de Luchon** (in former château of Lassus Nestier 1772). Archaeology, ethnography, Gallo-Roman remains.

BAYONNE

354 **Musée Bonnat** Leon Bonnat collection. Paintings by El Greco, Rembrandt, Rubens, Reynolds, Ingres; more than 2,000 drawings, mainly Italian school.

BONAGUIL

355 **Château** Important medieval fortress built 1485–1525 by Beranger de Roquefeuil, designed to resist artillery.

BORDEAUX

356 **Musée des Arts Décoratifs** Exhibits cover middle ages to 18th c. European ceramics, enamels, glassware, silverware, furniture.

357 **Musée des Beaux Arts** Paintings: French 18th and 19th c; Veronese, Rubens. Sculpture: Duplessis, Lemoine, Rodin.

LA BREDE

358 **Château de la Brède** Medieval castle still in possession of family of original owners.

CADILLAC

359 **Château de Cadillac** Built c. 1600 by the Duc d'Epernon. Painted ceilings; mantlepieces; funerary chapel.

CONQUES

360 **Conques Abbey** Romanesque pilgrimage church with Last Judgment portal. Ecclesiastical exhibits: Reliquary of Pepin d'Aquitaine (817–838); Statue of St Foy, portable altars; reliquaries.

LARESSINGLE

361 **Village and Castle** 13th c fortified village; in centre castle of Bishops of Condom. Being restored.

LECTOURE

362 **Musée** Roman altars.

MOISSAC

363 **St Pierre** Present form dates from 12th and 15th c. Superb portal of 12th c, originally on w façade, but removed to s when tower was fortified. Sculptures in porch represent Annunciation, Visitation and scenes from Childhood of Christ; tympanum group shows Christ surrounded by Elders of Apocalypse. Cloisters dating from c. 1100 among finest in France.

MONTAUBAN

364 **Musée Ingres** Paintings and over 4,000 drawings by Ingres, *Portrait of Madame Gonse*.

PAU

365 **Musée des Beaux Arts** Paintings: Tintoretto, Oudry, Boudin, Jourdains, Ribera, Romney, Degas *Cotton Bureau at New Orleans*. Some sculpture.

366 **Musée National Henri IV** In Pau castle 12th c to 16th c, birthplace of Henry IV. Rich collection of tapestries.

RODEZ

367 **Cathedral of Notre Dame** Built of sandstone between 1277 and 1535. Severe exterior, w front flanked by 2 massive towers; elaborate rose window and gallery crowned with Renaissance pediment. Tower (1510–26) to N of apse, square below with 3 octagonal storeys above, lavishly decorated and flanked with 4 turrets bearing statues of Evangelists. Fine Gothic screen.

SAINT BERTRAND DE COMMINGES

368 **Cathedral of Notre-Dame** Romanesque narthex 1120–40. Gothic aisleless building (1304–50). Rood loft; choir screen; bishop's throne. Ambulatory: glass of 1539; tomb of Bishop Hugues de Châtillon (1450); tomb of Bishop Bertrand de Miramont (d. 1258). E end: shrine of St Bertrand (15th, 16th c). Romanesque cloister. Treasury: medieval reliquaries and sacerdotal robes.

369 **Musée de Comminges and Galerie du Trophée** Roman exhibits.

TOULOUSE

370 **Cathedral (St Etienne)** Nave begun in 11th c, altered 1100. New choir started 1272 but never finished; Flamboyant portal (1449); 16th c tapestries in nave; stained glass in apse (1611–12); Arthur Legoust, statue of Antoine de l'Estang (d. 1617).

371 **Church of the Jacobins** Brick fortress church, built 1260–92. Used as barracks during 1st Empire, now being restored to original state. Large blind arches surmounted by oculi join buttresses; octagonal bell-tower. 2 equal naves divided by cylindrical columns.

372 **St Sernin** Largest and most perfect Romanesque church in France; started c. 1060; completed by 1271. Octagonal tower with short spire; twin doorways of s transept *Porte des Comptes* with capitals showing the deadly sins and triumphs of virtue; *Porte Miégeville* (c. 1120) in s side of nave with tympanum depicting the Ascension. Apse; 5 chapels; relief of the beardless Christ (late 11th c); Renaissance stalls in choir (1670). Treasury: gold and silver.

373 **Musée des Augustins** Situated in buildings of Augustinian priory; great cloister, late 14th c. Outstanding collection of Romanesque and medieval sculpture 11th c capitals from La Daurade. Paintings: Perugino; Rubens *Christ on the Cross*; Delacroix; Morisot; Toulouse-Lautrec.

374 **Musée Georges Labit** Arts of the Middle and Far East, some fine sculpture and rare Kan Sou neolithic vases (China).

375 **Musée St Raymond** Roman busts and marbles, Labours of Hercules; history of art; ceramics.

Provence

AIGUES-MORTES

376 **Tower of Constance and ramparts** The tower built by Louis IX mid-13th c. Ramparts built for Philip the Bold by Simone Boccanegra of Genoa 1272. Both in fine condition.

AIX-EN-PROVENCE

377 **Cathedral of St Sauveur** Romanesque, built 1175. 14th c tower; Flamboyant Gothic façade (1525); important 16th c doors of Gothic portal. Tryptych: Nicholas Froment *Burning Bush*.

378 **Musée Bibliographique et Archéologique** Provençal faience; paintings and sculpture.

379 **Musée Dobler** Country house built 1654–1669. Furniture of period.

380 **Musée Granet** Paintings: French, Italian, Flemish, Dutch; self portraits by Rembrandt; Ingres, Cézanne. Sculpture: Greek and Roman.

381 **Musée des Tapisseries et de l'Ameublement Ancien** (in former 17th and 18th c archbishop's palace). Important Beauvais tapestries of same period.

ANTIBES

382 **Château of Antibes** Residence of de Grasse family when princes of Antibes. Episcopal palace: residence of Grimaldi family, lords of Antibes 1385 to 1608.

383 **Musée Grimaldi** Modern paintings; works by Picasso.

ARLES

384 **Musée d'art Chrétien** Christian art, 4th and 5th c sarcophagi.

385 **Musée Lapidaire Païen** Important Roman remains.

AVIGNON

386 **Palais des Papes** Outstanding example of 14th c military architecture. N part built by Benedict XII 1334–41; w and s wings added by Clement VI with great audience chamber

(1352); Tour St Laurent added by Innocent VI. Extensively damaged during Revolution; subsequently used as barracks and prison; restorations in progress since 1920. Great audience chamber built by Jean de Loubières; vault painting by Matteo Giovannetti of Viterbo (c.1353). Pope's chapel; Tour de la Garde-Robe; important 14th c frescos.

387 **Musée Calvet** Paintings: 14th, 15th and 16th c primitives of Avignon and Rhône Valley schools; French: 17th to 18th c.

388 **Musée Lapidaire** Celtic, Roman and Gallo-Roman sculptures: Monster of Noves; Poumières Venus.

CARPENTRAS

389 **Musée d'Art Décoratif** Furniture, tapestries.

390 **Musée Duplessis** Paintings particularly French; 15th c *Rencontre à la Porte Dorée*.

CAVAILLON

391 **Musée Archéologique** Gallo-Roman remains.

CHATEAU GOMBERT

392 **Musée d'Art Provençal** Faience.

GRASSE

393 **Musée Fragonard** Paintings by Fragonard; history of art in lower Provence.

LOURMARIN

394 **Château de Lourmarin** 15th c fortress and Renaissance palace built 1540 for Blanche de Levis. Circular staircase and chimneypieces.

MARSEILLES

395 **Musée Archéologique** Greek ceramics; Phoenician, Greek and Gaulish items; Egyptian exhibits.

396 **Musée des Beaux Arts** Paintings of all periods, Flemish, Italian and French schools; works by Daumier.

397 **Musée Cantini** Marseilles and Provençal ceramics.

398 **Musée Grobet Labadie** Medieval sculpture; drawings; paintings.

MOUSTIERS-SAINTE-MARIE

399 **Musée de la Faience** Ceramics.

NICE

400 **Musée des Beaux Arts** 17th c Gobelin tapestries after frescos by Raphael at Vatican. Paintings: Italian and Spanish primitives; French School.

401 **Musée Massena** Works by Impressionists; objets d'art; faience; jewellery. Important library bequeathed by Chevalier de Cessole.

NIMES

402 **Musée des Antiques in Maison Carrée** Maison Carrée: Augustan temple, of outstanding workmanship, pseudoperipteral, with a colonnade which encircles the building and is partly engaged in the walls of the cellar; Corinthian capitals. Museum: Roman exhibits.

403 **Musée Archéologique** Roman and Gallo-Roman exhibits.

404 **Musée des Beaux Arts** Paintings: French, Flemish, Dutch and Italian.

ORANGE

405 **Arch** Roman triumphal arch with triple doors framed by Corinthian columns. Probably erected in reign of Emperor Tiberius in A.D.21.

406 **Musée** Roman exhibits; paintings by Sir Frank Brangwyn.

SAINT JEAN CAP FERRAT

407 **Musée l'Ile-de-France** Furniture; paintings; ceramics, especially Sèvres.

SAINT REMY

408 Important archaeological site. Gallo-Roman city of Glanum, destroyed in barbarian invasions of 3rd c. There remains a fine mausoleum and triumphal arch.

SAINT TROPEZ

409 **Musée de l'Annonciade** Modern paintings: Vuillard, Bonnard, Matisse, Braque.

TARASCON

410 **Château** Outstanding medieval fortress, very well preserved. Started in 12th c and continued until 15th c. King René of Sicily was particularly active in its construction during the 14th c.

TOULON

411 **Musée des Beaux Arts et d'Art Naval** Paintings: Italian Renaissance and French 17th and 18th c.

UZES

412 **Château d'Uzès** Medieval fortress with many Renaissance and later additions. Square 12th c keep built by Bermonde, first of Uzès family. 14th c buildings; Renaissance façade (c.1550) attr. to Philibert de l'Orme; early example of superimposition of the three orders; Gothic chapel (restored); Renaissance staircase with coffered ceiling.

VENCE

413 **Chapel of the Dominicans** Built 1950; decorated with painted ceramic tiles and stained glass by Henri Matisse.

VILLENEUVE LES AVIGNON

414 **Church of Notre Dame** Built 1333 to 1335. 10th c epitaph of St Casaria; high altar; figure of dead Christ by Duparc (1746). Sacristy: 14th c ivory Madonna.

415 **Fort St André** Built second half of 14th c by John the Good and Charles V. Outstanding entrance with 2 twin towers; curtain walls enclose 11th c Romanesque chapel, the town of St André and a Benedictine Abbey. Abbey includes main entrance and a vaulted building.

416 **Musée de l'Hospice** Paintings, including Enguerrand Charonton *Coronation of the Virgin* 1453.

Languedoc Roussillon

CARCASSONNE

417 **Musée des Beaux Arts** Paintings: 17th and 18th c French and some modern (Ernst, Dali, Picasso); faience.

418 **St Nazaire** Romanesque nave c.1095; Gothic transepts and apse c.1300–1320; stained glass windows 13th and 14th c. Statues in choir reminiscent of Rheims and Amiens.

419 **City Ramparts** Outstanding example of medieval military architecture; double row of ramparts. Restored by Viollet-le-Duc 1855.

CASTRES

420 **Musée Goya** Paintings by Goya include: *Sitting of the Royal Philippine company*. Spanish primitives and modern works.

CASTRIES

421 **Château de Castries** Built 1565; rebuilt in Neoclassical style; park laid out by Le Nôtre in 1666.

CERET

422 **Musée d'Art Moderne** Paintings, mostly Cubist.

MONTPELLIER

423 **Musée Atger** (in 14th c Benedictine convent). Paintings by Jordaens, Van Dyck, Raphael, Michelangelo, Tiepolo, Fragonard Fine drawing collection.

424 **Musée Fabre** Paintings: Italian and Dutch schools, French 18th to 20th c. Delacroix *Les Femmes d'Alger*; Courbet *Bonjour M. Courbet*. Over 2,000 drawings.

NARBONNE

425 **Cathedral of St Just** Gothic, consists of a large unfinished choir only; towers added in 15th c; 15th c chapter house contains ecclesiastical objects.

426 **Church of St Paul Serge** Built round tomb of an early Christian martyr, 12th c to 14th c; choir 1229.

427 **Musée des Arts et de la Céramique** Ceramics including Gallo-Roman pottery; enamels; paintings.

428 **Musée Lapidaire** In former 13th c church of Lamourguié. Roman monumental sculpture.

PERPIGNAN

429 **Le Castillet** Principal gateway of medieval defences, built of rose-red brick c.1360.

430 **Cathedral of St Jean** Started 1324, completed 1509. Nave very broad with series of altar pieces in the Catalan manner; altar by Bartolomé Soler of Barcelona (1620).

431 **Palace of the Kings of Majorca** 13th c. Courtyard with arched gallery of 2 tiers; Gothic doorway.

LE PUY EN VELAY

432 **Cathedral** Important Romanesque pilgrimage church. Arabic style façade with 6 Islamic domes. Romanesque fresco of St Michael in N transept. Chapel of Death: 16th c fresco *Arts Liberaux*. In cloister, mosaics of larva.

433 **Chapel of St Michel d'Aiguilhe** 6th c origin; 9th c early Romanesque portal; traces of Romanesque frescos.

434 **Museum of Crozatier** Painting *La Vierge au Manteau* anon. beginning 15th c.

ST MARTIN DU CANIGOU

435 **Abbey and Church** Abbey ruined; now reconstructed. 11th c Byzantine church with barrel vaulted nave.

SALSES

436 **Château de Salses** Only example of Spanish military architecture in France; built by Dom Sanche of Castille, on instructions of King Ferdinand, in 1497–1504; restored by Vauban in 17th c.

Corsica

AJACCIO

437 **Musée Fesch** Important collection of Italian paintings 14th to 18th c.

Acknowledgements

The numbers in heavy type refer to colour illustrations.

The publishers gratefully acknowledge the consent of the following for permission to reproduce subjects illustrated in this book:

© S.P.A.D.E.M., Paris 1968. 204, **214, 225,** **227, 228, 231,** 235, 240, 241, 242, **245, 249, 250.**

© A.D.A.G.P., 215, 237, **244, 246.**

Photographs were provided by the following:
Aerofilms, London 23; J. Allan Cash, London 110; Archives Photographiques, Paris 44, 80, 147, 148; Art et Industrie du Poitou 29; Atlasphoto, Paris 60; Bibliothèque Nationale, Paris **52, 53, 54,** **85, 97, 98, 99, 101**; Bildarchiv Foto Marburg 38, 43, 88, 111; B. Biraben, Bordeaux 18; E. Boudot-Lamotte, Paris **27, 28,** 40, 45, 55, 57, 61, 69, 86, 93, 112, **120,** 135, 159; Bulloz, Paris 128, 130, 154, 160, 169, 170, 174, 176, 177, 179, 204; Camera Press, London 243; J. Camponagara, Lyons 19; J. Dieuzaide, Toulouse 78, 95; French Government Tourist Office, London 46, 56, 104, **250**; Giraudon, Paris **frontispiece,** 15, 30, **31,** 36, 48, 49, 65, 76, **77,** **84,** 91, **119,** 124, 134, 136, 150, 152, **171, 185, 187, 195,** 199, 200, 201, 203, 209, **214, 225, 227,** 236, **b, d**; F. Guerard, Paris **122;** S. Guiley-Lagache, Paris **183;** Halin, Paris **i**; Hamlyn Archive 70, 178; André Held–Josph P. Ziolo, Paris **13,** 35; L. Hervé, Paris **121,** 241, **249;** H. Hinz, Basel **6,** 11, **14;** Hirmer Verlag, Munich 206; M. Holford, London 64, 67, 68, **83,** 89, 157, **196, 212, 226,** 234, 235, **a, f**; G. Karquel, St Denis 87, **184;** A. F. Kersting, London 58, **132, 161,** 193; R. Laniepce, Paris 208; E. Lessing/Time-Life **33**; Mansell Collection, London 126; Matignon, Paris 158; Musée des Arts Décoratifs, Paris 129, **142,** 168, **224;** Musée de l'Homme, Paris, 219; Musée Nissim de Camondo, Paris 166; Musée St Germain 2, 8, 10, 24; Roger Perrin, Arcueil 90; La Photothèque, Paris 144, 156; Rapho, Paris 192, 220, **246,** 247; Rapho/Ciccione 47; Rapho/Danese **163;** Réalités/Connaissance des Arts **143,** 153, **186, 194, g;** Réalités/R. Bonnejoy 189; Réalités/J. Guillot **51,** 167, **248;** Réalités/Ionesco **244;** H. Roger-Viollet, Paris 7, 9, 92, 103, 113, 123, 125, **139,** 240; J. Roubier, Paris 1, 16, 19, 21, 22, 25, 26, 37, 39, 41, 42, 59, 66, 81, 94, 216; Scala, Florence **front jacket, 71, 72, 74, 75, 96, 100, 102, 108, 109, 115, 117, 118, 131, 140,** 162, 165, 172, 173, **207, 211, 213,** 218, **245, c**; Service Photographique, Versailles **half-title, 73,** 79, 105, 106, **107,** 114, 116, 127, 133, **137,** 138, **141,** 145, 146, 149, 151, 155, **164,** 175, 180, 181, 182, **188, 190,** 191, **197, 198,** 202, 205, 210, 215, 217, 221, 222, 223, **228, 229, 230, 231,** 232, 233, 237, 238, 239, 242, **e;** Studio Remy, Dijon **32;** Editions Valoire, Blois **117a;** Jean Vertut, Paris **3, 4, 5, 12;** J.P. Viel/Hachette **50;** Yan, Toulouse 63, 82; Zodiaque, Yonne **62.**

Index

The numbers in heavy type refer to illustrations and those in italics to the Museums and Monuments index.

Abadie, P. *319*
Abaquesne, Masseot *81*
Abbate, Niccolò dell' 80,91,**128**
Abbeville *1,2,3*
Abstraction-Création *154*
Academy of Painting and Sculpture 101,119,120,142
Afro 157,161
Agen *350*
Aigueperse *290*
Aigues-Mortes *376*
Aix-en-Provence 27,*377–381*
Aix-les-Bains *332*
Ajaccio *437*
Albi 59,147,153,**78**,*351–2*
Alençon *16,17*; lace 103,*18*
Alesia 22,**24**
Aliscamps, les 27
Alise Sainte Reine *228–9*
Altar of Rome and Augustus 24,**19**
Amabilis of Bordeaux 25,**18**
Amberger *141*
Ambierle *333*
Amboise 74,75,*164–5*
Amboise, Cardinal Georges d' 74
Amiens 53,*4,5*
Amphitheatres 24,25,**23**
Ancy-le-Franc 79,*230*
Andelay, Jean d' 45
Anet 80,88,**113,122,130**,*52*
Angelico, Fra 65,133
Angers 61,*166–9*
Angoulême 39
Anguier, Michel 96
Anjony, Château de, Tournemire *329*
Anjou, Charles d' 73,*201*
Annunciation Master **69**
Antibes *382–3*
Appel, Karel 157,161
Aqueducts 25,**34**
Arches, Roman 22–3,25,**27**,*242,405,408*
Arles 7,23,24,25,26,36,39,**23**,*384–5*
Arp, Jean 157,161
Arras 6
Art Déco 141
Art Nouveau 141,153–4,**224,236**
Asnières 53
Aubert, J. 55
Aubusson tapestries 112,*213,308*
Audran, Claude 113,115
Autun 25,26,36,37,40,**20,42**,*231–3*
Auvergne-Romanesque *299,327*
Auxerre *234–5*
Aveyron *13,1*
Avignon 7,*59–60*,**95**,*386–8*
Avignon *Pietà* 65,147,**96**
Azay-le-Ferron *291*
Azay-le-Rideau 75,79,**105**,*170*

Baerze, Jacques de 61
Bagatelle, Château de la, Abbeville *1*
Bagnères de Luchon *353*
Balleroy *20*
Bandinelli, Baccio 76
Barbiere, Domenico del *81*
Barbizon school 144
Barge, Château de la, Courpière *302*
Baroque 95, 102, 103, 105, 113, **145, 146, 153, 159**, *105,112*
Bartolommeo, Fra 76
Basle altarpiece **212**,*117*
Bataille, Nicolas 166
Baudot, Anatole de *154,157*
Bayeux 39,**64**,*21–2*
Bayonne *59,354*
Bazaine, Jean 157,161
Bazille, F. 153
Beatus of Liebana **54**
Beaune 36,65,*236–9*
Beaurains, treasure of *6*
Beauregard, Château de, Cellettes *179*
Beauvais 34,*53*; tapestries, carpets **195**,*381*
Bec 39
Bedford, John of Lancaster, Duke of **99**
Beistegui, Carlos de 148
Belcayre *9*
Belleville Breviary 60
Bellay, Cardinal Jean du 80
Bérain, Jean 113
Beranger de Roquefeuil *355*
Bernard of Clairvaux (St Bernard) 40,*256*
Bernard de Soissons 53,*140*

Bernay *23*
Bernini, G. L. 102,103,105,**145**
Berry, John, Duke of 61,62,73,**83,84**,*57*
Berthouville, treasure of 26
Berzé la Ville 36,**49**,*240*
Besançon 25,26,*241–2*
Beynac *292*
Bibles 35,38,40,51,54,*151,249*
Biot *147*
Birague, René de 82
Biron, Château de, Monpazier *316*
Blois 74,75,94,**120,121**,*171–2*
Boccanegra, Simone *376*
Boffrand, G. 116,**183**,*135,136*
Boghem, L. van *243*
Bohier, Antoine 75
Bohier, Thomas 74,75,*183*
Bonaguil *355*
Bonnard, Pierre 153,155,**235**,*338,409*
Bonnat collection *354*
Bonneval, Château de, Coussac-Bonneval *303*
Bontemps, Pierre 80
Bordeaux 81,*356–7*
Bort-les-Orgues *293*
Botticelli, Sandro 148
Boucher, François 7,116,118,119,**171,185**,*28*
Boucicaut Book of Hours 62
Boudin, Eugène 156,*32,37,365*
Bougereau, A. W. 134
Boulle, André-Charles 103,**141,143**
Boulogne *7,8*
Bourdelle, A. 147,153,*114*
Bourg en Bresse *243*
Bourges 52,53,62,73,**75,83,92,93**,*173–7*
Brancion *260*
Brancusi, Constantin 155,156,**237**
Brangwyn, Sir Frank *406*
Braque, Georges 155,*126*,**409**
Brassaï 157,161
Brassempouy venus 10,**7**
Brécy *24*
Brède, Château de la *358*
Breton, Gilles le 76,**110**
Breton, Guillaume le *92*
Breton, Jean le *92,221,227*
Breuer, Marcel 157
Breughel 147,*243,288*
Brissac *93,178*
Broederlam, Melchior 61,*251*
Bronzino 133
Brosse, Salomon de 93,94,*98*
Brou *243*
Bruant, Libéral 95
Bruyas 134,**203**
Bullant, Jean 81,82,**104**,*57*
Bullet, J-B *56*
Burgundian Romanesque **42**,*231,233,236,270*
Bury 74
Bussy-Rabutin, Château de, Bussy le Grand *24,4*
Byzantine *270,280,435*

Cabanel, A. 134
Cabrières-d'Aygues 25
Cadillac *359*
Caen 39,40,**45**,*25–8*
Cahors 39,*294–5*
Caillebotte, G. 143,144,**214**
Calder, Alexander 157,161
Callot, Jacques 93,**157**,*28*
Cambrai 53
Cambrai, Jean de **83**
Camonde, Count Isaac de 143
Campana collection 133,134,**208,213**
Canaletto *338*
Cannes 153
Carcassonne 59,**90**,*417–9*
Carlingian 33–5,**47,51,52**,*40,192,348*
Caron, Antoine *133,172*
Carpaccio 129,**208**,*28*
Carpeaux, Jean Baptiste *15,209*
Carpentras 23,**25**,*389–90*
Carriera, Rosalba 116
Carrouges *29*
Castanet *9*
Castelnau *296*
Castres *420*
Castries, Château de *421*
Cavaillon *391*
Cellettes *179*
Cellini, Benvenuto 79,91,**126**,*112*
Celts, Celtic 13,21–22,**15,17,32**,*297,350,388*
Centula *see* St Riquier
Ceramics 21,79,81,101,103,119,**142,188**, *and see* Museums and Monuments index
Cerceau, Jean Androuet du **135**,*97,255*
Céret *422*
Cernon-sur-Coole *21*
Cessole library *401*
Cézanne, Paul 143,144,156,**227**,*380*
Chaâlis *55*

Chagall, Marc 155,156,**246**
Chalgrin, J. F. T. *94*
Challuau *76*
Châlons-sur-Marne 21,*128–9*
Chambéry *334–5*
Chambes, Jean de *207*
Chambiges, Martin *54,149,266*
Chambiges, Pierre *76,84,87*
Chambord 76,**119**,*180*
Champaigne, Philippe de 94,95,**133**,*101*
Champigny *181*
Champmol, Charterhouse of 61,**80**,*251*
Champs sur Marne *56*
Chantilly 81,115,*57*
Chardin, Jean-Baptiste 118,120,**175,187**
Charlemagne 33–4; talisman of 35,**51**
Charles I, King of England, collection of 94,103,**137, 138**
Charles V, King 60,61,62,**79**
Charles VII, King 62,65,73
Charles VIII, King 73
Charles IX, King 79,81; shield of **115**
Charleval 81
Charleville 93
Charonton, Enguerrand *416*
Charroux *272*
Chartres 7,36,51,52,53,**67–8,71,88**,*58–9*
Chassériau, T. 105
Châteaudun 60
Château Gombert *392*
Châteauneuf *245*
Châteauroux *297*
Châtillon sur Seine *246*
Chaufard 148
Chaumont sur Loire *182*
Chaux 120
Chenonceaux 75,82,**104**,*183*
Chéret, Jules 153
Chevalier, Etienne 65
Cheverny, Château de **156**,*184*
Chinese art **166**,*116,120,374*
Chinon, Château de *185*
Chiragan 25
Chocquet, Victor 144
Christine de Pisan 60,**101**
Cimabue 129,**207**
Citeaux 40
Classicism, Classical style 94,95,96,102,103,120,**144, 188**,*24,72,77,135,145,203,215,224*
Claude Lorraine 95,96,*164*
Clères *30*
Clermont-Ferrand *298–300*
Clos-Lucé *165*
Clouet, François 76,*57*
Clouet, Jean 76,**102**,*57*
Cluny 36,37,51,**39,40**,*247*
Cochin, Charles Nicolas 118
Coeur, Jacques 62,**92,93**,*175*
Colbert, Jean-Baptiste 101,103,104,105,**150**,*85*
Coligny d'Anderlot, François de *268*
Colmar *130*
Colombe, Michel 75,**103**
Combourg **154**
Commercy *131*
Compiègne 119,*61–3*
Conques 38,39,**44,50**,*360*
Constructivism 142
Contamin, Victor 154
Cordès-Orcival *301*
Cormatin *248*
Cormont, Thomas de *4*
Corneille de Lyon *172*
Corot, J. B. C. *141,147*
Correggio, Antonio 94,103,128,129,**137**,*258*
Corsica *437*
Cortona, Domenico da 76,**119**
Cosse-Brissac, Charles de *178*
Costa, Lorenzo 94
Cotte, Robert de 105,*71,89,105*
Coucy, Robert de *140*
Coucy-le-Château *10*
Cougnac 10,**3**
Courances *64*
Courbet, Gustave 133,134,148,153,**203**,*32,259,263, 424*
Courpière *302*
Cousin, Jean *52*
Coussac-Bonneval *303*
Cousteau, G. 95
Coutances 52,*31*
Couze *11*
Coypel, Antoine 105,114,**146**,*96,259*
Coysevox, Antoine 103,105,**132,150,159**,*112*
Cranach, Lucas 148,*141,340*
Craon, Château de, Haroué *135*
Cressent, Charles 116,**181**
Crozat, Pierre 115
Cubism *422* *and see under individual artists*
Culan *304*
Cunault *186*

Dada 141
Dali, Salvador *417*
Dammartin, Guy de *62*
Dampierre *65*
Dampierre-sur-Boutonne *273*
Dasypodius, Conrad *146*
Daumier, Honoré 148, *396*
David d'Angers *168*
David, Gérard *48*
David, J-L. 120, 127, 128, 130, 134, 148, **180**, **190**, *112*, *253*
Degas, Edgar 153, **204**, *365*
Delacroix, Eugène 129, 130, 133, 134, 148, **196**, *106*, *119, 163, 373, 424*
Delamaire, R-A. *114, 116*
Delaroche, Paul 133
Delaunay, Robert 142, **215**
Denis, Maurice 153
de Noailles culture 9, 10, **3**, **4**, **12**
Denon, Vivant 129, 130
Derain, André 155
Deschamps, Jean 59, *298*
Despiau, Charles 153
Desportes, A-F. 119, **170**, *56, 193*
'Diablotins' 12, **10**
Diaghilev, Serge 155
Dieppe *32*
Dijon 25, 36, 61, *249–54*
Dissay *274*
Douai *11*
Doyen, Gabriel François 119, *105*
Dreux *66*
Dubois *159*
Ducerceau, Jacques Androuet **129**
Duparc *414*
Durand-Ruel, Paul 144
Dürer, Albrecht 148, **222**, *28, 112, 243*
Dutch school of painting *6, 12, 168, 404, 424, and see individual artists*
Duvivier, Claude **168**
Dyck, Anthony Van 105, 148, *423*

Ebbo, Archbishop 34; Gospel Book of 34–5
'École de Paris' 148, *156*
Écouen 81, 82, 88
Écueillé *187*
Effiat, Château de *305*
Egyptian art 133, *63, 112, 169, 314, 342, 395*
Eiffel, Gustave 154, **216**
El Greco 148, *5, 112, 147, 340, 354*
Enamels **115**, **131**, *23, 34, 152, 218, 262, 300, 308, 314, 356, 427*
Entremont 22
Épernay *132*
Épinal *133*
Ermenonville *67*
Ernst, Max *417*
Étampes *68*
Étampes, Duchesse d' *79, 84*
Étruscan art *49*
Évreux *33–4*
Évreux, Jeanne d', Virgin of 60, **76**, *112*
Eyck, Jan van *65*

Faience *42, 48, 265, 300, 378, 392, 401, 417*
Falaise *35*
Fantin-Latour, H. *337*
Fareins *255*
Fécamp *75*
Fénelon, Château de, Sainte-Mondaine *326*
Fenouillet 22
Fère-en-Tardenois *81*
Flamboyant style 65, **86**, **87**, *2, 16, 27, 33, 41, 45, 54, 87, 149, 156, 157, 158, 164, 210, 217, 266, 317, 351, 370, 377*
Flemish school *6, 12, 13, 15, 133, 168, 251, 257, 396, 404 and see individual artists*
Fleury-en-Bière *69*
Fléville *134*
Folleville *75*
Font de Gaume 10, 11
Fontaine, P.F.L. *112*
Fontaine-Henry *36*
Fontainebleau 7, 76, 79, 80, 81, 93, **110**, **117**, **118**, *70*; School of 76, 79, 80, 82, **131**
Fontenay 40, **46**, *256*
Fontevrault 39, *190*
Fosse, Charles de la 105, *114, 115*
Fougères *155–6*
Fougères sur Bièvre *191*
Foullertorte, Château de, Saint-Georges-sur-Erve *215*
Fouquet, Jean 65, 73, **85**
Fouquet, Nicolas 95, 102, *76*
Fragonard, Jean-Honoré 119, 120, **173**, **177**, *5, 48, 168, 241, 253, 393, 423*
Francis I, King 75–6, 79, 80, 85, 86, **102**, **108**, **117**; style 75, **105**, **121**, *36*
Francis II, King, tomb of *159*
Franks, Frankish 27, 33, *315*
Fréjus 23, 25, 27
Frescos 25, 36, 59, 81, **49**, **117**, **118**, **146** *and see*

Museums and Monuments index
Froment, Nicholas *377*
Furniture 79, 96, 103, 114, 116, 118, 119, **105**, **129**, **141**, **181**, **186**, *and see* Museums and Monuments index

Gabillou *10*
Gabo, Naum 142, 155
Gabriel, Ange-Jacques 118, 119, *205*
Gabriel, Jacques 118, *61*
Gachet, Dr 143, **229**
Gaggini, Pace 75
Gailde, Jean **94**
Gaillard *19*
Gaillon 74, 75, **103**
Gallari, Claude *64*
Gallé, Emile 154, **224**
Gallo-Roman 24–7, **19**, **33**, **34**, **35**, *34, 144, 147, 228, 229, 237, 241, 242, 250, 267, 287, 297, 300, 318, 349, 353, 388, 391, 403, 408, 427*
Gamard *106*
Gap *336*
Garnier, Charles **193**
Garnier and Blanchard *204*
Gaston Phebus, Comte de Foix **97**
Gaucher de Reims 53, *140*
Gauguin, Paul 156, **228**, *340*
Geertgen tot Sint Jans 148
Géricault, Théodore 130, **205**, *253*
German school *12, 251 and see individual artists*
Germigny-des-Prés 34, **47**, *192*
Gérôme, J.L. 134
Giacommetti 162
Gien *193*
Gillot, Claude 115
Giocondo, Fra Giovanni 74
Giorgione *103*
Giovannetti, Matteo *386*
Girardon, François 103, 105, **148**, *101, 104*
Girart d'Orléans 60
Gisors, A. de *98*
Giusti, Antonio 74, **124**
Giusti, Giovanni **124**
Gobelins 101, 103, 113, **147**, *110, 400*
Godefroid de Claire 52
Godescalc Gospels 34, **52**
Gogh, Vincent van 143, 156, **229**
Goncharova, N. 155
Gothic 51–4, 59–62, 65 *and see* Museums and Monuments index
Gouffier, Arthur *277*
Goujon, Jean 80, 81, 82, 91, **112**, *47, 52*
Goya 148, **200**, *12, 350, 420*
Goyen, Jan van *259*
Graincourt-lès-Havrincourt *25*
Grand *25, 26*
Grasse *393*
Gray *257*
Greece, Greek art 21, **30**, **31**, **206**, **220**, **233**, *8, 49, 63, 112, 169, 246, 340, 344, 350, 380, 395*
Grenoble 33, *337–8*
Greuze, Jean-Baptiste 120, **178**, *161, 259*
Grignan *339*
Gris, Juan 155
Gros, J.A. 134, **201**
Grosbois *93*
Grünewald, Mathis 130
Guardi, Francesco 133, *161*
Guarrazar treasure 117
Guéret *308*
Guermantes *71*
Guibal *135*
Grignan *339*
Guimard, Hector 154
Guise family 80, 81

Hals, Frans 133
Hammerer, Jean *146*
Haras-du-Pin *44*
Haroué *197*
Harpignies, Henri *15*
Hautefort *309*
Haute-Goulaine *157*
Henniquin of Bruges *166*
Henry II, King 79–80, 81, 82, **111**, **123**, *83*
Henry III, King 80, 81
Henry IV, King 93, **152**;—style *200, 255*
Héré, E. 118, *122*
Hobbema, Meindert 133
Holbein, Hans *112, 141*
Hooch, Pieter de 133, **199**
Houdon, Jean-Antoine **176**, *112*
Huet, Paul *56*
Huvé, J. *99*

Illuminated manuscripts, Carolingian 34–5, **52**; Romanesque 38, 40, **54**; Gothic 52, 53, 54, 61–2, 65, **77**, **84**–5, *17–1, 101. See also 13, 57, 108, 132, 151, 249*
Impressionists 134, 142, 143, 144, 153, *123, 401 and see individual artists*

Indian art 120, *129*
Ingeborg psalter 52, 53, **77**
Ingres, J.A. 129, 130, 133, 134, 147, **191**, **197**, *65, 161, 354, 364, 380*
Isenheim Altar *130*
Isturitz *11*
Italian school *12, 168, 172, 354, 396, 400, 404, 411, 424, 437 and see individual artists*
Ivories 35, **2**, **4**, **7**, **91**, *32, 131, 266, 414*

Jabach collection 103, **137**, **138**
Jacquio, Ponce **123**
Japanese art 116, 120, *169*
Jean le Loup 53, *140*
Jewellery 33, 35, **51**, *401*
Jordaens, Jacob 162, *365, 423*
Josselin *158*
Jossigny *72*
Jouarre 33, **37**, *73*
Jourdain, C.R.F.M. 154
Jumièges 39, *39–40*
Juste, Jean *83*

Kahnweiler, D.H. 154
Kandinsky, Wassily 154
Keyser, Thomas de *147*

Labattut *9*
La Bouvandau *21*
La Brède *358*
La Caze collection 133, 134, **209**
Lace 103, *18*
La Charité-sur-Loire *36*
La Daurade *373*
La Ferté-Saint-Aubin *189*
Lamour, Jean **184**, *135*
Lanfranc, Abbot *39*
Langeais 36, *195*
Langres *258*
Lanquais *310*
Laon 51, 52, **89**, *74–5*
Lapalisse *311*
'La Poire' venus 10, **2**
Laressingle *361*
Largillière, Nicolas de *105*
Larionov, M. 155
Larivière *12*
La Rochefoucauld *283*
La Rochelle *284*
Lascaux 7, 9, 10, 11, 141, **6**, **11**, **14**
Lasgraisses *22*
Lassay-sur-Croisne *196*
La Turbie *23*
Laugerie *11*
Laurana, Francesco 73, *201*
Laussel 10, **12**
Laval *197*
Lavalée *130*
Leblanc, Abbé *118*
Le Brun, Charles 95, 101, 102, 103, 104, 105, 110, 130, **132**, **139**, **147**, **153**, **154**, *76, 85, 135*
Le Cateau *9*
Le Corbusier 155, 156, 157, **241**, **249**, *143*
Lectoure **362**
Leczinska, Maria 116, **169**
Ledoux, Claude-Nicolas 119, 120, 133
Léger, Fernand 147, 156, **250**
Legoust, Arthur *370*
Le Grand-Pressigny *194*
Le Havre 155, 156, *37*
Le Lude **200**
Lemaire *99*
Le Mans 52, 73, *201–2*
Lemercier, Jacques 94, *105, 107, 112, 212*
Lemoine, François 116, **182**, *20, 357*
Lemoine, Jean *16*
Lemoyne, J.B. *105*
Le Muet, Pierre *268*
Le Nain, Louis 95, 147, **155**, *75*
Lenoir, Alexandre 129, 130
Le Nôtre 102, 105, **163**, *64–5, 71, 76, 90, 244, 301, 421*
Leonardo da Vinci 74, 75, 94, 128, **107**, **127**, *112, 147, 165*
Le Plessis-Macé *210*
Leptolithic 9, 10, 12, **2–7**, **11**, **13**, **14**
Le Puy 38, *432–4*
Les Andelys *19*
Les Combarelles 10, 11
Lescot, Pierre 80, **112**, *112*
Lesdiguières mausoleum *336*
Les Egreteaux *306*
Les Eyzies *307*
Lespugue venus 10, 141, **4**
Le Sueur, Eustache 95
Le Vau, Louis 94, 95, 102, 105, **139**, **153**, **163**, *76, 84, 90, 106, 112, 312*
Liber S. Jacobi 38
Lignières *312*
Lille 128, *12*
Lillebonne 27, **35**
Limbourg brothers 59, 61–2, **84–5**

Limoges 38, *313–4*; Enamels **131**, *152, 218, 262, 300, 308, 313, 314*
Limosin, Léonard **131**
Llorens-Artigas, José **244**
Loches *198–9*
Loo, Carle van 116, 119
Lorenzetti, Ambrogio 60
Lothair 35, **53**
Loubières, Jean de *386*
Louis VI, King 45
Louis VII, King 45
Louis IX (St Louis) 40, 45, 53, 54, *86*; Bible Moralisée of 54; Crown of 54, **73**
Louis XI, King 40, 73
Louis XII, King 74, **124**, 83
Louis XIII, King 93, 94, 102; style *81, 189, 212*
Louis XIV, King 94, 95, 101, 103, 105, 113, **132**, **144**, **145**, **147**, **149**
Louis XV, King 105, 116, 118
Louis XVI, King 120
Louis XVIII, King 130
Louis-Philippe 130
Lourmarin *394*
Louviers *41*
Louvois, François 104
Lunéville *136*
Luxembourg Palace *98*
Luxeuil 33
Luzarches, Robert de *4*
Lyons 23, 24, 27, 79, 103, **33**, *340–3*

Mâcon *259*
Madeleine, la 10, 12
Madrid, Château de 76
Maeght foundation 156–7, **248**
Magdalenian culture 10–12, **8**, **10**, **11**, **13**
Maillol, Aristide 153
Maisons Laffitte 94, 96, **158**, *77*
Mallarmé, S. 147, 148
Malmaison **195**, *82*
Malraux, André 156, 162
Manet, Edouard 134, 144, 156, **198**, **202**, **226**, *123*
Mannerist style 80, 93, 94
Mansart, François 94–5, **158**, *20, 24, 77, 107, 171*
Mansart, Jules Hardouin 102, 105, 113, **132**, **161**, *44, 65, 84, 85, 90, 96, 216*
Mantegna, Andrea 94, **211**, *112, 223*
Marchant, Guillaume *84*
Marcilly-sur-Maulne *203*
Marly 105
Marseilles 9, 21, 73, 155–6, *395–8*
Martailly-les-Briancion *260*
Martini, Simone 59
Marville, Jean de 61
Massilia 9, 21, 22
Massol **147**
Master of Ambierle *333*
Master of the Death of the Virgin **91**
Master Erwin of Steinbach 146
Master Honoré 54, 60, **98**
Master of Moulins 148, *233*, *317*
Matisse, Henri 150, 153, 154, 155, 156, 157, **231**, **247**, *9, 338, 409, 413*
Matta 157, 161
Maurs 39
Mayeul 36
Mazarin, Cardinal 93, 94, 101, 103, **134**
Maze *204*
Mazzoni, Guido 74
Medici, Catherine de' 80, 82, **123**, *83, 183*
Medici, Marie de' 93, **152**
Megalithic 12–13, *9*
Mehun-sur-Yèvre *62*
Meillant *315*
Meissonier, J.A. 116, 133, 134, **168**
Memling, Hans *147*
Menars *205*
Menhirs 13, **1**
Mercoliano, Dom Pacello da 74
Merovingian 33, **37**, **48**, **90**, *49, 73, 144, 279, 348*
Mesnières-en-Bray *43*
Mesopotamian civilizations 147, **210**, **217**, **218**, **221**, *112 (3)*
Messilhac *322*
Metalwork 21, 35, 52, 53, 54, 60, **15**, **76**, **212**
Metz 25
Meudon 81
Michelangelo 74, 76, 81, 128, **125**, **194**, *12, 112, 423*
Mignard, Pierre 102, 104, *107*
Millet, Jean François 148
Mique, Richard **189**
Miró, Joan 157, 162, **244**
Moissac 38, **56**, **57**, *363*
Mondrian, Piet 154, 155
Monet, Claude 144, 154, **225**, *48, 123*
Monpazier *316*
Montabert, Paillot de 129
Montagu, Jean de *91*
Montal, Château de, Saint-Jean-les-Pinasse *325*
Montastruc rock shelter **8**
Montauban 93, *364*

Montbrison **344**
Montespan 11
Montcley *261*
Montfaucon 45
Montfort, Simon de 59
Montgeoffroy, Château de, Maze *204*
Montmaurin 25
Montmorency, Anne de, Constable of France 80, 81, **131**
Montor, Artaud de 129
Montpellier 153, *423–4*
Montreuil castle *206*
Montreuil, Pierre de 45, 53, 59, **55**, **72**, **74**, *84, 102*
Montsoreau *207*
Mont-St-Michel 40, **61**, **62**
Moore, Henry 157, **243**
Moreau, Gustaveer 147
Moreau-Nélaton 143
Morisot, Berthe *373*
Morosov, Ivan 154
Mosaics 25, 26, 27, 34, **33**, **47**, *192, 267*
Mosan 52, 53
Moulin, Philippe du *196*
Moulin, Château de, Lassay-sur-Croisne *196*
Moulins *317–8*
Moustiers 103, *265*
Moustiers-Sainte-Marie *399*
Murillo 128, 148, 161
Musée des Monuments Français *129–30*
Muséum Central des Arts 127, 128
Myneul **143**

Nancy 93, 118, **184**, *138–9*; Ecole de 153, 154, **224**, **236**
Nantes 51, *159–61*
Nanteuil, Robert **134**
Napoleon I 127, 130, **201**
Napoleon III 133, 134
Narbonne 25, 59, *425–8*
Natoire, Charles-Joseph 116, **183**
Nattier, Jean-Marc **169**
Neoclassicism 119, 120, 127, 129, 133, **189**, **191**, **197**, *136, 184, 268, 305, 421*
Neolithic 9, 12, 13, *9*
Nepveu, Pierre *331*
Nervi, Pier Luigi 157
Nevers 101, *262*
Niaux 10, 11, **13**
Nice *400–1*
Nîmes 23, 24, 25, 26, **34**, *402–4*
Niort *275–6*
Noguchi, Isamu 157, 161
Noves 22, **17**, *388*
Noyon 51, *78*

Obreri, Pierre 59
'Oculi *13*, *371*
Odo, Abbot of Cluny 36
Oeben, François **186**
Oiron *277*
Oppenord, Gilles-Marie 115
Orange 22–3, *405–6*
Orbais, Jean d' 53, *140*
Orbay, François d' *90*
Orléans *208–9*
Orme, Philibert de l' 80, 81, 82, **104**, **113**, *84, 52, 183, 224, 412*
Ornans *263*
Oudry, Jean Baptiste 116, *10, 365*

Pacherot, Jerome **103**
Pactius, Thomas *199*
Palissy, Bernard 81, *112*
Palla, Giambattista della 76
Paray-le-Monial 36, **41**, *264*
Parement de Narbonne 60
Paris 38, 51, 53, 54, 62, 93, *94–127*; Arc de Triomphe *94*; Church of the Visitation *95*; Cité de Refuge 155; Cluny abbey 130, **111**; Collège des Quatre Nations *95*; École des Beaux Arts 75, *109*; École Militaire 119; Eiffel Tower 142, 154, **215**, **216**; Grand and Petit Palais *111*; Hôtel Aubert de Fontenay *93*; Hôtel de Beauvais *93*; Hôtel de Carnavalet 93, 94; Hôtel de Guise 81, 114, *167*; Hôtel Lambert 93, 95, 96, **153**; Hôtel de Lauzun 93, 95; Hôtel de Mayenne 93; Hôtel Soubise 114, 116, **167**, *183*; Hôtel de Sully 93, **135**, *97*; Hôtel de Ville 153; Invalides 105, 113, **96**, *72*; Jeu de Paume 156, *123*; Les Arènes 24; Louvre 80, 93, 101, 105, 127, 128, 129, 130, 133, 147–8, 156, **139**, *112*; Luxembourg Palace 93, 104, *98*; Madeleine **192**, *99*; Musée National d'Art Moderne 156, *126*; Notre Dame 53, *74*, *100*; Notre Dame de Raincy 157; Opéra 156, **193**, **246**; Palais Royal 93, 94, 114; Pantheon 118, 153, *179*; St Catherine du Val-des-Ecoliers 82; Ste Chapelle 53–4, 60, *72, 102*; St Etienne-du-Mont *103*; St Germain-des-Prés *104*; St Jean de Montmartre 154; St Roch 96, 119, **174**, *105*; St Sulpice *106*; Sorbonne, church of the 94, 103, *101*; Théâtre des Champs Elysées 153; Tuileries 82, **159**; UNESCO building 156, 157,

243–5; Val-de-Grâce 94, 95, *107*
Pau *365–6*
Pechialet 10
Pech-Merle 10, **5**
Pellegrini, G. A. 116
Pellevoysin, Guillaume *174*
Penni, Luca **109**
Pépin d'Aquitaine **50**, *360*
Percier, Charles *112*
Périgueux 26, 39, *319–21*
Perpignan *429–31*
Perrault, Claude 102, 105, **139**, *85, 112*
Perret, Auguste 153, 155, 156, 157
Perrier, François 95
Perugino 94, *28, 48, 138, 161, 373*
Pevsner, Antoine 155
Philip IV, King 59
Philip the Bold, Duke of Burgundy 61, *251*
Philip the Good, Duke of Burgundy 65
Picasso, Pablo 141, 153, 154, 155, 156, 157, **242**, **245**, *338, 383, 417*
Pierrefonds *79*
Pilgrimage churches 38, 52, 53, 53, **44**, **63**, *432*
Pilon, Germain 82, 91, **111**, **114**, **123**, *209*
Pinaigrier, Robert *181*
Pisanello 148
Pissarro, Camille 144, *32*
Plessis-Bourré, Château du, Ecuéillé *187*
Poisson, Pierre 59
Poitiers 33, 39, 62, **60**, *278–82*; Minerva of 26, *29*
Poitiers, Diane de 74, 80, 81, **109**, **122**, **130**
Pompadour, Mme de 118, 119, **165**, *205*
Ponce-sur-le-Loire *211*
Pont Flavien 25
Pont-du-Gard 25, **34**
Pontormo, Jacopo 76
Porta, Antonio della 75
Portel, le *11*
Post-Impressionists 144, 156
Poumières Venus *388*
Pourbus, Frans, the Younger 93
Poussin, Nicolas 94, 95–6, 102, 103, 104, 147, **162**, *28, 57, 110, 253*
Prehistoric art 9–13, **1–14**, *3, 63, 72, 84, 139, 142, 147, 153, 194, 197, 241, 284, 307, 321, 335*
Primaticcio, Francesco 79, 80, 81, 82, **108**, **111**, **118**, **123**, *70, 83, 230*
Proudhon, P. J 134, **203**,
Prouvé, Victor **224**
Prud'hon, P. P. *257*
Psalters 52, 53, 54, **77**
Pucelle, Jean 60
Puget, Pierre 105, **160**
Puvis de Chavannes, Pierre 153
Puyguilhem, Château de, Villars *330*

Rambouillet *80*
Rambourg, Nicolas *309*
Raphael 76, 94, 102, 103, 104, 127, 128, 129, **108**, **151**, *400, 423*
Raulhac *322*
Ravel *323*
Rayonnant style *21, 45, 100*
Rembrandt 104, 105, 133, **209**, **238**, *28, 133, 354, 380*
Renaissance 65, *73–82 and see* Museums and Monuments index
Rennes 93, *162*
Renoir, Pierre Auguste 144, 153, **214**, *123*
Reynolds, Joshua *354*
Rheims 25, 26, 34, 51, 52, 53, 65, **51**, **65**, **69**, **70**, *140–2*
Ribera 133, *138, 365*
Richelieu 94, *212*
Richelieu, Cardinal 94, 96, 103, **136**, *101*
Riesener, Jean-Henri **186**, **189**
Riez 27
Rigaud, Hyacinthe 105, **149**
Rigny-Ussé *213*
Robbia, Girolamo della 76
Robert, Hubert 119, *67, 345*
Robin, Pierre *47*
Roche Courbon, Château de la, Sainte-Porchaire *285*
Rochechouart *324*
Rochefoucauld *283*
Rochier, Jean *336*
Rococo 113, 116, 118, 119, 120, **168**, **181**, **183**, **186**, *72*
Rodez 59, *367*
Rodier, Mathelin *159*
Rodin, Auguste 144, 147, 153, **240**, *125, 209, 332, 340, 357*
Rohan, Château des, Strasbourg *147*
Rolin, Nicolas 65, *238*
Roman 22–4, **18–20**, **23**, **25–9**, **32**, **34**, *49, 112, 169, 232, 344, 362, 369, 375, 380, 385, 388, 402, 403, 405, 406, 428*. *See also* Gallo-Roman
Romanesque 36–40, 45. *See also* Museums and Monuments index
Romano, Giulio 79, **108**, *70*
Romanticism 129, 134, **196**
Romney, George *365*
Ronchamp 156, 157, **249**, *143*
Roquepertuse 22, **16**

Rose windows 52, 53, 59, *33*, *58*, *100*, *140*, *146*, *149*, *201*, *367*
Rosny 93, *81*
Rosso Fiorentino 79, 81, **117**, *70*
Rothschild, Baron James de *133*
Roualt, Georges 155
Rouen 7, 25, 39, 65, 80, **86–7**, *45–9*; ceramics 81, 103, **142**, *23*, *48*
Rousseau, J. J. 120, **176**, *67*
Rousseau, Théodore 148
Roland le Roux *46*
Rubens, Peter Paul 93, 104, 105, 114, 128, 148, **152**, *28*, *138*, *258*, *354*, *357*, *373*
Rude, François *94*, *254*
Ruysdael, Jacob van *133*

St Baudime 39, **36**, *327*
St Benedict 34, 36, 37
St Benoît-sur-Loire 37, 38, *214*
St Bertin Gospels 40, *7*
St-Bertrand-de-Comminges *368–9*
St Cher, Hugues de 54
Saint-Colombe-sur-Seine *21*
St Denis 33, 34, 45, 51, 53, 54, 60, 74, 75, 80, 82, **55**, **123–4**, *83*
St Ebbo Gospel Book *132*
Ste .. y 39, **44**, *360*
Sai.. Georges-sur-Erve *215*
Sa.. Georges-sur-Loire *216*
St Germain 76, *84*
Saint-Germain-de-Livet *50*
Saint-Gilles-du-Gard 38, 39
St Hugh of Semur 36
Saint-Jean-Cap-Ferrat *407*
Saint-Jean-les-Pinasse *325*
Saint-Jouin-de-Marnes 39
St Louis *see* Louis IX
St Martial, Bible of 38
St Martin du Canigou **38**, *435*
St Maur-les-Fossés 80, 82
Sainte-Mondane *326*
St Nectaire 39, *327*
Saint-Omer *13*
Saint-Porchaire 81, *285*
St Quentin 53, *14*
Saint-Rémy 23, 27, **27–8**, *408*
St Riquier 34
Saint-Savin-sur-Gartempe *286*
St Sever Apocalypse **54**
St Stephen Harding 40, *249*
Saint Tropez *409*
Saintes 25, *287–8*
Salins de Montfort, Nicolas de *145*
Salins-les-Bains *265*
Salses *436*
Sambin, Hugues **129**
Sarcophagi 27, 33, **21**, **2**, *279*, *384*
Sarrazin, Jacques 96, **144**
Sarrebourg *144*
Sarto, Andrea del 76, **106**
Sassetta **232**
Saumur *217–8*
Saverne *145*
Sceaux *85*
Selles-sur-Cher *219*
Senlis 51, *86–7*
Sens 51, 53, *266–7*
Serlio, Sebastiano 79, 80, *230*
Serrant, Château de, Saint-Georges-sur-Loire *216*
Sert, José Luis **248**
Servandoni, J. N. *106*
Seurat, Georges 142, 156, **230**
Sèvres **188**, *88*, *299*, *407*
Shchoukin, S. I. 154
Sickert, W. R. *32*
Sireuil venus 10
Sisley, Alfred *32*
Sluter, Claus 61, **80**, *251*
Sohier, Hector 27
Soissons 51, 59, **66**, *89*
Solario, Andrea 74
Soler, Bartolomé *430*
Solesmes 74
Sommerard, A. and E. du 130, 139
Sorel, Agnes *198*
Soudain, Jehan *149*
Soufflot, J. G. 118, **179**, *205*
Souillac 38
Souvigny 51, *328*
Spanish school *12*, *400*, *420* and see *individual artists*
Stained glass 52, 53, 54, 81, **71–2**. *See also* Rose windows *and* Museums and Monuments index
Stein, Gertrude 154
Strasbourg **82**, *146–8*
Suger, Abbot of St Denis 45, 51
Sully, Maximilien de Béthune, Duc de 93
Sully, Maurice de **74**
Sully-sur-Loire *220*
Surrealism 141, 154, 155

Tal Coat, Pierre 162

Tamayo, Rufino 157, 161
Tanlay *268*
Tapestries 61, 95, 101, 103, 119, **64**, **100**, **122**, **147**, **156** *and see* Museums and Monuments index
Tarascon *410*
Taverna, Giulio **116**
Temple, Raymond du 60
Temples, Roman 22, 23, 25, 26, **26**, *347*
Teniers, David 114, *147*
Textiles 103, *343*
Teyjat 10, 11, 12, **10**
Theatres, Roman 23–4, 25, **23**
Theodochilde tomb **37**, *73*
Thomy-Thiery collection 148
Tiepolo, G. B. 133, *28*, *423*
Tintoretto *28*, *138*, *338*, *340*, *365*
Titian 94, 103, **138**, *112*, *259*
Tonnerre *269*
Toulon *411*
Toulouse 38, 59, **63**, *370–5*
Toulouse-Lautrec, Henri de 147, 153, **234**, *352*, *373*
Tour, Georges de la **140**, *133*, *161*, *162*
Tour, Maurice Quentin de la **165**, *14*
Tour-en-Sologne *221*
Tournai 33, 51
Tournemire *329*
Tournus **59**, *270*
Tours 33, 35, 38, *222–3*
Trémolières *116*
Très Riches Heures of the Duke of Berry 61–2, **84**, *57*
Tribolo 76
Trois Frères, les *11*
Troy, Jean François de 116, 118
Troyes **94**, *149–52*
Tura, Cosimo *161*
Tursac venus 10

Uccello, Paolo **213**
Usson, Château d', Les Egreteaux *306*
Utrecht Psalter 34
Uzès *412*

Vaison-la-Romaine 24
Valençay *224*
Valence *345*
Valenciennes *15*
Vallin, Eugène **236**
Vannes *163*
Varengeville *51*
Vasari, G. 127, 129
Vauban *436*
Vaux-le-Vicomte 95, 96, 102, **163**, *76*
Velasquez, Diego 133, 148, **48**
Velde, Henry van de *133*
Vence 156, 157, **247**, *413*
Vendôme *225–6*
'Venuses', prehistoric 9–10, **2**, **4**, **12**
Veronese 114, 129, 130, *28*, *48*, *112*, *162*, *357*
Versailles 7, 102, 103, 105, 113, 116, 119, 120, 133, **132**, **146**, **148**, **182**, **189**, *90*
Verteuil *289*
Vézelay 7, 37, 38, 51, **58**, *271*
Vien, Joseph-Marie 117, 119, **174**, *105*
Vienne 23, 24, **26**, *346–9*
Vignon, Pierre **192**, *99*
Villandry *227*
Villard d'Honnecourt 53, **69**, **70**
Villars *330*
Villeconin *91*
Villegongis *331*
Villeneuve-lès-Avignon *414–6*
Villers-Cotterets *92*
Vincennes 93
Vincent, F. A. 120
Viollet-le-Duc **90**, *79*, *102*, *298*, *419*
Viscardi, Girolamo 74, 75
Visitation Master **69**
Vix 21, **30**, **31**, *246*
Vollard, A. 154, 155
Vos, Marten de **48**
Vouet, Simon 95, 101, **156**, *184*
Vuillard, Edouard 153, *409*

Warin, Jean 96, **136**
Watteau, Antoine 7, 113, 115, 116, 119, 133, **172**, *15*, *168*
Werve, Claus de 61, *251*
Weyden, Roger van der 65, 148, *28*, *238*
Whistler, J. A. M. 148, **223**
Wicar, J. B. 128
Winckelmann, J. J. 127, 129
Wissembourg Head of Christ *148*
Witz, Conrad *147*

Zehrfuss, Bernard 157
Zola, Emile 134, 147, **202**

France is a country with one of the richest and most varied artistic heritages in the world. For the first time a survey has been produced of the treasures created and collected in France through the centuries. Over 250 carefully selected items are illustrated, more than 100 in colour. A team of specialists have collaborated on the text which traces the history of art and architecture, of taste and patronage in France from the cave paintings of pre-historic man to the architecture of Le Corbusier. The works which are familiar to us as examples of styles and periods in art are here examined in their historical setting. Who owned them and what was the climate of the periods in which they were produced? The Roman conquest of Gaul left magnificent theatres and temples which can still be seen at Arles and Vienne. During the eleventh and twelfth centuries it was the Christian church which undertook the major building projects and encouraged the development of all branches of art. These magnificent abbeys and churches, sculpture and reliquaries are rivalled only by the splendour of the Gothic cathedrals of the thirteenth and fourteenth centuries. The fifteenth century saw an awakening of artistic activity at court. The Renaissance monarchs built palaces and châteaux, looking to Italy for inspiration, artists and craftsmen and bringing back Italian works of art for their collections. The glorious age of the court of Louis XIV saw the culmination of the French classical style and the building of Versailles; the collections of the king and his ministers were enriched with works by Dutch, Flemish and Italian artists. The wealth and power of the court shifted in the eighteenth century to the aristocrats, financiers and bourgeoisie and grandeur changed to intimacy, a taste for frivolity and lavish decoration. After the Revolution in 1789 and the requisition of works of art from Italy, museums were formed to house these priceless treasures.

During the last hundred years Paris has been one of the centres of modern art, the home of Impressionism and the School of Paris. Her museums have been enriched with acquisitions from all countries and periods, forming collections which are among the most comprehensive in the world.

Such, briefly, is the story this book tells. It examines the masterpieces of each period, explains who were the key figures in each century, and describes their taste and collections. A list of the châteaux, palaces, town houses, churches and museums grouped geographically at the end of the book is an invaluable reference to tourist and art lover alike, giving brief histories of each building and mentioning the important works they house.

Unique in its approach this book has a threefold purpose, combining a history of the arts of France with the story of the country's collections and describing where these treasures can be found. It is beautifully designed, lavishly illustrated, fascinating to read and invaluable for reference.

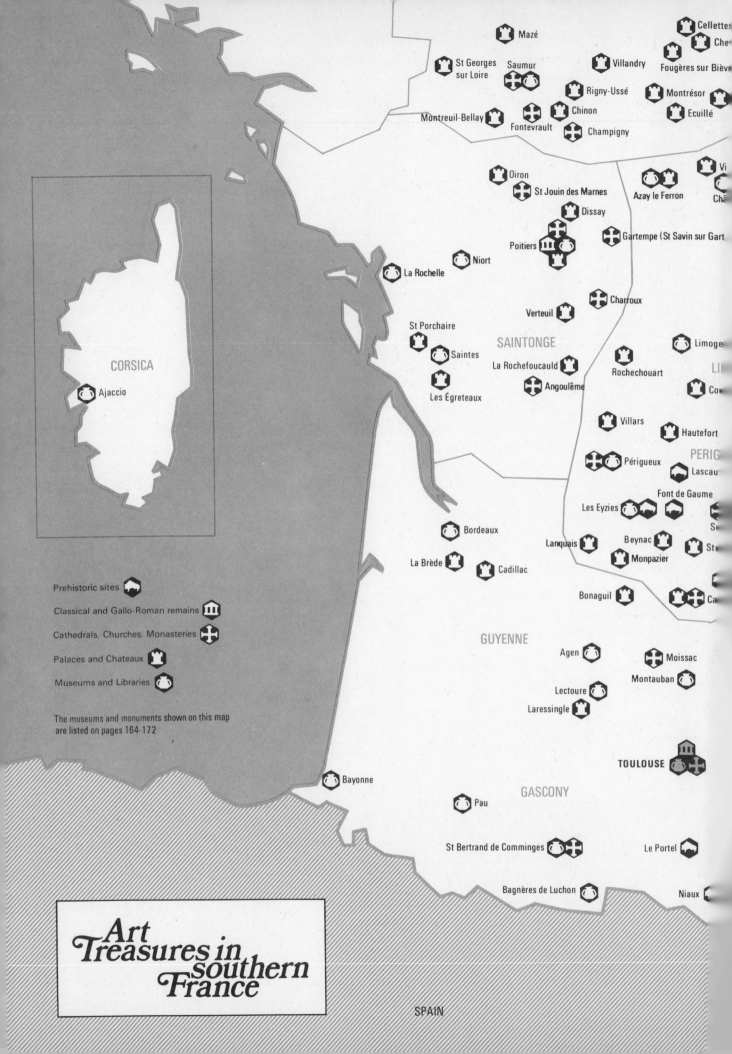

Art Treasures in southern France